ASPECTS OF

POVERTY

Selected Studies in Social Problems

Bernard Rosenberg
GENERAL EDITOR

Juvenile Delinquency
EDITED BY *Richard R. Korn*

Problems of Sex Behavior
EDITED BY *Edward Sagarin and Donal E. J. MacNamara*

Aspects of Poverty
EDITED BY *Ben B. Seligman*

The Social Control of Mental Illness
EDITED BY *Harry Silverstein*

ASPECTS
OF POVERTY

EDITED BY

Ben B. Seligman
University of Massachusetts

THOMAS Y. CROWELL COMPANY
NEW YORK
Established 1834

Editor's Foreword

A Chilean leader with much experience of the world once remarked that all political problems could be reduced to those that solved themselves and those for which there is no solution. Such limited wisdom applies, *pari passu*, to many so-called social problems. How often, if we only let them be, will they disappear. A thoughtful president of the United States may reflect that when he decides to stay out of Indonesia, things go his way; but when he plunges into Indochina, the results are disastrous. Spirited intervention might sometimes be required; but just as often, it boomerangs. Little problems or illusory problems suddenly become big and real for no other reason than that we have acted when it would have been advisable not to act. Prohibiting the consumption of alcohol or the ingestion of narcotics drives these substances inexorably into the organized underworld which battens on an illicit traffic that need never have existed in the first place. Outlaw prostitution, abortion, fornication and cohabitation, or legislate anywhere else in the sphere of private morals, or criminalize previously legal and possibly uncontrollable behavior, and you get a society of inveterate offenders. Ours is such a society. We, who like to believe that the American government is not one of men but of law, have piled law upon punitive law until countless inconsistent criminal codes produce juridical elephantiasis, and men become lawbreakers by definition. Our partially lawless police, trying, and then not trying, to contain "vice" are thrust into collusion with professional thieves, venal politicians, corrupt judges, and a wide assortment of reputable citizens similarly involved in the maladministration of criminal justice.

And all this accounts for only a fraction of the energy expended in unmaking problems initially made by misguided attempts to solve them. The impulse to do something, almost anything, in an apparently intolerable situation (which worsens as we proliferate our blunders) alternates with blindness, fatigue, indifference, and apathy.

Herbert Spencer, the founder of Anglo-American sociology, understood the desirability of inaction. His followers, inspired by that great proponent of laissez faire ideology, favored hands off a problem when the laying on of hands could only be fatal. These liberals, who did not wish to meddle with the economy, the polity, or the society at large, and who, when pushed, found themselves exposed as anarchists, were not in possession of the whole truth. Yet, that part of the truth which they did grasp seems largely to have been forgotten. We go on fatuously defining, and thereby creating problems beyond our capacity to solve except by generating even graver problems. Finally, the myth of absolute omnipotence yields to the myth of absolute impotence. Then, with neither action nor inaction as a purposive and effective principle, the world is allowed to drift. At that stage, things, as the Poles say, are worse than they were but better than they're going to be.

When to do something and when not to are the major questions of our time. They weigh heavily on the mind of this writer as he launches still another and, he hopes, better series of books, each devoted to a social problem.

And what, pray, is a social problem? Or better, in a totally problematic situation, what is *not* a social problem? As the categorical imperative within disappears and man literally reaches for the starry heavens above, while awaiting oblivion by self-destruction, anything and everything may be regarded as a problem. That, like all human enterprises, it is also social to some no doubt large extent, goes without saying.

If the editors and authors of this series are at all able to distinguish between remediable and irremediable problems, if they can admit the immense and universal ignorance that prevails as we all grope our way in darkness toward a little bit of light, if sociological arrogance is eschewed in favor of a more becoming modesty, and above all, if a hierarchy of values is sustained—such that well-subsidized trifles do not eclipse impoverished areas of investigation—then these books will have been worth our while. If not, let the reader beware.

BERNARD ROSENBERG

Contents

INTRODUCTION

The literature on poverty has grown to enormous proportions in recent years. This is quite understandable in light of the recent efforts of the federal government to deal with this problem through legislation. Yet, as Sar Levitan has suggested, federal activity essentially has been a supplement to the cumulative efforts of state and local governments to mitigate poverty. Unfortunately, most of this has turned out to be little more than a holding effort. Despite our vaunted affluence, poverty has remained with us, and promises to remain with us in the foreseeable future.

The student who wishes to study these issues today must find his way through a veritable jungle of data supplied by newspapers, journals of opinion, professional magazines, monographs, studies, research reports, government documents, symposia, readings, and books. Some accurately reflect the current state of affairs; others are little more than self-serving statements intended to camouflage meager results. Of data there are more than enough: the problem is to digest, understand, and to interpret. For example, Herman Miller—one of the nation's most eminent statisticians and an authority on income distribution—handles his materials with care and circumspection in his book *Rich Man, Poor Man*. In contrast, tendentious analyses by writers such as Rose Friedman, Gabriel Kolko, or Irving Kristol may mislead the unwary student.

1

Kristol has argued that one cannot associate poverty in America with a heartless *ancien régime* when 14 per cent of the families with yearly incomes under $3,000 buy a new car each year. Aside from the fact that a car is now a necessity for either working or seeking work in this country, the statistic itself is simply wrong. The survey Kristol cited actually reported that less than 2 per cent of low-income families bought new cars in 1960. Or take the example of Mrs. Friedman: She contends that no more than 10 per cent of the population should be classified as poor because the poor can *only* be defined in terms of inadequate diet. Such a standard implies a monetary income of less than $2,200 a year; anyone earning more than that would be classified "not-poor." The standard, of course, excludes any consideration of the human needs for clothing and shelter. Gabriel Kolko has attempted to demonstrate that no progress has really been made toward relieving poverty in the United States because, he says, income distribution has remained substantially the same since 1910. This is a misstatement of the facts, based on a false reading of inaccurate data (which were later corrected) from a government document.

While a statistical portrait is clearly essential, it is quite inadequate to describe the nature of poverty in the modern age. One needs to examine the quality of the lives of the poor, especially as contrasted with the expectations and standards generated by an affluent society. This is the focus of the present Reader. All the selections have appeared in larger works, and all have a common feature—they concentrate on the levels of living, the life style, the subculture of poverty in America. To be sure, there are other aspects of the problem, such as politics and the law, that press on the lives of the poor, and I have specifically included readings that explore these matters in detail. For how poor people get along in urban centers is much affected by what the police, the courts, and the politicians do to them.

Once again, the student is advised that the selections included in this Reader are not condensations: they are rather substantial sections taken from the original publications. Except for minor changes, such as the omission of a sentence or change of a word for smooth transition, the selections are reproduced as they first appeared. In some cases, line drawings, tables, and some footnote references have been omitted when they did not affect the flow of the argument. It is hoped that students will not limit their reading to these selections but will be encouraged to turn to the parent works and also to follow, with some care and diligence, the wide variety of discussions that frequently appear elsewhere. Otherwise, this Reader will fail in its major objective —to stimulate exploration of one of the most exacerbating social problems of the day.

The books and sources from which the selections have been taken are identified at the beginning of each section, with appropriate acknowledgments. For titles, I have used particular chapter headings to emphasize the main ideas under discussion. For example, Jules Henry is primarily concerned with the forces that contemporary culture brings to bear *against* man. Our attitude toward the aged is one of these forces. Since it leads to poverty among the aged and creates human obsolescence, it is indeed an important aspect of poverty. The materials from my own book on poverty, consisting of two chapters dealing with national and local politics, have been consolidated to underscore the issue of power more sharply.

Gunnar Myrdal, the noted Swedish social scientist, has described our concern with poverty as an intellectual and moral catharsis. We can no longer conceal the fact that there are large groups of poor people in urban and rural slums. Even if we tried to disguise or hide this, we should be reminded of it by the unrest in the ghettos of our major cities. It is hoped that this Reader will further the moral catharsis and help the student begin his own evaluation and analysis of the nature of poverty.

THE POOR ARE STILL HERE

Herman P. Miller

The problem of counting the poor can be a most troublesome one. When the War on Poverty was announced by President Johnson in January, 1964, his Council of Economic Advisers (CEA) declared that 20 per cent of the population of the United States could be counted as poor. To arrive at its estimate the CEA had used a $3,000 annual income as a yardstick. However, the CEA figure was considered by many economists to be too conservative and too crude. The $3,000 a year cut-off point seemed entirely arbitrary, for it failed to account for family size, age of the family head, or geographic location.

It was argued by many—among them Herman P. Miller, special assistant to the director of the Census Bureau—that the CEA's use of a single figure to define the boundaries of poverty distorted the analysis of poverty, overstating it for certain groups and understating it for others. Dr. Miller suggested that a variable standard centered around a figure of $3,000 would be more realistic.

This variable concept creates a band with upper and lower limits and has been used by such analysts as Oscar Ornati, then at the New School for Social Research, and by Mollie Orshansky of the Social Security Administration (SSA). Miss Orshansky also

Source: Herman P. Miller, *Rich Man, Poor Man*, pp. 56–120. Copyright © 1964 by Thomas Y. Crowell Company, New York, publishers.

argued that a poverty profile should be based on accepted standards of consumption allowing for the different needs of families of various sizes. Toward this end, she developed a measure of poverty known as the SSA Index, using consumption data from the Department of Agriculture. She defined the poverty line in terms of a family income less than three times the cost of an "economy diet" ($4.60 a week per person). The average income of families whose economic position was defined by this approach was only about 65 per cent of what was required to remove them from poverty.

Dr. Miller finds, in *Rich Man, Poor Man*, that the disparity in income between the haves and have-nots has been increasing in recent years—a dramatic reversal of the trends initiated by FDR's New Deal in the 1930's. True, the position of the lowest income groups has been upgraded in absolute dollars, but this is simply a reflection of the different standards used to define poverty in any given society and stage of development. The basic concept of what a person needs to remove him from poverty is subject to change.

There is an extraordinary amount of information in Dr. Miller's book. I have selected only a small part for this Reader. As Professor Lewis Coser noted in reviewing *Rich Man, Poor Man*, the book ". . . conveys a sense of urgency about poverty amidst affluence," yet it does this with the quiet tone of the dispassionate statistician. A certain degree of caution should be expressed, however; a bare recital of the list of material goods possessed by the poor would be misleading. It can be argued that a telephone or radio are not luxuries, but rather functional necessities, particularly for elderly persons who are often physically isolated. We must update traditional notions of subsistence, broadening our idea of how much a person needs in the way of material goods to rise above the level where he is considered deprived.

Dr. Miller, who has written widely on problems of income distribution and poverty, has taught at the American University and the University of California at Los Angeles.

◄§§►

"Ye have the poor with you always." So it says in the Bible and so it is. Truer words were never written. The proof can be found right here at home. One report found that in this, the richest of all countries, 40 per cent of the families live in poverty or deprivation. In fact that is the title of a study published in 1962, *Poverty and Deprivation in the U.S.—The Plight of Two-Fifths of a Nation.* This is no phony Communist propaganda, nor the wild charges of a radical reformer. These are hard-boiled statistical "facts" prepared by Leon Keyserling, chief economic counselor to President Truman and former head of the Council of Economic Advisers.

Does it seem strange that in 1962 Keyserling found that two-fifths of the families were poor when even during the depression President Roosevelt found that only one-third of the nation was ill-housed, ill-clothed, and ill-fed. The amount of goods and services per capita has doubled since the early thirties. How then can there have been an increase in the proportion of families living at substandard levels? The answer is quite simple. It all depends on how high you set your standard. In 1889, a study was made of poverty in London, *Life and Labour of the People*. It showed that about one-third of the people lived in poverty. During the depression a similar study was made in the United States. It also showed that about one-third of the people lived in poverty. Recent statistics for American cities prepared by the Bureau of Labor Statistics also point to the conclusion that about one-third of the people have incomes insufficient to maintain a decent level of living. The clear meaning of these findings is that as incomes go up "needs" also go up, evidently in such a way as to leave a large proportion of the population at substandard levels.

The term "poverty" connotes hunger; but this is not what is meant in discussions about poverty in America. Harlan County, Kentucky, is about as poor a county as you will find in this country. If you remember the depression, you're almost sure to remember Harlan County, Kentucky. It was the scene of many bloody mine union battles during the thirties. These battles are commemorated in a union song that goes something like this:

> They say in Harlan County
> There are no neutrals there.
> You either be a Union man
> Or a thug for J. H. Blair.
>> Which side are you on?
>> Which side are you on?

Harlan County was poor in the thirties and it still is. The clearest sign of its poverty is the fact that people are leaving in droves. Half the people who lived there in 1950 were gone by 1960. And those who remained did not live well by any means. Two-thirds of the homes were substandard. Half lacked baths, inside toilets, and other conveniences that are regarded as essential for modern living. One-fourth even lacked running water in the home. By present-day American standards they are poor, poor, poor.

But let's probe a little deeper:

> 88% have washing machines
> 67% have TV
> 42% have a telephone
> 59% have a car

It is quite evident that even in this poor American community there are many of the trappings of an affluent society. Some families have washing machines but no running water. They carry water from a well to a machine to get their clothes washed. Three-fifths of the families have cars. Many of the cars may be jalopies, but even a jalopy costs $500 or more a year to run. Two-thirds of the families have TV sets. They may not be the latest models. The fact that they are there, however, immediately points to a distinction between the American poor and the starving poor in India and China.

There are many different definitions of poverty. According to Keyserling's definition in the study cited above, an American family faces stark poverty if its income is under $4,000 and it is deprived with an income of less than $6,000. [The poor have also been] defined as the families in the bottom fifth of the income distribution. In 1960, these families had cash incomes under $3,000. (Since Keyserling's figure includes noncash income, the two numbers are not as different as they might at first appear.) This definition of poverty is arbitrary. It includes among the poor some families that do not really belong there and it excludes some that should be counted. One justification for the use of this definition is its use by a congressional committee, which concluded that in 1957 the lowest fifth of the families were in "low-income status." There is no reason to believe that this proportion would have changed by the time the census was taken in 1960. The term "poor" as employed here is synonymous with "low-income status," "bottom income groups" and other euphemistic phrases that are often used to describe poverty.

WHO IS POOR?—A SUMMARY VIEW

Who are the American poor? How did they get that way? How have their characteristics changed over time? At this point, the problem will be examined broadly. A more detailed appraisal is presented in the following section. There are many reasons for poverty, but some are much more important than others and they appear with remarkable regularity in the studies that have been made. [In studying some of the most significant characteristics of the poorest fifth of the families in 1951 and 1960] the key fact to notice is how little these characteristics have changed in the past decade. Of course, this does not mean that those who were poor in 1951 were still poor in 1960. If tags could be put on people so they could be followed through life, you would surely find that some who were higher up on the income scale in 1951 have dropped down relative to others because of retirement, widowhood, divorce, illness, and many other factors. Conversely, many who were poor in 1951 have undoubtedly moved up. This would be particularly true of young couples that were just starting out ten years earlier.

The kinds of forces involved in the movement of families in and out of poverty over a period of time can be seen in a particular case—Mr. and Mrs. Bacon of New York City. In 1950, the Bacons (the name is fictitious but the case is real) were interviewed by a welfare agency in New York City as one of one hundred poor families, for the Joint Committee on the Economic Report. The facts stated here are those shown in the report *Making Ends Meet on Less Than $2,000 a Year*.

Mr. Bacon at age thirty-eight was a temporary postal worker who made $1,820 in 1949. This was the total income he had to support his wife and three children aged six, four, and one. The family lived in a low-income housing project, where they had a two-bedroom apartment costing $38 a month, utilities included. They were eligible for a three-bedroom apartment but did not apply for it in order to save on the rent. The parents' bedroom was shared by their year-old daughter; the two boys had the other bedroom.

Mr. Bacon had quit school at sixteen. At seventeen he had been convicted of a petty theft and put on probation. He had knocked about from job to job, working as a construction laborer before he took the temporary job in the post office. He was a heavy drinker and, according to the social worker who reported the case, an unstable person who occasionally deserted his family.

Mrs. Bacon was more responsible than her husband, but she was having a very difficult time keeping the family together. She was a high school graduate but was unable to fulfill her plans for a nursing career. She had worked in a factory and in a hospital for a few years before her marriage. She was basically healthy, but at age thirty-seven all her upper teeth had been removed and she could not afford dentures. According to the social worker, Mrs. Bacon did a good job as a housewife, but she did not fully appreciate the seriousness of her plight. The apartment was described as pleasant and clean, with colorful curtains hanging on the windows. Mrs. Bacon managed her money well, although with only $20 a week to spend on food, cheese often had to be substituted for meat. The relationship between the parents was strained, but Mrs. Bacon thought her husband would stay home more if they could only get a television set.

The tension between the parents seriously affected the oldest child. He was asthmatic and had to miss school one day each week to go to a clinic for treatments. At his young age, he had already been labeled a problem child in school and had to be taken to a psychologist.

What happens to a family like the Bacons? The seeds of poverty were planted here, not only for the present generation, but for future generations as well. Unfortunately, the family was not followed over the years, so there is no way of knowing just what became of them. Still it is interesting to speculate. Mr. Bacon had little schooling, no vocational training or skill, and he drank. None of these traits are conducive to regular employment or high income and it is likely that he has had neither.

The Bacons may well be one of those families that would be counted among the poor at any time, but this is not necessarily the case. Life is complex and almost anything is possible.

In the years since the Bacons were first interviewed, much could have happened. The oldest child was twenty in 1963 and he could have been out working and contributing to the support of the family. If he had a factory job, he could be adding substantially to the family income. Moreover, the youngest Bacon child would be fifteen in 1963, if no other children were born. This would leave Mrs. Bacon free to accept employment and even a part-time job could pull the family above the poverty line. By considering only a few of the things that might have happened to this one family, you can see the factors that might cause the movement of families into or out of poverty over a period of time. [During the decade] 1951 and 1960 some families entered the ranks of the poor and others moved up the income ladder but on the average the same *kinds* of people were poor throughout the period.

.   .   .   .   .

Perhaps the most distinctive characteristic of the poor is their low productivity. Most of these families are headed by persons who cannot command a high income because of age or lack of training or work experience. The aged are a case in point. They form the single largest block at the bottom. Since most of them are in retirement and are living on pensions, it is to be expected that their incomes will lag behind the working population.

The economic problems of broken families are not too dissimilar from those of the aged. These families are the product of divorce, desertion, illegitimacy, or the death of a husband. In a very large proportion of these cases, there are young children present in the home. The mothers are unable to work at all or can only work part time because they must stay home to take care of their babies. Of course, even when they work, many are employed in low-paying jobs because of their lack of training, skill, or work experience.

A third major group at the bottom are the nonwhites, the great majority of whom are Negroes. Overall they represent only about 10 per cent of all families; but they are 21 per cent of the poor.

Herman P. Miller

MORE ABOUT THE POOR—AN INVENTORY

A good deal is known about the characteristics of poor families from small surveys that are made each year. But the 1960 census provides a much closer look at this group. At the time of the last census, there were nearly ten million families with incomes under $3,000. They were the poorest fifth of all families. What were they like? A very detailed statistical profile is provided in Table 1. To these numbers must be added several million unrelated individuals with very low incomes and very poor prospects, who are not shown in this table.

TABLE 1
Families with Income Less than $3000 in 1959

CHARACTERISTIC	TOTAL	WHITE	NONWHITE
Total families	9,650,000	7,615,000	2,035,000
Husband-wife	7,207,000	5,910,000	1,297,000
Head under 35	1,582,000	1,230,000	352,000
Head 35 to 64	3,264,000	2,555,000	709,000
Head 65 and over	2,361,000	2,125,000	236,000
Other male head	368,000	282,000	86,000
Head under 35	47,000	32,000	15,000
Head 35 to 64	178,000	131,000	47,000
Head 65 and over	143,000	119,000	24,000
Female head	2,075,000	1,423,000	652,000
Head under 35	530,000	318,000	212,000
Head 35 to 64	1,096,000	747,000	349,000
Head 65 and over	449,000	358,000	91,000
URBAN AND RURAL NONFARM			
All families	8,080,000	6,279,000	1,801,000
Husband-wife	5,810,000	4,709,000	1,101,000
Head under 35	1,366,000	1,051,000	315,000
Head 35 to 64	2,392,000	1,810,000	581,000
Head 65 and over	2,053,000	1,848,000	205,000
Other male head	299,000	223,000	75,000
Head under 35	43,000	28,000	14,000
Head 35 to 64	138,000	98,000	40,000
Head 65 and over	118,000	97,000	21,000

TABLE 1 (CONT.)

CHARACTERISTIC	TOTAL	WHITE	NONWHITE
Female head	1,971,000	1,347,000	625,000
Head under 35	522,000	314,000	209,000
Head 35 to 64	1,039,000	708,000	332,000
Head 65 and over	410,000	325,000	84,000
RURAL FARM			
All families	1,570,000	1,336,000	234,000
Husband-wife	1,397,000	1,201,000	196,000
Head under 35	216,000	179,000	37,000
Head 35 to 64	872,000	744,000	128,000
Head 65 and over	309,000	278,000	31,000
Other male head	70,000	59,000	11,000
Head under 35	5,000	4,000	1,000
Head 35 to 64	40,000	34,000	7,000
Head 65 and over	25,000	21,000	3,000
Female head	103,000	76,000	27,000
Head under 35	8,000	4,000	3,000
Head 35 to 64	57,000	40,000	17,000
Head 65 and over	38,000	32,000	7,000

U.S. *Census of Population: 1960, Detailed Characteristics, United States Summary,* Table 224.

Much about the American poor can be pinpointed by lumping the detailed figures of this table into five major groups. In this classification, each family with a 1959 income less than $3,000 is counted only once, although the classification factors seem to overlap. That is, all farm families—whether or not they are aged, fatherless, or nonwhite—are counted in Group I. All families that are aged but *not* farmers are counted in Group II, whether or not they also are fatherless or nonwhite, and so on.

This technique is a useful sieving process that might be compared to the selection of hotel rooms for the different families. Imagine a series of five rooms lined up consecutively and each connected by a door. A family enters the first room. If it is headed by a farmer, it stays in that room regardless of any other characteristic it may have, otherwise it goes into the second room. The family remains in the second room only if the head is sixty-five years old or over, otherwise it goes into the third room. It stays in the third room only if it is headed by a woman, otherwise it goes into the fourth room. It stays in the fourth room only if it is nonwhite, otherwise it goes into the fifth room and remains there. After one family has been assigned to a room, a second one starts the procedure all over again and keeps going from room to room until it too finds its proper place. In this way all of the 9,650,000 families with incomes under $3,000 are classified into each of the five groups.

Before examining the groups individually, a word should be said about the reason for selecting them. If every family is to be counted in only one category, a decision must be made regarding the relative importance of each of the reasons why families are poor.

Consider, for example, the case of an elderly Negro farmer trying to scratch a living out of an unwilling plot of land. Why is he poor? Well, there are several reasons. In the first place, the land he is working is unproductive and could not provide a livelihood even for a younger and more energetic man. Secondly, he is old and feeble and may be unable to work efficiently even if he had productive land. Finally, he is a Negro and has probably never had the opportunity to obtain sufficient education to permit him to take full advantage of the most recent developments in agricultural science.

To assign a man like this to one group, some decision must be made regarding the relative importance of his many handicaps. The decision is subjective; but anyone who wants to can go back to the detailed figures and recast the numbers to suit himself. It probably will not make too much difference because the number of crucial variables is quite limited.

In the present grouping it was decided that farm residence takes precedence above all others. One reason for this judgment is that the cash income figures used here have less meaning for the farmers than for nonfarm groups because farmers often receive food and lodging in addition to their cash income. Also, trying to eke a living out of barren soil is probably a more important cause of poverty than any personal characteristics an individual may have. Moreover, if you live on a farm, the opportunities for more profitable employment elsewhere are often quite limited, although many farmers do have some nonfarm employment.

Age was used as the second major category. Most people over sixty-five years old are either unable to work or they cannot find jobs under current conditions of employment. The resident of a city who is too old to work must live on savings, pensions, or handouts. It does not matter much if the individual is a man or a woman, white or nonwhite. The income will be quite low in any event.

The fatherless family was used as the third major category. The women who head these homes generally have trouble as a constant companion. They have responsibilities at home that prevent them from working full time; they lack the training that commands good wages. The family income will be low.

Families headed by a nonwhite male under sixty-five years old were classified in the fourth category. These families live in non-farm areas, generally central cities, where jobs are available. They are also headed by men who are still in their productive ages. Their incomes should be high, but they are not. It is presumed that discrimination is one important reason why they are poor. In many cases, however, their poverty may be unrelated to the fact that they are nonwhite.

Finally, there are those families who are poor even though they do not seem to suffer from any of the obvious factors that cause poverty. Many of these families are Puerto Ricans and Mexicans, who are technically white but do not get the advantages that "whitehood" brings. Many other families are headed by men who are disabled, younger men who are just getting started, or by men who never did get started and never will because they simply lack what it takes to rise above minimum levels of living in this society. There are millions of fine, respectable, honest men whose native intelligence is quite low and who lack training to do any but the most menial work. They are poor because their productivity is low. This type of individual is likely to become an increasingly serious social problem. The situation was clearly stated by the editor of *Harper's* magazine in September, 1962: "It is perfectly clear to me, at least, why Mr. Kennedy hasn't been able to find jobs for our three or four million unemployed. The human race—or anyhow that sample of it located in North America—no longer fits the kind of society it has to live in. Our society just doesn't have any jobs for certain types of people. If it continues to develop along its

present course, the number of such unemployables seems likely
to grow rather rapidly."

Low-Income Farmers

There were about one and a half million farm families with
cash incomes under $3,000 in 1959. The great majority of these
families had incomes under $2,000, so they would be considered
poor even if a generous allowance were made for the imputed
value of rent and food produced and consumed on the farm.

Only about one-quarter million of these families were nonwhite, so that the low-income farm population is no longer
dominated by Negro sharecroppers. That was the case twenty
years ago. Since then the Negroes have largely left the farms and
they are more highly clustered in the centers of large cities.

Broken families are also scarce on farms. If a farm woman is
left without a man, she will more likely than not remarry or
give up the farm and seek other quarters. Thus the great bulk
of the low-income farm residents are white families consisting
of a husband, wife, and in many cases children. About half of
these family heads are between thirty-five and sixty-four years old
and an equal number are under thirty-five or over sixty-five. At
one time, this type of farm probably contained a much larger
segment of the poor than it does today. The northward migration of the Negro and the magnetism of better job opportunities
in the big cities have acted as a constant drain for the younger
population on these farms. As a result, marginal farmers are
dwindling as a proportion of the poor.

About one-half of these low-income farm families live in the
South. In Alabama and Mississippi, half of the farm families
have incomes under $2,000 a year. Farmers in the other parts of
the South are not much better off. Michael Harrington in *The
Other America* has aptly described rural areas in the South as "a
belt of misery that runs from the Middle Atlantic coast to the
South and to the West."

The reasons for farm poverty are about as varied as the poor
themselves. There is no such thing as a "typical" case. And yet

there are some aspects of farm poverty that can best be understood only in the context of a particular case (real but disguised).

In 1950, Jason and Luella Wood were interviewed in Kansas for the Joint Committee on the Economic Report. At the time, they operated a hundred-acre farm that they rented for one-half the crops. Mr. Wood raised corn and prairie hay, getting around twenty bushels of corn to the acre. He did not sell his share of the crops but kept it as livestock feed. For cash income, Mr. Wood raised chickens and sold cream to a local produce station. His net income after farm-operating expenses was $800.

The Woods raised almost all of their own foodstuff and spent only $125 during the year for store groceries. Their home was a forty-year-old seven-room house, livable but in need of many minor repairs. Wood and coal stoves were used for heating and cooking in winter, and kerosene was used in the summer. A pitcher pump in the kitchen supplied soft water from a cistern while a well some distance from the house provided drinking water. They had no electricity and used kerosene and gasoline lights and a battery-operated radio. Mrs. Wood made most of her clothes, many of them from feed bags, which were also used for tablecloths and curtains. The Woods did own a good car, bought secondhand.

Despite their very frugal living, the Woods spent every cent of the $800 they made. The only reserves they had were $300 in bonds and $1,000 in cash, part of which they had inherited. The Woods were getting by in the sense that they managed to live from year to year, they ate reasonably well, and they were adequately sheltered. Yet there can be little doubt that they were poor according to any reasonable standards of living for this country.

The Aged

One of the largest groups among the American poor is the aged. About two and a half million low-income families, living for the most part in large metropolitan areas, are headed by a person over sixty-five years of age. They are predominantly white.

Most of the aged poor are couples. There were two million of them in 1960. An additional half million were elderly women, largely widows living with their children.

As in the case of the farmers, the money incomes of the aged often fail to tell the whole story. Many older people have their homes paid for or are living on savings which do not show up in their current incomes. There are some elderly people whose income is only $1,000 a year but who manage to get to Florida every winter by drawing on their savings. These are undoubtedly the exceptions rather than the rule. Most of the aged depend on social security or other pensions. While these have gone up, they have not risen sufficiently to keep the incomes of the aged on a par with those of the rest of the population. Younger men can always take on a second job when they feel they are falling behind—and millions do. They also can send their wives out to work—and millions do that too. The aged have no such option and so they tend to fall behind in a booming economy. In view of this fact, it is surprising indeed that the aged have not increased as a proportion of the poor.

One of the striking facts revealed in any examination of the financial situation of the aged is the extent of their dependence on forms of income other than earnings. In 1960, about 36 per cent of all families headed by a person sixty-five years old or over derived all of their income from social security payments, private pensions, and public assistance. About 60 per cent of those with incomes under $3,000 did no paid work. These facts, of course, only confirm what nearly everyone knows: large numbers of older people do not work.

Families headed by persons over sixty-five are much smaller, on the average, than those headed by younger people. Their "needs" are also less, on the average. Therefore, a poverty line of $3,000 for them may seem unreasonable. An examination of the figures below suggests, however, that the total number included among the poor might not be changed greatly if an alternative definition of poverty had been used. About three-fourths of all aged families at all income levels were couples. About 60 per cent of them had incomes under $3,000 in 1960. If $2,500 had been used as the poverty line, about 50 per cent would have been included and even a $2,000 income limit would have included 36 per cent. But there were also quite a few larger families headed by persons over sixty-five and for them even $3,000 as the poverty line may be unreasonably low. About 28 per cent of the aged families with four persons had incomes under $3,000. A poverty line of $4,000 might have been more reasonable for this group and that would bring the proportion up to 33 per cent. Similarly, about 30 per cent of the aged families with five or more persons had incomes under $3,000. The proportion would have been raised to 38 per cent had a poverty line of $4,000 been used.

A large proportion of the aged have very limited resources to fall back on in case of emergency. About 30 per cent of all aged families have no liquid assets whatever and another 20 per cent had less than $1,000 in 1960. Most of the assets of the aged are tied up in their homes or in life insurance rather than in forms that can be readily converted into cash in case of emergency.

TABLE 2

Income of Families Headed by a Person Aged 65 or Over, in 1960

INCOME LEVEL	ALL FAMILIES	TWO PER- SONS	THREE PER- SONS	FOUR PER- SONS	FIVE OR MORE PERSONS
Under $2,000	31%	36%	20%	18%	18%
Between $2,000 *and* $3,000	20	24	13	10	12
Between $3,000 *and* $4,000	12	12	16	6	8
$4,000 *and over*	36	29	52	67	62

U.S. Senate, Special Committee on Aging, *Background Facts on the Financing of Health Care of the Aged,* 87th Congress, 2nd Session, p. 36.

Broken Families

The broken family, sometimes referred to as the fatherless home, is another major segment of the poor. There were one and a half million families like this in 1960, and virtually all concentrated in large metropolitan areas. About one million of these families were white and one-half million were nonwhite.

The large proportion of nonwhites within this group reflects the instability of family life among the Negroes. Every fifth Negro child is born out of wedlock and mothers of many of these children are left to fend for themselves in a hostile world. Even if they were accepted by society their economic lot would not be much better than it is because of their lack of skill or experience. Desertion, which is the poor man's divorce, may also be a greater cause of broken families among Negroes than among whites.

The women who head broken families are almost equally divided into three age groups: under thirty-five, thirty-five to forty-four, and forty-five to sixty-four. The half million or so who are over sixty-five were counted with the aged population.

Many of the problems that face the fatherless home were found in the home of Mrs. Scilaro and her family in Philadelphia, when her case was reported to the Joint Economic Committee in 1950. Mrs. Scilaro was born in Italy and came to this country to marry her husband. She could neither read nor write. She had seven children, two of whom died. The five children living with her in 1950 ranged from twelve to seventeen. Her husband died shortly after the birth of her youngest child.

Upon the death of her husband, full responsibility for the support of the family fell on Mrs. Scilaro's shoulders. She went to work in a garment factory as a seamstress; her take-home pay was $30 a week or about $1,500 in 1950. Her oldest son quit school at seventeen and went to work in a restaurant, where he earned $5 a week plus some of his meals. He was promised a better job as soon as he turned eighteen. The other Scilaro children also planned to quit school when they reached seventeen.

The Scilaros lived in a little house on a very narrow street in the old part of Philadelphia. On the first floor were a living room and a tiny kitchen. Winding stairs led to three small bedrooms on the second floor. There was running cold water in the kitchen but no other plumbing. The toilet was outside in the backyard. A single coal stove in the kitchen supplied heat for the whole house in the winter. The kitchen also had a gas cook stove and an electric refrigerator that was purchased for $50. Mrs. Scilaro paid for it at the rate of $1 a week.

The family was constantly in debt. All purchases were made in neighborhood stores on credit and the bills were paid whenever Mrs. Scilaro could pay them. Very little clothing was purchased and that largely from a secondhand clothing store in the neighborhood. The only saving grace for this family was that they were all basically healthy and there were no medical bills.

The family was very close-knit. The boys all played together and refused to separate to play with others of their own age. Occasionally they would earn money shining shoes and would go to the movies together. Most of their time was spent playing on their own narrow street.

Nonwhite Families

In 1960 there were about one million nonwhite families (over 90 per cent Negroes) living in or near large cities and headed by a man sixty-five years old. Much has been written and said about the plight of the Negro. Their overrepresentation among the poor should surprise no one. There are undoubtedly many factors that keep the Negro at the bottom, but there can be little doubt that racial discrimination is a key cause.

In 1962, President Kennedy's Council of Economic Advisers prepared an estimate of the economic loss to the United States resulting from racial discrimination in employment. This study showed that if the education and training of the Negro population were fully utilized by the elimination of racial barriers in employment, our national product might rise by as much as 2½ per cent each year. In 1961, this would have increased our income as a nation by $13 billion. These wasted skills amounted to one-fourth of the total that was spent for national defense in that year. The monetary loss in national income is, of course, only a small part of the total social burden of discrimination. When the costs of higher crime rates, poor health, urban decay, and many other problems that stem directly or indirectly from discrimination are added, the amount becomes astronomical.

An examination of the jobs held by heads of nonwhite poor families makes obvious the reason for their poverty. One-fourth of them are laborers and an additional third work as domestics or in the service trades. About three out of every five of these family heads work in these three low-paying occupations. When the semi-skilled factory workers are added, about 85 per cent of the nonwhite poor families are accounted for.

Other Groups among the Poor

Finally, there is the fifth group, whose poverty has no apparent explanation in census statistics—white families living in or near large cities and headed by a man in his productive years. What are these three million families like? Explanations based on personal or environmental factors could be made for the farm poor, the aged poor, the widowed and divorced poor, and the Negro poor. What is there to say about the white poor?

First of all it must be recognized that these three million families come from a total of thirty million who have the same characteristics—that is, they are white, live in the city, and are headed by a man under sixty-five. In the normal course of events, some of these families would be expected to be poor. Some of the men heading these families are bound to be ill or disabled and the families suffer as a result. Others may lack the intelligence to learn a trade or to hold down a responsible job. As a result they are cast into the most menial and lowest paying occupations. Still others get bad "breaks." Their employer goes out of business or has a bad year and their incomes suffer as a result.

The diversity of this group is reflected in the kinds of work they do. The heads of nonwhite poor families were very highly concentrated in the labor, service, and semiskilled factory trades; about 85 per cent of them were employed in these occupations. Only one-half of the white poor family heads worked in these occupations. An additional 20 per cent were craftsmen and 30 per cent were white-collar professional or managerial workers. Some of those in the better-paying occupations may have just been starting out on their careers and could look forward to higher incomes in the future. Nearly half of the total were over forty-five, and while they were still too young for the "scrap heap," they may have had difficulty in getting good jobs because of their "advanced age."

Many different kinds of families are included in this group. For some, like the Duncans of Portland, Oregon, and the Mahoneys of Pittsburgh, poverty is only temporary. In 1950, when Mr. Duncan was interviewed for the Joint Economic Committee, he was twenty-nine years old and was working as an auto repairman. His income was only $2,000, but he had just started working at his trade. Frank Mahoney and his wife were in much the same position. Their income in 1950 was $1,900, but Mr. Mahoney was only twenty-eight years old and was working for his master's degree under the G.I. Bill. They would not be poor for long.

For others equally young, however, the future prospects were not so good. Frank Petrov, age twenty-five, his wife Maria, age twenty, and their four-year-old son also lived in Pittsburgh. In 1950, when this case was reported, Mr. Petrov was working as a messenger for a telegraph company. His earnings were $1,500. This employment climaxed a long line of poor jobs. He quit school in the seventh grade and was in the service during World War II, but was discharged because of poor health. After his discharge he went to work in a steel mill, but he quit this job because he was too nervous to stand the work. He then went to work in a pants factory, where he earned $18 a week. About this time he met his wife, who was employed in a suitcase factory and also earned $18 a week. Shortly after their marriage, Mrs. Petrov became pregnant and had to leave her job.

Maria's background is not too different from her husband's. She is one of ten children of Italian immigrants. She also quit school in the seventh grade, when she was fifteen years old. She was sixteen when she married Frank. Despite their poverty and uncertain future, both parents were very anxious to have more children. The social worker reported that when the inadvisability of increasing their family was mentioned Maria replied, "Whether you can afford children or not, you sometimes just decide to have them."

Frank and Maria were both in poor health. Maria suffered from indigestion, obesity, and other ailments which required regular treatment at a public clinic. Frank was nervous. He could not do physical work. His wife reported that if anything disturbed him, such as a reprimand for taking too long to deliver a telegram, he would come home and kick the furniture, sometimes breaking it.

The family moved very often, a total of ten times during five years of marriage. At the time of the interview, they were living in a public housing project which they regarded as the best home they had ever had. The home was well kept and neatly furnished with secondhand pieces. The most valued possession was the television set.

The financial prospects for this family were clearly not good. Uneducated, unskilled, and in poor health, Frank could hardly expect ever to move out of the ranks of the poor. The tensions caused by financial pressures would undoubtedly increase in time as children came and bills mounted. But the pleasures were bound to increase too. They had a large, close-knit family and many friends. There would be poverty; but there would also be parties, evenings spent in loud discussion, weddings, picnics, and all the other pleasures that make life bearable for some of the poor.

SUMMARY

Poverty is nothing to joke about. It is real, serious, and important. But it is also one of those emotionally charged words that can trap you if you are not careful. Much needless soul searching can be avoided if it is recognized at the outset that there is no objective definition of poverty any more than there is an objective definition of art or beauty. The standards of poverty are established by society. They can be arbitrarily defined for a given time and place; but they vary from place to place and they differ from time to time for a given place. Professor Dorothy Brady, who has devoted a lifetime to this field of study, once wrote: "When faced directly with the problem of determining [poverty] for a given time and place, the theorist will deny the possibility of a unique answer and the propagandist will settle for one of many solutions if the result suits his purposes." The prophetic wisdom of this remark is most clear when you see the way in which politicians and propagandists manipulate income figures to meet their particular needs.

Many people refuse to recognize a simple statistical fact. If a distribution has a middle and a top it must also have a bottom and somebody must be there. The important question is why they are there and how much they get. People are not all equally endowed with good health, intelligence, creativity, drive, etc. In any society a premium will be paid to those who are most productive.

The individual can legitimately demand from a democratic society that he be given the chance to develop his God-given talents. Society, in turn, must place a floor beneath those who fall to the bottom so as to minimize their suffering.

On the first point, there is still a long way to go in America. There is still much evidence of discrimination, neglected talent, and the transmission of poverty from one generation to the next. The picture is, of course, not all black. Millions of immigrants who came to this country with only the clothes on their backs have lived to see their children outgrow the filthy slums of the Lower East Side, Hell's Kitchen, and other choice spots that match the worst you would find today. But there is still a long road ahead, particularly for the Negroes, Puerto Ricans, and other minorities.

On the second point, there is much to be proud of in the United States. As previously stated, in 1929 about half of the families and individuals had incomes below $3,000 (in 1962 dollars). That number has been more than cut in half. At the current rate of progress perhaps only about 10 per cent of the population will be below this poverty line in 1980.

Does this mean that poverty will be virtually eliminated in the next fifteen years? The historical evidence points strongly against such a conclusion. The chances are that our standards will be lifted a little higher, our belts will be opened another notch, and there will still be a large block of families living under new and higher substandard conditions.

The Bureau of Labor Statistics has estimated that the cost of a "modest but adequate" level of living (excluding taxes) for a working-class family of four persons in New York City was about $4,000 in 1947 and about $5,200 in 1959 (both figures in terms of 1961 purchasing power). In other words, the "modest but adequate" level of living rose by 28 per cent in New York City in this twelve-year period. At this rate of growth, a working-class family living in New York City will be considered poor in 1975 if its income is under $7,000 (in 1961 dollars). Even families making considerably more than this will be considered poor if allowance is made for normal inflation and taxes.

Do these numbers seem unreasonably high? Well, they are no more unreasonable than the present standard of living seemed a few years ago. How far this nation has come from that bleak day in January, 1937, when President Roosevelt stated in his second inaugural address: "I see millions of families trying to live on incomes so meager that the pall of family disaster hangs over them day by day." There still are families like that, to be sure. There always will be. But abject poverty of this type is dwindling. When you speak of the millions of poor today, you mean something entirely different.

THE INCOME OF MINORITIES: THE NEGRO

"One hundred years of delay have passed since President Lincoln freed the slaves, yet their heirs, their grandsons are not fully free. They are not yet freed from the bonds of injustice. They are not yet freed from social and economic oppression." These are not the remarks of a rabble rouser or a soap-box orator. They were made by the President of the United States in a nationwide address on June 12, 1963—the eve of the admission of two Negro youths to the University of Alabama.

All figures collected in the census—on housing, education, occupation, income—show that the Negro still ranks among the poorest of the poor. His lowly position has been documented so many times and in so many ways that presenting the evidence seems like proving the obvious. Yet what is obvious to some is not even apparent to others. Facts form the only solid basis for the discussion out of which justice and truth may emerge. Though "redress is being sought in the streets, in demonstrations, parades, and protests," it is not yet too late for facts.

There is a general impression that the Negro has largely left the South. This is not the case. In 1960 there were 18.9 million Negroes in the United States. About 11.3 million, or 60 per cent, lived in the South, 3 million lived in the Northeast, 3.5 million lived in the North Central states, and only 1 million lived in the West. Within the South, a large proportion of the Negroes have migrated to urban areas. Three major concentrations of Negroes can be identified in the United States. About one-third live in southern cities, about one-fourth live on southern farms, and the remainder live in the North and West.

The Income They Receive

Income is one of the best measures of economic status. By this standard, the position of Negroes is quite low in comparison with whites in most states. More disturbing is this sad fact: in many states their situation relative to the whites has grown *worse*, not better. The income gap between the races generally widened during the fifties. Shown below is a comparison of the median income of white and Negro males by state for 1949 and 1959. The figures are restricted to states with 100,000 or more Negroes.

The income position of Negroes relative to whites is most favorable in the North and in California. In most northern states, except New Jersey, the average income of Negroes was

TABLE 3

The Income Gap—Regional Differences in the Incomes of White and Negro Males in 1949 and 1959*

STATE	1949			1959		
	WHITE	NEGRO		WHITE	NEGRO	
		Amount	Per cent of white		Amount	Per cent of white
United States overall	$2,582	$1,356	53%	$4,337	$2,254	52%
			NORTHEAST			
Massachusetts	2,630	1,944	74	4,452	3,063	69
Connecticut	2,809	2,023	72	5,033	3,545	70
New York	2,929	2,097	72	4,812	3,372	70
New Jersey	3,033	1,977	65	5,172	3,375	65
Pennsylvania	2,638	2,073	79	4,369	3,246	74

Herman P. Miller

TABLE 3 (CONT.)

			NORTH CENTRAL			
Ohio	2,852	2,146	75	4,903	3,492	71
Indiana	2,696	2,211	82	4,483	3,520	79
Illinois	3,030	2,260	75	5,056	3,651	72
Michigan	3,039	2,659	87	4,983	3,768	76
Missouri	2,224	1,611	72	3,863	2,616	68
			SOUTH			
Maryland	2,782	1,601	58	4,880	2,769	57
District of Columbia	3,242	2,182	67	4,694	3,376	72
Virginia	2,255	1,220	54	3,758	1,907	51
North Carolina	1,872	1,002	54	3,040	1,318	43
South Carolina	2,043	801	39	3,224	1,140	35
Georgia	1,870	919	49	3,420	1,510	44
Florida	2,239	1,185	53	3,769	2,080	55
Kentucky	1,701	1,197	70	2,938	1,787	61
Tennessee	1,685	1,141	68	2,939	1,637	56
Alabama	1,809	957	53	3,409	1,446	42
Mississippi	1,462	605	41	2,796	904	32
Arkansas	1,423	759	53	2,553	990	39
Louisiana	2,228	997	45	4,001	1,609	40
Oklahoma	2,041	992	49	3,489	1,704	49
Texas	2,272	1,202	53	3,756	1,916	51
			WEST			
California	2,966	2,121	72	5,109	3,553	70

* For states with 100,000 or more Negroes in 1960.

U.S. Census of Population: 1960, Detailed Characteristics, Table 133; and U.S. Census of Population: 1950, Vol. II, Table 87.

about 70 per cent or more of the white average in 1959. The situation for Negroes was best in states such as Michigan, Pennsylvania, and Indiana, where unionized heavy industries are concentrated. In these states, the median income of Negroes was about three-fourths of that received by whites.

Negroes do not do as well in the South as in the North. In the District of Columbia, the average for Negroes was 72 per cent of the white average, about the same as in many northern states. This relatively high ratio is due partly to the influence of the federal government, which is the major employer in the District of Columbia. It also reflects the fact that many of the higher paid federal employees—who are white—live in the suburban areas outside the District and are not counted in the comparisons with Negroes living within it.

Except for the District of Columbia, which most Southerners do not regard as the South, Kentucky was the only southern state in which the average income of Negroes reached 60 per cent of the white average. In some states of the old Confederacy —Virginia, Florida, Tennessee, and Texas—the Negro average was about half of the white average. In the deep South, the Negro average was well under half the white average, dropping to as low as one-third in Mississippi and South Carolina.

Out of a total of twenty-six states (including the District of Columbia) for which data are shown, the ratio of Negro to white income increased slightly between 1949 and 1959 in two states (District of Columbia and Florida) and it was unchanged in two others (New Jersey and Oklahoma). In every other state there was a widening of the gap between the incomes of whites and Negroes and in some cases it was fairly substantial. In Michigan, for example, the ratio of average Negro income to white income dropped from 87 per cent in 1949 to 76 per cent in 1959. In several southern states, notably Kentucky, Tennessee, Alabama, and Mississippi, there was also a marked reduction in the relative income position of Negroes.

How They Live

The low income of the Negro shows up very clearly in the kind of housing he has. A very large proportion of Negro children are reared in homes that are inadequate by modern standards. The situation is better than it was ten years ago, but it is still poor in many parts of the country. The figures in Table 4 tell the story better than words.

For the country as a whole, nearly half of the nonwhite families live in homes that are either already so run-down that they are hazardous to live in or are badly in need of repair. Between 1950 and 1960 the proportion living in dilapidated housing was cut in half; but much of the change seems to have been a shift from dilapidated to deteriorating homes. Even in 1960 only two nonwhite families out of every five lived in sound structures with hot and cold running water, a bath or shower, and a flush toilet.

TABLE 4

Nonwhite Housing Conditions in 1960 and 1950, by Region

YEAR AND CONDITION OF HOUSING	UNITED STATES	SOUTH	NORTH AND WEST
1960			
Sound			
With all plumbing facilities	43%	30%	58%
Lacking plumbing facilities	11	15	7
Deteriorating	29	32	25
Dilapidated	17	23	10
1950			
Not dilapidated			
With all plumbing facilities	28%	13%	53%
Lacking plumbing facilities	39	47	26
Dilapidated	33	39	21

U.S. Bureau of the Census Press Release, March 23, 1961.

Housing conditions for nonwhites are worse in the South than in the rest of the country. In 1950, only 13 per cent of the nonwhite families lived in sound structures with all facilities. Despite vast improvements, only 30 per cent of the nonwhites in the South had this kind of a home in 1960. The proportion was about twice as great in the North and West. Over half of the nonwhite families in the South continue to live in dilapidated or deteriorating structures.

Employment and Earnings

The price that Negroes pay for their dark skins is nowhere more obvious than in employment. In almost every group of jobs they earn less money than whites because they hold the lowest paying jobs in that group. They are clerks instead of managers, laborers instead of bricklayers, machine operators instead of toolmakers. But that is only part of their disadvantage. They often get lower pay even when doing exactly the same work as whites. White men earn more simply because they are white, regardless of the job. The details of facts and figures paint this pathetic picture in stark detail.

About 3,600,000 Negro men were employed in April, 1960. One million worked as laborers; an additional half million were employed in the service trades as janitors, porters, cooks, elevator operators, and the like. Together, these two very low-paying occupation groups accounted for about 40 per cent of all jobs held by Negro men. Even within these low-paying jobs, Negroes earned far less than whites. Among farm laborers, whites averaged 35 per cent more than nonwhites; the medians were $1,300 and $800 respectively. Among nonfarm laborers the differential was 25 per cent in favor of the whites (the average was $3,200 for whites and $2,400 for nonwhites); and among service workers average earnings for whites was 29 per cent higher ($3,600 as compared with $2,500). Not all service workers are low-paid. Within this occupation group, average earnings for Negroes range from about $4,300 for policemen and firemen to about $2,500 for janitors and porters. Only about 4 per cent of the firemen and policemen were Negro; 37 per cent of the janitors were.

A large proportion of Negro men work as factory hands or in other semiskilled jobs ranging all the way from parking lot attendants to truck drivers. About one-fourth of the total fall in this occupation group. Earnings there are somewhat higher than in the service trades, averaging about $3,000 in 1959; but still the Negroes made about 32 per cent less than the whites, who averaged $4,400. The main reason for the lower than average earnings of nonwhite workers within this broad occupation group is their concentration in its lower paid jobs, and very often in its lower paying industries. For example, about one-fourth of all semiskilled Negroes are truck drivers or deliverymen. Whites in this occupation averaged $4,500, nonwhites only $2,600, a differential of about 42 per cent. The difference is probably due to the fact that most nonwhites in this occupation work as lower paid deliverymen rather than as truck drivers. Relatively large numbers of semiskilled Negroes also work at such low-paying jobs as parking lot attendants, packers and wrappers, laundry and dry-cleaning workers, and taxi drivers and chauffeurs. About one-third of all men employed by laundry and dry-cleaning plants were Negro. Their earnings averaged only $2,600, about the same as janitors and porters. This fact is significant and disheartening. Even when Negroes succeed in "getting ahead in the world" and become truck drivers and semiskilled factory workers, who have higher status than janitors and porters, their earnings do not increase appreciably, and in some cases not at all.

Only about 10 per cent of the Negro men worked as craftsmen. Their average earnings were $3,500 as compared with

TABLE 5
Jobs and Pay of Negro Men in 1960

OCCUPATION*	NUMBER OF NEGRO WORKERS	PER CENT OF OCCUPATION THAT IS NEGRO	MEDIAN EARNINGS WHITE	NON-WHITE
Negro men employed	3,644,000	8.4%	$4,855	$2,703
Professional and technical workers	113,000	2.5	6,693	4,563
Engineers	4,000	0.5	7,452	7,076
Medical and other health workers	12,000	3.4	7,953	4,642
Schoolteachers	28,000	6.8	5,701	4,450
Farmers and farm managers	154,000	6.5	2,324	788
Managers, officials, and proprietors	63,000	1.4	6,719	3,869
Salaried	31,000	1.0	7,025	4,433
Self-employed	32,000	1.9	5,831	3,318
Clerical workers	179,000	5.9	4,848	4,072
Mail carriers	20,000	10.4	5,309	5,101
Sales workers	47,000	1.6	5,036	2,809
Craftsmen and foremen	357,000	4.2	5,316	3,480
Construction craftsmen	120,000	5.5	4,839	2,855
Foremen	16,000	1.5	6,651	4,791
Mechanics and repairmen	117,000	5.3	4,798	3,478

TABLE 5 (CONT.)

Semiskilled workers	887,000	10.3	4,445	3,040
Trucking	248,000	12.7	4,539	2,638
Laundry and dry cleaning	36,000	33.3	3,253	2,600
Durable goods manufacturing	147,000	9.8	4,695	3,749
Nondurable goods manufacturing	114,000	9.1	4,465	3,272
Nonmanufacturing industries	77,000	14.6	4,496	2,859
Private household workers	27,000	44.7	956	1,216
Service workers	508,000	19.5	3,582	2,529
Janitors	265,000	37.2	2,833	2,543
Police and firemen	25,000	3.8	4,932	4,276
Waiters, cooks, and bartenders	81,000	15.8	3,267	2,759
Farm laborers	257,000	21.4	1,256	816
Nonfarm laborers	745,000	24.9	3,210	2,394

* This table does not include all occupations.

U.S. Census of Population: 1960, Detailed Characteristics, United States Summary, Tables 205 and 208.

$5,300 for whites, a differential of about 35 per cent. Negro craftsmen were about equally divided into three occupational categories: construction workers, mechanics, and all others. Their average earnings in construction were $2,900, only about $400 more than the average earned by janitors or porters. In contrast, white craftsmen in the construction trades averaged about $4,800. Among mechanics, whites averaged $4,800, nonwhites, $3,500.

Within the white-collar fields, relatively few Negroes are employed as managerial or sales workers. In 1960 there were a total of 31,000 salaried managers who were Negro, 32,000 owners of unincorporated businesses (small retail stores for the most part), and 47,000 salesmen. Salaried managers who were Negro averaged $4,400, 37 per cent below the $7,000 received by whites. Negro businessmen averaged only $3,300, or about 43 per cent below the white average. The average income received by Negro salesmen ($2,800) was about 44 per cent below the white average and only several hundred dollars more than that of porters and janitors.

Clerical work is a major source of white-collar employment for Negro men, and their earnings in this occupation compare more favorably with those of whites than in most other occupations. About 179,000 Negro men were employed as clerical workers in 1960 and their average earnings ($4,100) were only 16 per cent below the white average. One reason for the relatively small differential is that a large proportion of Negro clerical workers are employed by the U.S. Post Office, where their average earnings do not differ appreciably from those received by whites.

Professional and technical work, the highest paid of all, was relatively unimportant among Negroes and it paid them substantially less than it did whites. A total of about 113,000 Negro men had professional and technical employment in April, 1960. The two largest categories were schoolteachers and clergymen, who accounted for about 40 per cent of the group. Partly because of their heavy concentration in these two relatively low-paying professions, their earnings averaged only $4,600, about 32 per cent below the white average of $6,700.

Like the men, Negro women are highly concentrated in low-paying jobs. Unlike the men, however, the earnings differential between the races was not appreciable in most occupations.

Nearly 900,000 Negro women, or over one-third of the total employed in April, 1960, were private household workers, a dignified title for women who clean other women's homes. These women averaged only $700 in earnings in 1959, about the same as the average for white women in this occupation. The average annual figure is very low partly because household workers, even more than other women, so often have part-time jobs.

The second major source of employment for Negro women was the service trades. Over 500,000 women, or about one-fifth of the total who were employed in April, 1960, worked as waitresses, cooks, charwomen, hospital attendants, and practical nurses. The average earnings of nonwhite women in this occupation was $1,400, the same as that received by white women in the service trades.

Factory work was a third major source of employment for Negro women. About 310,000 were engaged in semiskilled jobs in April, 1960. Somewhat more than half of these women worked in manufacturing plants, but about 100,000 worked in low-paying laundry and dry-cleaning plants. It was partly for this reason that their overall average earnings were only $1,800 in 1959, or about 23 per cent below the white average of $2,400. Nonwhite women who worked in durable-goods manufacturing plants made an average of $2,500 as compared with $2,900 for white women; nonwhite women employed in soft-goods factories averaged $2,000 as compared with $2,300 for white women.

Relatively few Negro women had white-collar employment in April, 1960. About 180,000, less than 10 per cent of the total, were clerical workers. About 50,000 were secretaries and typists, while most of the others did general clerical work. The average earnings of nonwhite women who were clerical workers was $3,000 in 1959, about the same as that received by white women in this occupation.

The number of professional and technical workers among Negro women was about the same as the number of clerical workers, 175,000. About 100,000 were schoolteachers and more than 30,000 were professional nurses. These two occupations accounted for 75 per cent of all Negro women employed in professional and technical jobs. The average earnings of nonwhite professional women was $3,600, the same as that received by white women.

Is the Negroes' Lot Improving?

The figures [in Tables 5 and 6] document the shocking facts of American economic life. Though the shackles of slavery have been removed and the whip of the taskmaster has been broken, their effect remains and the Negro exists on the crumbs of U.S. affluence. With few exceptions he cannot get a well-paying job.

There is a general impression that this situation has improved in recent years. Senator Jacob Javits of New York, for example, states in his book, *Discrimination U.S.A.*: "The tremendous progress of the last three decades in increasing equality of opportunity of employment must be credited to the influence of the federal government, to FEPC legislation, to the labor unions, and to civic and community relations organizations. This is

Herman P. Miller

dramatically shown by the gains scored for the Negro worker, the chief victim of discrimination." The Department of Labor reports that "occupational differences between Negroes and whites are still large, but Negroes have raised their occupational

TABLE 6
Jobs and Pay of Negro Women in 1960

OCCUPATION*	NUMBER OF NEGRO WORKERS	PER CENT OF OCCU- PATION THAT IS NEGRO	MEDIAN EARNINGS	
			WHITE	NON- WHITE
Negro women employed	2,455,000	11.6%	$2,393	$1,219
Professional and technical workers	175,000	6.4	3,641	3,571
Medical and other health workers	44,000	5.7	3,126	3,057
Schoolteachers	94,000	8.5	4,161	3,790
Clerical workers	182,000	2.9	3,018	2,993
Secretaries, stenographers and typists	52,000	2.4	3,241	3,231
Sales workers	36,000	2.2	1,496	1,562
Semiskilled workers	310,000	9.5	2,371	1,829
Laundry and dry cleaning	99,000	35.9	1,667	1,542
Durable goods manufacturing	27,000	6.9	2,948	2,549
Nondurable goods manufacturing	76,000	9.1	2,346	1,964
Nonmanufacturing industries	18,000	17.9	2,001	1,440
Private household workers	888,000	53.4	661	704
Service workers	520,000	18.3	1,391	1,365
Charwomen	51,000	25.0	1,325	1,354
Practical nurses	32,000	16.3	1,805	2,031
Waitresses and cooks	135,000	11.2	1,148	1,158

* This table does not include all occupations.

U.S. *Census of Population: 1960, Detailed Characteristics, United States Summary,* Tables 205 and 208.

levels appreciably faster, in the past 22 years, than whites." This conclusion is valid as a generalization for the country as a whole. However, most of the improvement in the occupational status of the Negro since 1940 has been due to his movement from the rural South to the urban industrial areas rather than to any major improvement in job opportunities. The problem can be seen more clearly, perhaps, in the following perspective.

There has been a general upgrading of occupational skills for both whites and Negroes as the American economy has moved away from agriculture and become more complex and industrialized. As a result, Negroes who were once highly concentrated in sharecropping and farm labor have now moved up to unskilled and semiskilled factory jobs; some have moved into white-collar employment. But there has been a parallel upgrading of jobs held by whites. The real question is whether the relative upward movement has been faster for nonwhites than for whites. The answer, based on statistical tests that have been applied to the data collected in the past three censuses, seems to be no. Although the occupational status of nonwhites relative to whites has improved for the country as a whole, in most states the nonwhite male now has about the same occupational distribution relative to the whites that he had in 1940 and 1950. The results show that there have been few significant changes in the occupational distribution of nonwhite males relative to whites during the past twenty years.

· · · · ·

Puerto Ricans

Puerto Ricans represent one of the newer minority groups in the United States. There were about 856,000 Puerto Ricans living in this country at the time of the last census. Nearly three out of every four lived in New York City, for the most part in Manhattan, the Bronx, and Brooklyn. It is reasonable to turn to the census results for New York City for a cross section of their economic status.

Income

The Department of Labor estimated in 1959 that a family of four living in New York City and its suburbs needed an income of about $6,000 [including taxes] to maintain a "modest but adequate" level of living. . . . About 60 per cent of the Puerto Rican families in New York City have four or more persons. How many achieve this $6,000 figure?

Half the Puerto Rican families in New York City had incomes under $3,800 in 1959. The median for nonwhites (99 per cent Negro) in the city was $4,400, $600 greater, while the median for whites was $6,400. Four out of every five Puerto Rican families had incomes under $6,000 in 1959. Keeping in mind the fact that many of these families are quite large and that they pay exorbitant rents for substandard homes, you can begin to appreciate their plight.

Education

Without education the opportunity to rise above the lowest levels is slim indeed. Perhaps because many Puerto Ricans are recent immigrants to this country, their educational attainment is far below that of the whites and even below that of Negroes in New York City. The average Puerto Rican in the city had only 7½ years of schooling as compared with 9½ years for Negroes and nearly 10½ years for whites. One out of every two adult Puerto Ricans in New York City had not gone beyond the seventh grade and nearly three out of every four had no formal education beyond the eighth grade. What chance do people with this little schooling have to make a decent living in a society where one-third of the salesmen and one-fourth of the office clerks have college training? You can see the transmission belt of poverty operating at full steam. The children will suffer because there is generally a very close association between an individual's own educational attainment and his plans to educate his children.

Housing

The poverty of Puerto Rican families in New York City is reflected in the poor quality of their housing. Only 60 per cent of the Puerto Ricans in New York live in sound units, whereas 40 per cent live in units that are either deteriorating or dilapidated. Evidently Puerto Ricans who live in the Bronx have higher economic status than those who live in Manhattan or Brooklyn. This pattern is reminiscent of that followed by the Jewish immigrants to New York in the early part of this century. The first sign of having "arrived" in the new world was a move away from the Lower East Side to the Bronx.

TABLE 7

Puerto Rican Housing Conditions in New York City: 1960

CONDITION OF HOUSING	ALL OF NEW YORK CITY	MAN-HATTAN	BROOKLYN	THE BRONX
Sound	60%	52%	55%	72%
Deteriorating	30	35	33	22
Dilapidated	10	13	13	6

U.S. *Censuses of Population and Housing: 1960*, Census Tract Report for New York City.

The higher economic status of Bronx residents is reflected in the figures on educational attainment and family income. Median years of school completed was about one-half year greater in the Bronx (8.0) than in Manhattan. Moreover, family incomes were also somewhat higher in that borough. One-half of the Puerto Rican families in the Bronx had incomes over $4,100 in 1959. The median in Brooklyn was [about] $300 lower ($3,900) and in Manhattan it was $600 lower ($3,500).

You might think there would be a substantial rent differential for the inferior housing, but that was not the case at all. The average rent paid by all Puerto Rican families in the city was $62 a month. Those living in sound units paid $64. In deteriorating units the average monthly rent was $59 and in dilapidated units it was $56. In each case, this rental amounted to about one-fifth of the annual income received by the average family. However, one Puerto Rican family out of every five in the city paid a third of their income for rent; in a large proportion of the cases it was rent for a substandard unit.

In New York City, Puerto Rican housing is inferior to that of nonwhites. Both are far inferior to that of whites. Indeed, Ne-

groes and Puerto Ricans occupy about one-half of all the dilapidated units in the city even though they account for only about
one-fifth of all households.

Has there been any improvement since 1950 in the economic
status of Puerto Ricans relative to nonwhites (Negroes) in New
York City? The tentative answer is "No."

According to the census results, the Negro has increased his
schooling by one full year on the average, whereas there was a
drop of one-half year in the average years of schooling for
Puerto Ricans (due undoubtedly to the low educational attainment of recent immigrants). In 1950, the average income of
Negro men and women was $100 more than that received by
Puerto Ricans. In 1960, the differential, on a family basis, rose
to $400 in favor of the Negro. Conceivably the figures for Puerto
Ricans are depressed by immigrants who must go through the
process of Americanization.

Were They Better Off in Puerto Rico?

A report issued several years ago by the Bureau of Applied
Social Research at Columbia University argued that the average
Puerto Rican "would prefer living on his island if he were able
to find there the kind of economic opportunity which exists in
New York." It does seem that Puerto Ricans come to New York
primarily because of anticipated economic gain. They leave
their island voluntarily, and in numbers that accelerate when
times are good in the States and jobs are plentiful. To what
extent are their expectations realized?

There are many opinions on the subject, but few objective
answers. Christopher Rand in *The Puerto Ricans* reports: "One
often hears that Puerto Ricans can earn twice as much in New
York as on their island, and that living costs in the two places
differ little except for the items of fuel and warm clothes in the
New York winter." He recognizes this as a probable exaggeration
but concludes that "by and large more can be made in New
York (in good times)—and more can be saved, too, or spent on
TV sets or washing machines." This judgment is not supported
by the census results. The census was taken in Puerto Rico at
the same time as in the States, using roughly the same definitions and procedures. This provides a comparison between

Puerto Ricans living in New York City and those living in San Juan, the largest city on the island.

It turns out that family income is higher in New York by 60 per cent: $3,800 against $2,300 (see Table 8). But rents are also much higher—70 per cent—and the quality of housing is much worse. On this basis it seems unlikely that *real* incomes—money incomes adjusted for differences in the cost of living—actually are higher in New York.

TABLE 8

Puerto Rican Family Incomes: New York City vs. San Juan in 1959

INCOME LEVEL	NEW YORK	SAN JUAN
Under $2,000	16%	43%
Between $2,000 and $4,000	38	28
Between $4,000 and $6,000	27	13
$6,000 and over	20	15
Median income	$3,800	$2,300

U.S. *Census of Population*: 1960, Census Tract Report for New York City; and *Detailed Characteristics, Puerto Rico,* Table 119.

Housing is not only a major item in the cost of living, but also an excellent indicator of levels of living. It also happens to be one of the few items for which objective comparisons can be made between New York and San Juan. Therefore it may prove worthwhile to examine the results carefully. All but a handful of Puerto Ricans living in New York reside in rented units and 40 per cent of these units have one or more major defects. In San Juan, only about half of the families live in rented units and an equal number either own their homes or are in the process of buying them. These homes, incidentally, are not shacks by any means. The great majority of them are in sound condition and contain complete plumbing facilities. Even if home ownership is ignored and only the total picture is examined, it appears that Puerto Ricans in San Juan have better housing than those in New York. About the same proportion in both places live in dilapidated homes; but nearly three-fourths of the San Juan residents live in sound structures as compared with only 60 per cent of the New Yorkers.

The census findings are confirmed by impressions of on-the-
spot observers. Christopher Rand reports: "New stucco or ce-
ment dwellings can be seen everywhere, and public-housing
projects galore can be seen in the towns—San Juan, with its
suburbs, is sometimes called the world's best-endowed city now
in regard to public housing."

TABLE 9
Puerto Rican Housing: New York City vs. San Juan in 1960

CONDITION OF HOUSING	NEW YORK	SAN JUAN			
			OWNER OCCUPIED		
		TOTAL	LAND AND BUILDING	BUILDING ONLY	RENTER OCCUPIED
Number of units	156,000	96,000	29,000	18,000	49,000
Sound	60%	72%	91%	45%	70%
Deteriorating	30	18	7	32	19
Dilapidated	10	10	2	23	11

U.S. Censuses of Population and Housing: 1960, Census Tract Report
for New York City; and *U.S. Census of Housing: 1960, Advance Reports,* Puerto Rico, HC (A2)—53, Table 1.

Those who rent get a better deal in San Juan. The overall
average is $36 per month, against $62 in New York. And San
Juan rents are more responsive to the quality of the housing,
covering a wide range: $48 for sound housing, $26 for deteriorating units, $18 for dilapidated units. In New York, Puerto Ricans
paid high rentals for all grades of housing; the comparable figures
were $64, $59, and $56.

Other costs of living may also be higher in New York. Clothing requirements are undoubtedly greater, and the expense of
establishing a foothold in a new environment must be counted.

These comparisons seem to downgrade the economic explanation for Puerto Rican immigration. There appears to be no great
immediate advantage in moving from San Juan to New York.
The figures don't tell the complete story, however.

Only *average* real income seems to be about the same in both
places. Many families are below the average. These may be the
ones who migrate. To the extent that this is true, New York is

getting selected immigrants—people who could not make the grade in their own home towns.

Another fact to remember is that San Juan has a population of about 600,000 out of nearly 2½ million on the island. About half the people live in rural areas where incomes are very low. A substantial portion of the migrants undoubtedly come from these rural areas. They may move to New York rather than to San Juan because they have only unskilled services to offer and New York may provide a better market for those services.

Thus, while real income levels may be the same, *on the average*, in both places, the income levels among prospective migrants may be substantially worse on the island. To test this theory, much more information—and more comparable information—about conditions in Puerto Rico and New York would be needed.

SPANISH-AMERICANS

Those of us who live on the Eastern Seaboard—and this still includes about one out of every three Americans—know very little about the three and a half million people who are identified by the Census Bureau as "persons with Spanish surname." These people live in the southwestern part of the United States and in 1960 were distributed as follows: Arizona 194,000; California 1,400,000; Colorado 157,000; New Mexico 269,000; and Texas 1,400,000.

Early in the sixteenth century, the Spaniards conquered the territory that is now the American Southwest. The largest and earliest settlements were in New Mexico, but there were also others in California and Texas. This group, sometimes identified as Spanish-American or Hispano, lived in the territory that came under the American flag by the annexation of Texas, the Treaty of Guadalupe Hidalgo, and the Gadsden Purchase. Beginning about 1910, a second major group, consisting of immigrants from Mexico and their children, was added. Direct immigration from other Spanish-speaking countries has been negligible.

Ethnically, the population of Spanish-American and Mexican descent ranges from Indians to those of unmixed Spanish ancestry. Indians and the part-Spanish, part-Indian Mestizos are particularly frequent among the recent immigrant generation, the Mexican-Americans.

Special recognition of the interest in the Spanish-American and Mexican-American population of the United States was first given in the collection and publication of data on "Mexicans" in the 1930 census. These figures were collected largely because of the heavy immigration from Mexico during the twenties. Somewhat related data were collected in the 1940 census. In 1950 and 1960 white persons of Spanish-American and Mexican-American origin were identified on the basis of their Spanish surname. This procedure was limited to the five southwestern states referred to earlier.

Not as Well-off as Whites

Unlike the Puerto Ricans, who have a common origin and are concentrated in New York City, the Spanish-Americans are widely scattered and have diverse backgrounds. Over four-fifths of them are native Americans and more than half have mothers and fathers who are both native American. Thus, to a very large extent, this is an indigenous population rather than recent immigrants.

Unlike other parts of the country, nonwhites in the five southwestern states are not always predominantly Negro. In New Mexico, for example, three-fourths of the nonwhites are Indians, and in Arizona nearly two-thirds are Indians. In Texas, nonwhites are almost entirely Negro; but even in California and Colorado only three-fourths of the nonwhites are Negro. Table 10 has been arranged so that the incomes of Spanish-Americans can be compared separately with whites, Negroes, and other racial groups in each state. The "other" groups are predominantly Chinese and Japanese in California, American Indians in New Mexico and Arizona, and about equal numbers of American Indians and Orientals in Colorado and Texas.

The incomes of Spanish-Americans are far below those of whites in all states. In 1959, they fared poorest in Texas, where their median ($1,500) was only 58 per cent of the white median, and best in California, where they had 79 per cent of the white median. In the other three states their median was about 65 per

TABLE 10

Regional Comparison of Median Incomes in 1959:
White—Nonwhite—Spanish-American

COLOR	ARIZONA	CALI-FORNIA	COLORADO	NEW MEXICO	TEXAS
White	$2,996	$3,583	$2,876	$2,961	$2,632
Negro	1,622	2,528	2,289	1,751	1,167
Other nonwhite	1,034	3,014	2,361	1,378	1,943
Spanish-American	1,944	2,835	1,929	1,912	1,536

U.S. *Census of Population: 1960, Detailed Characteristics,* report for each state, Table 133 and Vol. II, *Persons of Spanish Surname.*

cent of that received by whites. The relationships in 1959 were not much different from those which prevailed ten years earlier. Although the situation was not static, no major changes appear to have taken place. During the fifties there was a slight increase in the income of Spanish-Americans relative to whites in California and Colorado and a slight decrease in Arizona.

Four-fifths of the Spanish-Americans live in California and Texas. Their relative economic position appears to be far better in California than in Texas. What factors account for the difference? Part of it is accounted for by the fact that a larger proportion in California live in urban areas where job opportunities are better and wages are higher. The "typical" Easterner thinks of Spanish-Americans as migrant farm workers. This may have been the case at one time, but it was far from true in 1960. Spanish-Americans in California and Texas are predominantly urbanites—85 per cent in California and 79 per cent in Texas live in urban areas.

Another factor that helps account for the higher incomes in California is the greater opportunity for employment in industry. This is particularly true for women. In California, 61 per cent of the employed Spanish-American women worked in offices or in factories. In Texas, only 38 per cent worked in these kinds of jobs. A much larger proportion of the women in Texas worked in the low-paying service trades. Many of them were domestics. The occupational distribution of the male labor force was much the same in both states; but it is likely that there was less discrimination in pay in California because a large proportion of the work in that state is done under government contract.

The lower incomes of Spanish-Americans in Texas may also be due to their low educational attainment in that state. Table 11 shows that Spanish-Americans were four and a half years behind whites in years of school completed in Texas, but only three years behind in California. Their lack of education in Texas, combined with language difficulties, may have made them ineligible for some of the better paying jobs.

TABLE 11

Regional Comparison of Median Years of Education in 1960:
White—Nonwhite—Spanish-American

COLOR	ARIZONA	CALI-FORNIA	COLORADO	NEW MEXICO	TEXAS
White	11.3	12.0	11.9	11.1	10.7
Nonwhite	7.7	10.8	11.2	7.9	8.7
Spanish-American	8.0	9.0	8.6	8.4	6.2

U.S. *Census of Population: 1960, Detailed Characteristics,* report for each state, Table 103 and Vol. II, *Persons of Spanish Surname.*

Better Off than Nonwhites

Spanish-Americans are poorer than whites. That is a well-known fact. They are also better off than most nonwhites. That is also a fact, but it is not so well known. Spanish-Americans have generally had a very good press in the eastern part of the country. Their plight has been well publicized and considerable sympathy—well deserved—has been engendered. In the process, unfortunately, the impression has been created that their plight is worse than that of Negroes and other minority groups on the West Coast. Lyle Saunders states: "Not all Spanish-speaking are poor, but in general more of them are poor than is true for any other group. . . . While not all Spanish-speaking people live in slums . . . more of them do proportionately than any other population group." These statements were not true in 1949 when they were written, nor are they true today.

What are the facts as revealed in the census? They can be summarized as follows. Although Spanish-Americans are not as well off as whites, they are better off than Negroes (except in Colorado, where both are few in number) and Indians, and nearly as well off as Japanese and Chinese. These relationships not only existed in 1960 but they were also much the same ten years earlier.

In California, the median income of Spanish-Americans ($2,800) was about $300 above the Negro median even though Spanish-Americans were about two years behind in their schooling. In Texas, the other state with a large concentration of Negroes, the Spanish-Americans were $400 ahead of the Negro in median income—a differential of 32 per cent. Here again the economic advantage of the Spanish-American was maintained despite a two-and-a-half-year disadvantage in schooling.

The difference between the incomes of Spanish-Americans and Indians is even greater than that cited above. Despite a doubling in the average income of Indians in Arizona during the fifties, the Spanish-American was still $900 ahead in 1959. In New Mexico the average income of Indians also doubled during the fifties, but the Spanish-American was still $500 ahead in 1959.

Orientals were the only large minority group on the West Coast that had higher incomes than Spanish-Americans. But the difference was not very great. The median for Japanese and Chinese in California was $3,000; for Spanish-Americans it was $2,800.

Quality of Housing

The low economic status of Spanish-Americans and non-whites in the western states is reflected in the poor quality of their housing. Conditions were best in California, which is considered one of the most progressive states with respect to social services. Yet even in this state two out of every ten Spanish-American and nonwhite families were living in homes that were either badly run-down or dilapidated. Only one out of ten whites in the state resided in homes this bad. Conditions were much worse in Texas. There four out of every ten families in these minority groups lived in substandard homes.

Living conditions for Spanish-Americans and nonwhites were somewhat better in Colorado and New Mexico than in Texas; but the housing in Arizona was far worse than in any of the other states shown. Five out of every ten Indian families in this state lived in deteriorating or dilapidated homes. This was over three times the rate shown for white families. The low incomes and poor housing of the Indians in Arizona suggest that the opening sentence of the Meriam Report is as valid in 1960 as it was thirty-five years ago, when it was written: "An overwhelming majority of the Indians are poor, even extremely poor, and they are not adjusted to the economic and social system of the dominant white civilization."

TABLE 12

Regional Comparison of Housing in 1960:
White—Nonwhite—Spanish-American

CONDITION OF HOUSING	ARIZONA	CALI-FORNIA	COLORADO	NEW MEXICO	TEXAS
White					
Sound	86%	91%	87%	87%	83%
Deteriorating	10	7	10	9	12
Dilapidated	4	2	2	4	4
Nonwhite					
Sound	49%	80%	69%	68%	61%
Deteriorating	26	15	27	18	27
Dilapidated	25	5	4	14	12
Spanish-American					
Sound	62%	78%	66%	71%	61%
Deteriorating	24	16	26	18	26
Dilapidated	14	6	8	11	13

U.S. *Census of Population: 1960,* Summary of census tract reports for Standard Metropolitan Statistical Areas for each state.

FOR FURTHER READING

There are a number of classic works that are quite useful in providing an historical background for a study of poverty. These include Robert H. Bremner, *From the Depths* (New York: New York University Press, 1956); Charles Booth, *Life and Labour of the People of London* (London: Macmillan and Co., 1903); Benjamin S. Rowntree, *Poverty: A Study of Town Life* (London: Longmans, 1922); Brian Tierney, *Medieval Poor Law* (Berkeley: University of California Press, 1959); Harold L. Wilensky and Charles N. Lebeaux, *Industrial Society and Social Welfare*, paperback ed. (New York: Free Press, 1965); and Robert Hunter, *Poverty* (New York: Harper Bros., 1904). For some recent studies providing an overall view, the student may wish to consult Gabriel Kolko, *Wealth and Power in America* (New York: Praeger, 1962); Michael Harrington, *The Other America* (New York: Macmillan, 1962); and James N. Morgan *et al.*, *Income and Welfare in the United States* (New York: McGraw-Hill, 1962). As suggested before, the Kolko book should be read with caution. Much of the material on measuring poverty is to be found in publications of the Council of Economic Advisers, in *Monthly Labor Review*, and in the *Social Security Bulletin*. Mollie Orshansky has published her valuable studies in the latter journal. Herman P. Miller's "The Dimensions of Poverty," in Ben B. Seligman, ed., *Poverty as a Public Issue* (New York: Free Press, 1965) is a good introduction. Also useful are Oscar Ornati, *Poverty Amid Affluence* (New York: Twentieth Century Fund, 1966) and Leon Keyserling, *Poverty and Deprivation in the United States* (Washington: Conference on Economic Progress, 1962).

THE SOCIAL

DYNAMICS

OF THE GHETTO

Kenneth B. Clark

Kenneth B. Clark, Professor of Psychology at the City University of New York, worked with Gunnar Myrdal on a study of the Negro in the United States. This study led to the 1944 classic *An American Dilemma*. In 1954, the Supreme Court's school desegregation decision relied heavily on evidence from Dr. Clark concerning the effects of prejudice on children. And, more recently, Dr. Clark was a founder and prime supporter of the New York antipoverty agency HARYOU (Harlem Youth Opportunities Unlimited).

His book *Dark Ghetto*, from which the following selection is taken, has done much to expose the conditions of life in Harlem. Some critics have argued that, as a partisan in the antipoverty war, Dr. Clark exaggerates the situation of the Negro. This is doubtful, and it is also difficult to challenge Dr. Clark's conclusions. *Dark Ghetto* is a factual study of the political, religious,

Source: Kenneth B. Clark, *Dark Ghetto*, pp. 21–62. Copyright © 1965 by Kenneth B. Clark. Reprinted by permission of Harper & Row, Publishers.

and economic leadership of Harlem which grew out of a report Dr. Clark prepared for HARYOU.

The author is not impartial. He writes as a committed person, deeply involved in one of the most critical issues of the time. He believes that the style of life in Harlem reveals a pathological condition. He has serious questions about our traditional methods of dealing with social problems—for these methods only perpetuate the pathology. And once and for all, Dr. Clark disposes of the notion that the Negro poor are responsible for their situation. In this he performs a notable service.

White America is basically a middle-class society; the middle class sets the mores and the manners to which the upper class must, when it wishes influence, seek to conform, at least in appearances, and which the lower class struggles to attain or defensively rejects. But dark America, of the rural and of the urban Negro, has been automatically assigned to be a lower-class society; the lower class sets the mores and manners to which, if the Negro upper class wishes influence, it must appeal; and from which the Negro middle class struggles to escape. As long as this chasm between white and dark America is allowed to exist, racial tensions and conflict, hatred and fear will spread. The poor are always alienated from normal society, and when the poor are Negro, as they increasingly are in American cities, a double trauma exists—rejection on the basis of class and race is a danger to the stability of society as a whole. Even though Negroes are a minority in America—approximately one-tenth of the population—a minority that is sick with despair can poison the wellsprings from which the majority, too, must drink. The social dynamics of the dark ghettos can be seen as the restless thrust of a lower-class group to rise into the middle class.

The problem of the American Negro, once predominantly Southern, has gradually over the past few decades become predominantly a Northern problem. Millions of Negroes have come North seeking escape from the miasma of the South, where poverty and oppression kept the Negro in an inferior caste.

Three out of every four Negroes live in cities; approximately one of two lives in Northern cities. A million and a half left the South in the years 1950–1960, the largest number heading for California, New York, Illinois, and Michigan. Of the Negroes who live in the North, 95 per cent now live in cities (in 1890 it was 65 per cent).

There are Negro residential areas in such Southern cities as Atlanta, Birmingham, and New Orleans, but the Negro ghetto in America is essentially a Northern urban invention. There are racially mixed residential areas in a number of Southern cities, few in Northern cities. Although the South often criticizes the North for its urban segregation and explains its own comparatively mixed residential patterns as illustrative of a more intimate and more tolerant relationship to the Negro, the fact is that in the South mixed neighborhoods are permitted only so long as Negroes are not seen as a threat. In Charleston, South Carolina, for example, racial residential patterns reflect slavery days, and whites and Negroes tend to live in the same area as they did before Emancipation. Negro servants can come into any area and live in white homes without a lifted eyebrow. Racial problems have not been problems of racial contact—despite the implications of those who refuse to join Negroes at a college dormitory table or to use a common washroom in a factory. It is not the sitting next to a Negro at a table or washing at the next basin that is repulsive to a white, *but the fact that this implies equal status.* Historically, the most intimate relationships have been approved between Negro and white so long as status of white superiority versus Negro inferiority has been clear. Trouble comes only when Negroes decide not to be servants or mistresses and seek a status equal to that of whites. When Negroes start to assume symbols of upward mobility, then a pattern of residential segregation develops in the South, too. In Little Rock and Pine Bluff, Arkansas, and Atlanta, Georgia, to illustrate, as the status of Negroes improved, housing segregation increased. The South is today becoming more "Northern" in its discriminatory pattern. As its economic level rises, it will steadily become more and more like the North. Then urban ghettos will be created, and the Negro will be forced to deal with a different kind of rejection. Part of the

TABLE 1

Residential Concentration of Negroes

CITY	TRACTS WITH 90 PER CENT + NEGRO POPULATION	IN CITY	IN TRACTS 90 PER CENT + NEGRO	PERCENTAGE IN TRACTS 90 PER CENT + NEGRO
Chicago, Ill.	122	812,637	533,214	65.6
Baltimore, Md.	31	325,589	184,992	56.8
Cleveland, Ohio	27	250,818	134,142	53.5
Washington, D.C.	29	411,737	200,380	48.7
St. Louis, Mo.	10	214,377	94,041	43.9
Houston, Texas	8	215,037	87,222	40.6
Philadelphia, Penn.	27	529,240	207,627	39.2
New Orleans, La.	17	233,514	85,968	36.8
New York, N.Y.	71	1,087,931	362,370	33.3
Detroit, Mich.	45	482,223	140,546	29.1
Los Angeles, Calif.	19	334,916	68,715	20.5

Source: U.S. Census of Population: 1960. The data presented in Tables 1 through 3 were prepared by James A. Jones, research director of Haryou.

social dynamics of the ghetto is the tension between those Negroes who wish to resist and eventually to destroy the ghetto and those whites who seek to maintain and strengthen it.

Eleven metropolitan areas have Negro communities of between 200,000 and one million: New York, Chicago, Los Angeles, Detroit, Philadelphia, Washington, D.C., St. Louis, Baltimore, Cleveland, Houston and New Orleans. (See Tables 1, 2, 2A, 3.) In Washington, D.C., Negroes are in the majority; in Philadelphia, one in four persons is Negro. In the half century between 1910 and 1960 when the nation's Negro population doubled, New York City's Negro population multiplied ten times over.[1] Now the largest concentration of Negroes in an urban ghetto area is in Chicago; the largest number of Negroes lives in New York; and the largest percentage of Negroes (of total population) is in Washington, D.C.

In every one of these cities, Negroes are compelled to live in concentrated ghettos where there must be a continuous struggle to prevent decadence from winning over the remaining islands of middle-class society. A possible exception to this picture of creeping blight seems to be the Bay Area of San Francisco, Berkeley, and Oakland, where the Negro residential areas do not stand out from the other middle-class areas; the usual signs of congestion, deterioration, dirt, ugliness are not yet present there. In all of these ghettos whites had lived before and, as Negroes came, gradually moved away. The origin of Harlem—symbol of Negro ghettos everywhere—is, in many ways, typical of the blight that has already affected almost all.

In the early years of the century an upper-class community of luxury, Harlem by World War I became a moderately populated area of middle-class Jews, Italians, Irish, Germans, and Finns and then, during the twenties and thirties, was transformed into one of the largest and most densely populated Negro communities in the country.

The Negro came to Harlem, as all migrants do, seeking better living conditions and expanded economic opportunities. Harlem became the center of Negro culture and talent. It is here

---

[1] E. Franklin Frazier noted in *Condition of Negroes in American Cities*, that when the first federal census was taken, Negroes constituted 13.1 per cent of the New York City population and 5.7 per cent of Philadelphia's.

TABLE 2
Cities with 200,000 or More Negroes

CITY	TOTAL POPULATION	TOTAL	NEGROES MALES	FEMALES	PER CENT NEGRO
New York, N.Y.	7,781,984	1,087,931	498,167	589,764	%14.0
Chicago, Ill.	3,550,404	812,637	387,718	424,919	22.9
Philadelphia, Penn.	2,002,512	529,240	250,256	278,984	26.4
Detroit, Mich.	1,670,144	482,223	232,829	249,394	28.9
Washington, D.C.	763,956	411,737	196,257	215,480	53.9
Los Angeles, Calif.	2,479,015	334,916	160,118	174,798	13.5
Baltimore, Md.	939,024	325,589	157,130	168,459	34.7
Cleveland, Ohio	876,050	250,818	120,873	129,945	28.6
New Orleans, La.	627,525	233,514	110,096	123,418	37.2
Houston, Texas	938,219	215,037	103,471	111,566	22.9
St. Louis, Mo.	750,026	214,377	100,159	114,218	28.6
A Sampling of Other Cities					
Pittsburgh, Penn.	604,332	100,692	48,670	52,022	%16.7
Kansas City, Mo.	475,539	83,146	39,723	43,423	17.5
Boston, Mass.	697,197	63,165	30,081	33,084	9.1
Rochester, N.Y.	318,611	23,586	11,491	12,095	7.4
Minneapolis, Minn.	482,872	11,785	5,792	5,993	2.4

that most Negro artists and intellectuals lived, drawing their ideas and inspiration from the life of the community. But the Negro in Harlem found himself increasingly isolated culturally, socially, and economically by a wall of racial prejudice and discrimination. He was blocked from the training necessary to prepare himself for the highly skilled jobs in private industry or government, and he was pushed into the most menial occupations. His housing and schools deteriorated, and he was forced to pay more for less. He discovered that his new neighbors resented his presence, his aspirations, and his talents. They left in droves, and Harlem became a prison of its new residents. During the thirties Harlem seethed with discontent and racial strife, gaining an exaggerated reputation as a center of vice and crime. White persons ventured into the community only in search of exotic primitive glamour. Today, Harlem, no longer the mecca

TABLE 2A

Cities with 200,000 or More Negroes in Terms of Percentages of Negroes

CITY	PER CENT NEGRO
Washington, D.C.	%53.9
New Orleans, La.	37.2
Baltimore, Md.	34.7
Detroit, Mich.	28.9
Cleveland, Ohio	28.6
St. Louis, Mo.	28.6
Philadelphia, Penn.	26.4
Chicago, Ill.	22.9
Houston, Texas	22.9
New York, N.Y.	14.0
Los Angeles, Calif.	13.5
Sample Cities in Terms of Percentage of Negroes	
Kansas City, Mo.	%17.5
Pittsburgh, Penn.	16.7
Boston, Mass.	9.1
Rochester, N.Y.	7.4
Minneapolis, Minn.	2.4

Source: U.S. Census of Population: 1960.

TABLE 3

Negro Residential Concentration by Areas of Cities

CITY AND AREA	POPULATION	NEGROES	PER CENT
New York, N.Y.			
Brooklyn ghetto	91,391	87,654	%95.9
Queens ghetto	20,324	19,091	93.9
Manhattan ghetto	241,125	236,051	97.9
Los Angeles, Calif.			
Area I	48,806	46,865	96.0
Area II	15,489	14,990	96.8
Baltimore, Md.			
Area I	149,197	143,849	96.4
Washington, D.C.			
Area I	120,060	115,552	96.2
Area II	66,043	64,196	97.2
Cleveland, Ohio			
Area I	70,060	68,700	98.1
Area II	49,815	46,863	94.1
St. Louis, Missouri			
Area I	97,144	93,807	96.6
New Orleans, Louisiana			
Area I	45,111	44,044	97.6
Chicago, Illinois			
Area I	347,806	340,599	97.9
Area II	105,307	102,096	97.0
Area III	21,133	20,401	96.5
Area IV	22,168	21,347	96.3

Source: U.S. Census of Population: 1960.

for white bohemia, is a center both of trouble and potential talent, the fountainhead of Negro protest movements. Despite the apathy and despair of many of its residents, it is a vibrant, exciting and, all too frequently, a turbulent community.[2]

In most important ways—social and economic structure, community culture, quality of education, and the like—all urban

[2] The name "Harlem," as used in this book, refers to that section of Manhattan sometimes referred to as Central Harlem, and excluding Spanish Harlem. Its boundaries are: 110th Street on the south; Third Avenue on the east; Harlem River, northeast; the parks bordering St. Nicholas, Morningside, and Manhattan avenues on the west.

ghettos in America are similar. As one Negro told a Haryou interviewer: "I don't limit the black man to Harlem alone. Harlem is only one of the accidents in time that have beset the
children along the way. Problem of the black man is universal,
the world over."

Economic and Social Decay

The symptoms of lower-class society afflict the dark ghettos of
America—low aspiration, poor education, family instability, illegitimacy, unemployment, crime, drug addiction and alcoholism,
frequent illness and early death. But because Negroes begin
with the primary affliction of inferior racial status, the burdens
of despair and hatred are more pervasive. Even initiative usually
goes unrewarded as relatively few Negroes succeed in moving
beyond menial jobs, and those who do find racial discrimination everywhere they go.

The most concrete fact of the ghetto is its physical ugliness—
the dirt, the filth, the neglect. In many stores walls are unpainted, windows are unwashed, service is poor, supplies are
meager. The parks are seedy with lack of care. The streets are
crowded with the people and refuse. In all of Harlem there is no
museum, no art gallery, no art school, no sustained "little the-
ater" group; despite the stereotype of the Negro as artist, there
are only five libraries—but hundreds of bars, hundreds of
churches, and scores of fortune tellers. Everywhere there are
signs of fantasy, decay, abandonment, and defeat. The only constant characteristic is a sense of inadequacy. People seem to
have given up in the little things that are so often the symbol of
the larger things.

The dark ghetto is not a viable community. It cannot support
its people; most have to leave it for their daily jobs. Its businesses
are geared toward the satisfaction of personal needs and are
marginal to the economy of the city as a whole. The ghetto
feeds upon itself; it does not produce goods or contribute to the
prosperity of the city. It has few large businesses. Most of the
businesses are small, with what that implies in terms of degree
of stability. Even the more substantial-appearing businesses (e.g.,

real estate and insurance companies) are, by and large, marginal. Of 1,617 Harlem businesses listed in the yellow pages of Manhattan's telephone directory, 27 per cent are barber shops, beauty shops, or cleaning establishments—all devoted to tidying up, a constantly renewable service. Thirty-five per cent are involved in the consumption of food and drink (bakeries, caterers, grocery stores, liquor stores, luncheonettes, restaurants, bars, and taverns). In general, a ghetto does not produce goods of lasting worth. Its products are used up and replaced like the unproductive lives of so many of its people. There are 93 funeral homes in Harlem.

Even though the white community has tried to keep the Negro confined in ghetto pockets, the white businessman has not stayed out of the ghetto. A ghetto, too, offers opportunities for profit, and in a competitive society profit is to be made where it can.

In Harlem there is only one large department store and that is owned by whites. Negroes own a savings and loan association; and one Negro-owned bank has recently been organized. The other banks are branches of white-owned downtown banks. Property—apartment houses, stores, businesses, bars, concessions, and theaters—are for the most part owned by persons who live outside the community and take their profits home. Even the numbers racket, a vital and indestructible part of Harlem's economy, is controlled by whites. Here is unproductive profit-making at its most virulent, using the Negro's flight from despair into the persistent dream of quick and easy money as the means to take from him what little money he has.

When tumult arose in ghetto streets in the summer of 1964, most of the stores broken into and looted belonged to white men. Many of these owners responded to the destruction with bewilderment and anger, for they felt that they had been serving a community that needed them. They did not realize that the residents were not grateful for this service but bitter, as natives often feel toward the functionaries of a colonial power who, in the very act of service, keep the hated structure of oppression intact. Typical of this feeling are the following views expressed to Haryou investigators in 1962 and 1963. None who heard their

contempt, their anti-Semitic overtones, would have been surprised at the looting of 1964—rarely does a social revolt occur
without decades of advance warning.

That Jew, he's got a wagon out here, and he will send his son
through college, you understand? Nothing but a wagon, selling to
these people in this junky neighborhood right here, and he's got a
house in the Bronx, and he's paying for it, and the child is going to
college, and he's selling you stringbeans at fifteen cents a pound.

—Man, age 27

Another thing I am sick and tired of, I am sick and tired of all these
Jew business places in Harlem. Why don't more colored business
places open? This is our part of town. They don't live here but they
got all the business and everything.

—Woman, age 38

Negroes have left business in the ghettos to whites not from
a dislike of business but for a complex of other reasons. In those
Southern cities like Birmingham, Atlanta, and Memphis, where
the pattern of segregation is so complete that the dark ghettos
must be almost self-sufficient, there are a number of Negro-
owned stores, restaurants, and banks. But, in the North, the
Negro is allowed to involve himself partially in the total city,
and whites are willing to open businesses within the ghetto,
sensing a profit among the tenements. The white power structure has collaborated in the economic serfdom of Negroes by
its reluctance to give loans and insurance to Negro business.
Eugene P. Foley, administrator of the Small Business Administration, told a meeting called in August 1964 to encourage
economic investment among minorities that, before its field
office opened in Philadelphia in that year, "I am ashamed to
admit that my agency had made seven loans to Negroes in ten
years." The situation has somewhat improved since then; in the
six months after the field office opened fifty-five loans were
granted and sixteen new businesses opened; new field offices
were organized, also, in Harlem and in Washington, D.C.
    There are insufficient economic resources within the ghetto
to support its future development. Therefore any economic
growth—as in fact is true of suburbs—must be supported and
developed from without. But unlike the suburbs, where residents

have high income and good credit, the ghetto has inadequate resources to command the attraction of economic power outside and cannot lure capital into its limits. Most ghetto residents are permitted only menial jobs and marginal income. The suburbs drain the economy of the city—through subsidized transportation, housing development, and the like. The economy of the ghetto is itself drained and is not replenished.

Housing Decay

Another important aspect of the social dynamics of the Northern urban ghettos is the fact that all are crowded and poor; Harlem houses 232,792 people within its three and one half square miles, a valley between Morningside and Washington Heights and the Harlem River. There are more than 100 people per acre. Ninety per cent of the 87,369 residential buildings are more than thirty-three years old, and nearly half were built before 1900. Private developers have not thought Harlem a good investment: Few of the newer buildings were sponsored by private money, and almost all of those buildings erected since 1929 are post-World War II public housing developments, where a fifth of the population lives.

The condition of all but the newest buildings is poor. Eleven per cent are classified as dilapidated by the 1960 census; that is, they do "not provide safe and adequate shelter," and thirty-three per cent are deteriorating (i.e., "need more repair than would be provided in the course of regular maintenance"). There are more people in fewer rooms than elsewhere in the city. Yet the rents and profits from Harlem are often high, as many landlords deliberately crowd more people into buildings in slum areas, knowing that the poor have few alternatives. The rent per room is often higher in Harlem than for better-equipped buildings downtown. Slum landlords, ready enough when the rent is due, are hard to find when repairs are demanded. Even the city cannot seem to find some of them, and when they go to trial for neglect, they are usually given modest and lenient sentences—compared to the sentences of Harlem teen-agers who defy the law. Cruel in the extreme is the landlord who, like the store owner who charges Negroes more for shoddy merchandise, exploits the powerlessness of the poor. For the poor are not only poor but unprotected and do not know how to seek redress. One is reminded of the Biblical admonition: "For whosoever hath, to him shall be given, and he shall have more abundance: but whosoever hath not, from him shall be taken away even that he hath."

The effects of unsafe, deteriorating, and overcrowded housing upon physical health are well documented and understood.[3] The multiple use of toilet and water facilities, inadequate heating and ventilation, and crowded sleeping quarters increase the rate of acute respiratory infections and infectious childhood diseases. Poor facilities for the storage of food and inadequate washing facilities cause enteritis and skin and digestive disease. Crowded, poorly equipped kitchens, poor electrical connections, and badly lighted and unstable stairs increase the rate of home accidents and fires. Nor is the street any safer. Harlem's fourteen parks, playgrounds, and recreational areas are inadequate and ugly, and many of the children play in the streets where heavy truck traffic flows through the community all day. Far more children and young adults are killed by cars in Harlem than in the rest of the city (6.9 per 100,000 population compared to 4.2 per 100,000 for New York City as a whole).

The physical health of the residents of the ghetto is as impaired as one would expect based on knowledge of its housing conditions. The best single index of a community's general health is reputed to be its infant mortality rate. For Harlem this rate in 1961 was 45.2 per 1,000 live births compared to 25.7 for New York City. For Cleveland's Hough area the infant deaths are also about double that of the rest of the city. Poor housing

[3] Among others, see D. M. Wilner, R. P. Walkley, and M. Tayback, "How Does the Quality of Housing Affect Health and Family Adjustment?" *American Journal of Public Health*, June 1956, pp. 736–744; "Report of the Subcommittee on Housing of the Committee on Public Health Relations," *Bulletin of the New York Academy of Medicine*, June 1954; M. Allen Pond, "The Influence of Housing on Health," *Marriage and Family Living*, May 1957, pp. 154–159; Alvin L. Schorr, *Slums and Social Insecurity*, Social Security Administration, Division of Research and Statistics, no date; D. M. Wilner, R. P. Walkley, T. Pinkerton, and M. Tayback, *The Housing Environment and Family Life: A Longitudinal Study of the Effects of Housing on Morbidity and Mental Health*, Baltimore, John Hopkins Press, 1962.

conditions, malnutrition, and inadequate health care are undoubtedly responsible; where flies and maggots breed, where the
plumbing is stopped up and not repaired, where rats bite help-
less infants, the conditions of life are brutal and inhuman. All
are symptoms of the underlying fact of poverty. Perhaps even
more extraordinary than the high rate of disease and death is the
fact that so many human beings do survive.

The effect of housing upon the social and psychological well
being of its occupants is much discussed but less well documented. The most careful of the few relevant studies (those by
Wilner, Walkley, Pinkerton and Tayback) on the psychological
effects of poor housing have produced findings less dramatic
than one would expect. The link between housing and mental
health is not clearly established, but residents of public housing
do have higher morale and greater pride in their neighborhoods
than those who live in slums, and they are more likely to say
that they have improved their lot in life and are "rising in the
world." Nevertheless, their pride is generally not followed by
genuine aspiration. They often express hope, but it usually is,
alas, a pseudohope unaccompanied by an actual struggle to win
better jobs, to get their children into college, to buy homes.
Real hope is based on expectations of success; theirs seems
rather a forlorn dream. Wilner and Walkley point out that "for
all the housing improvement, many other circumstances that
would be expected to affect the way of life [of these families]
remained substantially the same. These were still families at
the lowest end of the economic scale; practical family situations
remained materially unimproved; in one-third of the families
there was no husband present; and one-third were on public
welfare."[4] Housing alone does not lead to sound psychological
adjustment, for to build new housing or to spruce up the old is
not to abolish the multiple pathology of the slums. Still, at the
very least, good housing improves health, lifts morale, and
thereby helps to generate a restless eagerness for change, if not
in the adult generation then in their children; a fact, incidentally, that might give pause to some of those in society who

[4] Daniel M. Wilner and Rosabelle Price Walkley, "Effects of Housing
on Health and Performance," in *The Urban Condition*, L. J. Duhl, editor,
New York, Basic Books, 1963, p. 224.

support aid to public housing believing it will decrease the demands of Negroes. It will, in fact, stimulate them to further demands, spurred by hope for a further identification with middle-class society. Housing is no abstract social and political problem, but an extension of a man's personality. If the Negro has to identify with a rat-infested tenement, his sense of personal inadequacy and inferiority, already aggravated by job discrimination and other forms of humiliation, is reinforced by the physical reality around him. If his home is clean and decent and even in some way beautiful, his sense of self is stronger. A house is a concrete symbol of what the person is worth.

In Harlem, a Haryou interviewer had a conversation with a little girl about her home that revealed both the apathy and the hope of the ghetto:

INTERVIEWER: Tell me something about you—where you were born, you know, where you grew up, how everything went for you?

GWEN D: When I was born I lived on 118th Street. There was a man killed in the hallway, and a man died right in front of the door where I lived at. My mother moved after that man got killed.

I liked it in 97th Street because it was integration in that block. All kinds of people lived there.

INTERVIEWER: Spanish people? White people?

GWEN D: Spanish people, Italian people, all kinds of people. I liked it because it wasn't one group of whites and one group of Negroes or Spanish or something like that; everybody who lived in that block were friends.

INTERVIEWER: How come you moved?

GWEN D: Well, my mother she didn't like the building too well.

INTERVIEWER: What didn't she like about it?

GWEN D: Well, it was falling down!

INTERVIEWER: In your whole life, has anything happened to you that you really got excited about?

GWEN D: I can't remember.

INTERVIEWER: Tell me about some real good times you've had
               in your life.

GWEN D: In Harlem?

INTERVIEWER: In your life, that you've really enjoyed.

GWEN D: One year we was in summer school, and we went
               to this other school way downtown, out of Har-
               lem, to give a show, and everybody was so happy.
               And we were on television, and I saw myself,
               and I was the only one there with a clean skirt
               and blouse.

INTERVIEWER: And you really got excited about that. Anything
               else ever happen to you that you had a really
               good time?

GWEN D: No.

INTERVIEWER: What kind of changes would you want to make?
               Changes so that you can have a better chance,
               your sisters can have a better chance and your
               brother?

GWEN D: Well, I just want a chance to do what I can.

The Dynamics of Under-Employment

The roots of the pathology of ghetto communities lie in the
menial, low-income jobs held by most ghetto residents. If the
occupational level of the community could be raised, one would
expect a corresponding decrease in social pathology, in dependency, disease, and crime.

With the growth of the civil rights movement, Negroes have
won many footholds earlier forbidden to them, and it would
seem logical to conclude, as many do, that Negroes are better off
than ever before in this gradually desegregating and generally
affluent society. But the fact is that in many ways the Negro's
situation is deteriorating. The Negro has been left out of the
swelling prosperity and social progress of the nation as a whole.
He is in danger of becoming a permanent economic proletariat.

About one out of every seven or eight adults in Harlem is unemployed. In the city as a whole the rate of unemployment is half that. Harlem is a young community, compared to the rest of New York, and in 1960 twice as many young Negro men in the labor force, as compared to their white counterparts, were without jobs. For the girls, the gap was even greater—nearly two and one-half times the unemployment rate for white girls in the labor force. Across the country the picture is very much the same. Unemployment of Negroes is rising much faster than unemployment of whites. Among young men eighteen to twenty-four, the national rate is five times as high for Negroes as for whites.

An optimist could point to the fact that the average family income of Negroes has increased significantly within the two decades 1940–1960, but a more realistic observer would have to qualify this with the fact that the *discrepancy* between the average family income of whites and that of Negroes has increased even more significantly. The real income, the relative status income, of Negroes has gone down during a period when the race was supposed to have been making what candidates for elective office call, "the most dramatic progress of any oppressed group at any period of human history."

The menial and unrewarding jobs available to most Negroes can only mean a marginal subsistence for most ghetto families. The median income in Harlem is $3,480 compared to $5,103 for residents of New York City—a similar gap exists in the country as a whole. Half the families in Harlem have incomes under $4,000, while 75 per cent of all New York City residents earn more than $4,000. Only one in twenty-five Negro families has an income above $10,000, while more than four in twenty-five of the white families do.

Nor do Negroes with an education receive the financial benefits available to whites. Herman P. Miller in his book, *Rich Man, Poor Man*,[5] states that Negroes who have completed four years of college *"can expect to earn only as much in a lifetime as whites who have not gone beyond the eighth grade."* This is true both in the North and in the South. The white high school graduate will earn just about as much as a Negro who has gone

[5] New York, Thomas Y. Crowell Co., 1964.

through college and beyond for graduate training. One young man in Harlem asked: "What is integration into poverty?" The question is not easy to answer.

Both the men and the women in the ghetto are relegated to the lowest status jobs. Sixty-four per cent of the men in Harlem compared to only 38 per cent of New York City's male population, and 74 per cent of the women, compared to 37 per cent for New York City, hold unskilled and service jobs. Only 7 per cent of Harlem males are professionals, technicians, managers, proprietors, or officials. Twenty-four per cent of the males in the city hold such prestige posts.

An eighteen-year-old Negro boy protested: "They keep telling us about job opportunities, this job opportunity, and that, but who wants a job working all week and bringing home a sweat man's pay?" Most of the men in the dark ghetto do work for a "sweat man's pay," and even *that* is now threatened by the rise of automation.

Many of the jobs now held by Negroes in the unskilled occupations are dead-end jobs, due to disappear during the next decade. Decreases, or no expansions, are expected in industries in which more than 43 per cent of the labor force in Harlem is now employed (i.e., transportation, manufacturing, communication and utilities, and wholesale and retail trades). Employment in those industries and occupations requiring considerable education and training is expected to increase. As the pressure of unemployed white workers in the few expanding areas of unskilled jobs grows, the ability of ghetto residents to hold on to such jobs becomes doubtful. And by 1970 there will be 40 per cent more Negro teen-agers (16–21) in Harlem than there were in 1960. The restless brooding young men without jobs who cluster in the bars in the winter and on stoops and corners in the summer are the stuff out of which riots are made. The solution to riots is not better police protection (or even the claims of police brutality) or pleas from civil rights leaders for law and order. The solution lies in finding jobs for the unemployed and in raising the social and economic status of the entire community. Otherwise the "long hot summers" will come every year.

By far the greatest growth in employment in New York City is expected in professional, technical, and similar occupations—

some 75,000 to 80,000 jobs by the end of the present decade.[6] Of the 3 per cent of Harlem residents in this group, the major portion are in the lower-paying professions: clergymen, teachers, musicians, and social welfare and recreation workers. A substantial increase of 40 per cent in the number of managers, officials, and proprietors is expected in business and government, but the Negro has made few advances here. This will be offset by declines expected in retail business, where the trend toward bigness will result in fewer small store proprietors, another prophecy with grim implications for Negroes since the only business where Negro ownership exists in number is small stores. The number of clerical positions is due to grow in New York by 35,000 to 40,000 jobs. Approximately 14 per cent of the residents of Harlem have such jobs, but most of them are in the lower-paying positions. Electronic data-processing systems will soon replace many clerks in routine and repetitive jobs, such as sorting, filing, and the operation of small machines—the kind of jobs Negroes have—while workers in jobs requiring contact with the public, such as claim clerks, complaints clerks, and bill collectors—usually white—will be least affected by office automation. The number of sales workers will decline as self-service increases, and here too, Negroes who have been successfully employed will lose out.

Jobs for skilled workers are due to grow in New York State by 28,000 yearly. Building trades craftsmen will be particularly in demand. But the restrictions to apprenticeship training programs in the building trades industry have kept Negroes from these jobs. Semiskilled and unskilled jobs (excluding service workers) will decrease by 70,000 to 80,000 jobs between 1960 and 1970. Thirty-eight per cent of the Negro male workers living in Harlem have such jobs now. If present employment patterns persist, Negro and white workers who might ordinarily qualify for semiskilled jobs will undoubtedly be pushed into the unskilled labor force or become unemployed in the face of increasing competition with those who are better trained. Negro unemployment will rise as the unskilled labor supply exceeds the demand.

[6] *Manpower Outlook 1960–1970*, New York City Department of Labor, 1962, pp. 1 and 12, provides the projections that pertain to job expectations.

The only jobs that will increase, and in which Negroes now dominate, are jobs as servants, waitresses, cooks—the traditional service jobs which have added to the Negro's sense of inferiority. But as the requirements for skilled jobs grow stiffer and as semi-skilled jobs decline, Negroes will face strong competition from whites to hold even these marginal jobs.

It is illegal in New York to deny a job to anyone on the basis of skin color, but it is common practice anyway. First, Negro applicants are often said to lack the qualifications necessary for a particular job. Who can prove this to be disguised racial discrimination? Like any charge with some truth, the extent of the truth is hard to determine. Second, often working against the Negro applicant, though sometimes in his favor, are ethnic quotas applied to certain types of jobs, employed with the conscious intent of maintaining an "ethnic balance" in the work force. When the quota is filled, the Negro applicant, no matter how well qualified, is told that there are no openings. Third, and much more subtle, although no less discriminatory, is the practice employed by some unions of requiring that a member of the union vouch for an applicant. When the union has no Negro members, the possibility of finding someone to vouch for a Negro applicant is extremely remote.

Through historical processes certain ethnic or religious minority groups come to predominate in certain kinds of jobs: in New York, the waterfront for the Italians, the police force for the Irish, the school system for the Jews, and the personal services for Negroes.[7]

A study by the Bureau of Social Science Research, Inc., showed a fourth technique of exclusion; that employers tend to label some jobs, usually the lowest, as "Negro jobs"—Negroes are hired by many firms, but at "Negro jobs," with menial status, minimum wages, and little if any security.

Furthermore, many Negroes are discouraged before they begin. Guidance counselors often in the past advised Negro students not to prepare for jobs where employment opportunities for Negroes were limited. Doubtless they believed they did so

[7] A similar conception has been formulated by Eli Ginsberg in A Policy for Skilled Manpower, New York, Columbia University Press for the National Manpower Council, 1954, especially p. 249.

in the best interests of the youth—better not to encourage him
to pursue a career which is likely to end in bitter frustration and
unemployment. There is some evidence that this form of root
discrimination is now being reduced under persistent pressure
from groups like the Urban League and the National Scholar-
ship Service and Fund for Negro Students. The plethora of
ineffective antidiscrimination and equal opportunities legislation—contrasted with the clear evidence of actual exclusion—
leads one to suspect that this type of discrimination works in
such a way as to be relatively immune to laws. It would appear
that effective techniques for reducing discrimination in employment must, therefore, be as specific, subtle, and as pervasive as
the evil they seek to overcome.

It has been charged over and over again that Negro youth lack
motivation to succeed. To the extent that this is true, it is largely
a consequence of ghetto psychology. Teen-age boys often help to
support their families, and they have neither the time nor money
nor encouragement to train for a white-collar job or skilled craft.
Negroes often dread to try for jobs where Negroes have never
worked before. Fear of the unknown is not peculiar to one racial
group, and Negroes have had traumatic experiences in seeking
employment. The Negro youth is caught in a vicious cycle: Poor
preparation means poor jobs and low socio-economic status. Low
status and poor jobs result in poor preparation for the next
generation to come.

A comprehensive employment program for the youth of dark
ghettos everywhere must be geared toward revamping the various
systems which feed upon one another. It must upgrade the educational system which spawns functional illiterates and which
helps perpetuate personnel practices which exclude Negro
youth. Even if a personnel officer is free of racial prejudice, the
majority of Negro applicants can be rejected for jobs which
require basic educational skills. Inferior schools, which discriminate against the masses of Negroes, have made Fair Employment Practices regulations virtually irrelevant. A crash program
of rehabilitation with specific skill training is imperative. So,
too, is a systematic procedure to inform ghetto youth about the
occupations for which they might qualify. A realistic and comprehensive occupational training and employment program

would include a counseling service not only to develop motivation and self-respect but also to help young people with concrete problems related to getting and keeping a job—many do not know how to apply for a job, how to speak to an employer, how to fill in an application blank. Many must learn the importance of promptness, appropriate dress and speech, and to modify habits that had been appropriate in the menial jobs to which Negroes had been relegated in the past. They must learn to appear and to behave like other middle-class applicants with whom they will be required to compete.

The Haryou proposal[8] to the City of New York included such a many-pronged attack. Over a three-year period, 7,000 Harlem youths, ages 16 through 21, were to receive job training. In on-the-job training the youth was to be paid the standard wage of the job for which he was being trained, with the employer and the project sharing the cost. As he improved, the employer would assume more of the salary costs. Also part of the Haryou plan was to establish a special counseling and guidance program for high school dropouts, for those who could be encouraged to re-enter high school. Those who chose not to return to school were to be referred to training programs appropriate to their specific needs and interests. High school graduates with marketable work skills were to be referred for employment through the program placement services. Graduates in need of further training would get it.

The young people associated with Haryou during its planning stage (the Haryou Associates) pointed out that Negro youth in Harlem did not have the opportunity to learn how to manage even a small business or store since, unlike other lower-middle-class groups in the city, their parents did not own stores. They believed that this was a major handicap and suggested the organization of a Harlem Youth Enterprises, Unlimited, which would sponsor a cluster of local business enterprises owned by youth so as to provide them with on-the-job training opportunities.

For those who have been so severely damaged that they are

---

[8] See author's introduction and *Youth in the Ghetto, A Study of the Consequences of Powerlessness and a Blueprint for Change*, Harlem Youth Opportunities Unlimited, Inc., New York, 1964.

not at present able to profit from organized job training and not able to benefit from the small-business management program, Haryou proposed to recruit in the poolrooms and other hangouts for a Community Service Corps, designed to perform various needed community services at whatever level of competence these young people had. The corps would try to raise their level of competence so that they would eventually be able to move into a more demanding job training program. Since each corps trainee would get enough money to meet his normal living needs, it might turn out that in a time of severe job scarcity, young people would "make a career" of job training. The alternative—larger welfare rolls, more jails, bigger police force to constrain hordes of desperate, jobless young people—is clearly more expensive. But the emphasis in all these programs would not be on "make-work" jobs designed to provide pocket money or to keep youths out of trouble during the stormy adolescent years. Rather, they would concentrate on providing young people with salable skills and insure a boost to the socio-economic status of ghetto residents of all America's urban ghettos, crucial if the pathology rooted in social and economic inferiority is to be remedied. One man expressed to a Haryou interviewer the view of many in the dark ghettos of America:

Most of all, I am trying to impress on them that the people are not chaining themselves to posts, that demonstrations are not being held, that people are not exposing themselves to dogs and tear gas so they can go on being delivery boys forever.

And another said with wistfulness:

If you go down and say well, man, I want a job, and showed that you really want to work and were given a job, then that's hope.

The main hope, however, may be that stated by Gunnar Myrdal in his book, *Challenge to Affluence*.[9]

. . . at this juncture of history there is a striking convergence between the American ideals of liberty and equality of opportunity on the one hand, and of economic progress on the other. Indeed, the chief policy means of spurring economic progress will have to be huge reforms that are in the interests of social justice.

[9] New York, Pantheon Books, 1963.

White Unions, Black Proletariat

America does not like to admit—seldom does admit—that it is divided by social and economic classes. This fantasy has persisted in large measure because of the presence of Negroes, without whom low-income and low-status whites would see they themselves have been relegated to the lower rungs of the ladder; and that for many the ladder is not a ladder at all: The presence of the Negro obscures the facts.

The white worker has felt much less a proletariat psychologically than his counterpart in Europe because of the existence of a black proletariat in subjugated status beneath him. From a psychological point of view it was correct that he should. Whites will have to risk their own status if Negroes are to be admitted into the world of work as peers, and the white worker has understood this instinctively. The white worker is vulnerable because he has only the reality of his wish to give some security to his assumed status. When the Negro starts moving he threatens almost total collapse of white status and of the white worker's world. This is a matter of bread and butter and self-respect to the white worker. Unlike so many who have opposed the Negro —in the churches and elsewhere—the worker is really vulnerable. He feels his own job is at stake, that his family's future is endangered, that in an automated society there will be fewer jobs for the white man as well as the black. He has no time for a stereotyped liberal response in behalf of civil rights.

Racism has been one of the persistently debilitating facts in the American labor movement. After Eugene Debs, the American labor movement was never really a solid force, a movement in which the total rights and concerns of all workingmen were protected. The American Federation of Labor's position was one of no direct involvement in politics and one of apology when it did hesitatingly enter the political arena. It refused to become a significant part or core of any labor party. The Congress of Industrial Organizations was more politically active but also uninterested in a labor party. After the initial stages the labor movement organized itself in terms of respectable nonproletarian models. As it grew strong it took on the appearance and manner of management, with large salaries, palatial offices, and privileges and prerogatives for leadership competing with the luxury symbols of management. The American labor movement is basically a vehicle by which the workingman seeks to realize his aspirations to be a boss. It is a ringing refutation of the Marxian premise of categorical cleavages between economic classes. It is inextricably bound up in the American dream of success, of upward mobility. Unions are seen as escalators to management, not just as the protector of the workingclass. The presence of Negroes on the American scene has given some objective support to this belief, for whites have moved up—in large measure —by excluding Negroes from the competition, from the unions, and hence from the better-paying jobs.

In the highest levels of labor unions, the status of Negroes is weak and almost invisible. In New York City no Negro holds a position of primary power in organized labor. Negroes have been effectively segregated in American labor, much as in American churches, with their "own" unions, such as the railroad Brotherhood of Sleeping Car Porters, for workers in jobs almost exclusively reserved for Negroes. Where Negroes are singled out as labor representatives, they hold these posts at the pleasure of white leadership. Even in unions where most workers are Negro or Puerto Rican, the actual top leadership is predominantly white and often seems responsive more to the wishes of management than to the people they allegedly serve.

A significant example of the powerlessness of the Negro worker in a major trade union with a "liberal" reputation is found in the status of Negroes in the International Ladies' Garment Workers Union in New York City. The ILGWU is unique in many respects. The ILGWU is probably the most decisive force in the ladies' garment industry in New York City because it rationalized and stabilized industry practices and established union control over a scattered multiplicity of small, highly competitive shops. Both employers and the workers regard the union as the major power in the industry.

The ILGWU and its leaders are important politically in New York City and state through their pivotal position in the Liberal party and the role of the Liberal party in city and state democratic politics. The ILGWU is generally considered to be a major liberal social and political force. This liberal image, however justified in other respects, does not extend to the protection of the economic status of Negro and Puerto Rican workers in the garment industry. Although there are thousands of Negroes employed in garment manufacturing in New York City, they are concentrated, with few exceptions, in the low wage, unskilled classifications and with very little job mobility. For example, Negroes are concentrated in such categories as "push boys" and shipping clerks in what amounts to a segregated ILGWU "auxiliary unit" known as 60–A and which operates under the control of the predominantly white Pressers Local 60.

Herbert Hill, National Labor Secretary of the National Association for the Advancement of Colored People, in testifying before a subcommittee of the House Committee on Education and Labor on August 17, 1962, referred to 60–A as the "Jim Crow auxiliary of local 60" and stated that:

The racial practices of the ILGWU are seen most clearly in relationships to the Cutters and Pressers locals. Local 60, the Pressers local, controls jobs within its jurisdiction that on an hourly rated basis are the highest paying jobs in the entire garment industry in New York City. The average wage being almost $5.00 an hour. Local 60 has an all-white membership. On the other hand, there is 60-A which is simply an appendage to Local 60 and which has a membership which is almost entirely Negro and Puerto Rican. The members of 60-A are shipping clerks, push boys and delivery men. These workers earn in the vicinity of $50.00 per week. Yet, 60-A with twice the membership of Local 60 has never been chartered by the International as a separate local and the manager of 60, who is a presser, functions also as the manager of 60-A. One must ask, why should a local of shipping clerks and push boys, whose members are paid extremely low wages, be attached as an auxiliary unit to the pressers local whose members make the highest wages in the garment industry?

Hill has charged that:

—there is not a single Negro who is an officer of the international union;
—there is not a single Negro on the twenty-three member General Executive Board;[10]
—there is not a single Negro or Puerto Rican vice president of the union;

[10] Until recently, there was not a Puerto Rican on the Board. In March 1964, however, as a result of exposure and pressure, a Puerto Rican was appointed to the ILGWU General Executive Board.

—there are no Negro or Puerto Rican local managers;
—only 11 per cent of the unionized garment workers in New York earn enough to maintain a "modest but adequate" standard of living;
—the wages of workers in the New York City ladies' garment industry have declined relative to the total manufacturing average.

None of these charges was denied or refuted by the top leadership or spokesmen of the ILGWU.

Daniel Bell, sociologist of Columbia University, said in an article in the *New Leader* (January 21, 1963):

. . . The fact is—and this is the "bite" in Hill's charges—that the Negroes are underrepresented in the leadership of many of the unions where they form a significant proportion of the membership. In the case of these unions, what the Negroes want is "recognition" at the level of top leadership and a growing share of the spoils of office. . . . For one thing, the realistic political process in the United States, at least in the northern urban centers, has been one of ethnic groups advancing themselves precisely in this fashion; by organizing on bloc lines, electing their own kind, and using the patronage system to enhance the wealth and status of their group. . . .

Bell concludes:

. . . In economic and educational opportunity, the Negro is in a position of inequality, and the government is bound to help him move ahead. But doesn't the trade union movement have a *special* obligation to help redress the balance . . . ?

The predicament of Negroes and Puerto Ricans in the ILGWU reflects the powerlessness of their general educational, economic, political, and social status. Earlier immigrants have used labor unions, public schools, and the control of political organizations as ladders of economic and social mobility. As they became successful through the use of these institutions and instruments of power, they tended to assume leadership positions and dominate them. As the numbers of Negroes and Puerto Ricans increased in the city as a whole to a "significant proportion" of the voting strength and union membership, older ethnic groups who had already consolidated their educational, economic, and political power are reluctant to share this with Negroes and Puerto Ricans. As the sheer weight of numbers of these new minorities increases, older minorities are required to set up institutional, bureaucratic, or even moral and ideological blocks to the fulfillment of the demands of Negroes and Puerto Ricans for a share in the spoils and patronage power. Within the conflict between the past and the present lie the seeds for serious social problems and tensions of the future.[11]

There are a few indications that labor unions are beginning to re-examine the role of Negroes. A. Philip Randolph, one of the AFL–CIO vice presidents, has played a crucial part in bringing the problem to the attention of labor leadership. So, too, the pressures of Hill, labor secretary of the NAACP, have been effective. The early resistance of George Meany seems to be giving way to recognition of the fact that inclusion of Negroes in the labor movement will, in fact, not be a threat but will strengthen it. If this is a new positive development in American labor it matches the recognition by leaders of business and industry that exclusion of Negroes from full participation in the economy saps the strength of the economy, artificially restricts the skilled labor supply, and thereby grants to labor unions control over that supply. The cooperation of management in the President's Committee on Equal Employment in opening job opportunities for Negroes is based on the knowledge that as one provides better jobs for Negroes one increases the number of consumers, one expands the domestic markets and the national productivity and the general level of prosperity. Labor, too, will be strengthened because as long as Negroes are kept out of labor unions they remain a vast reservoir of cheap labor which, in effect, is more of a threat to the workingman than Negro competition could be within the union. Bringing Negroes in will make the unions morally and pragmatically more powerful.

If labor unions do not fully let down the barriers of apprenticeship and membership to Negroes on an open and free competitive basis, management and ownership will have to bring pressure to bear. If management transforms its own policies, compensating for past injustice by more active hiring of Negroes

[11] For a documentation of the status of nonwhite workers in the ladies' garment industry in New York City and in the ILGWU see Herbert Hill, Testimony Before the House Committee on Education and Labor, 88th Congress, 1st Sess. 1569–72 (Jan. 31, 1963 Congressional Record House pp. 1496–1499); see also Hill, *The ILGWU, Fact and Fiction*, New Politics, Winter, 1963, pp. 7–27.

at higher status levels, the labor unions themselves will heed the demands of social change. But if Negroes gain at the expense of whites, racial hostility will increase and force a regression. It is incumbent upon economic power to supply jobs for all who need and wish them. The consumer potential of the urban Negro is, in this effort, an untapped resource. The American economic society is vigorous and can respond imaginatively to threats against its own security and the stability of society itself.

The resistance of labor to automation can be tolerated up to a point, but when the economic imperatives are clear, neither management nor labor can hold the clock back in automation and in civil rights. The total economy is threatened by the decay of the heart of American cities, long the creative centers of industry, transportation, communication, and education, and by the dangers of Negro unemployment, and Negro concentration in low-status menial service jobs. No longer can the potential consuming power of one-tenth of the American people be ignored, and the power of consumption be artificially limited by the low wages of Negroes and the heavy load of Negro welfare dependency, a product of broken families caused in turn in large part by male unemployment.

The Cycle of Family Instability

One of the inevitable results of the unemployment and menial job status of urban Negroes is family instability. Family breakdown occurs among the white poor, too, but inferior racial status that makes escape seem impossible and damages the core of personality adds impetus to the problem. Once again, the Negro poor are forced to be different. As the Haryou report indicated, approximately one out of every five men in Harlem is separated from his wife, and about two out of every seven women are separated from their husbands. In the city as a whole, only one in thirty men is separated from his wife, and approximately one in sixteen women from her husband. Only about half of the children under eighteen in the Harlem community are living with both parents, compared with 83 per cent in New York City as a whole. The child without a secure family life is often forced either into aggression and delinquency or into apathy and despair. As one mother said to a Haryou interviewer:

When you see an obedient child, he will come home when you tell him to be home in an hour or two. But when he comes home, the mother has the door locked and the father is gone someplace half drunk. The child can't come home like he wants to. Maybe the child wants to say something to his parents, but his parents are not home. He has no one to talk to but perhaps an older brother. When the parents are not home, the children are lost. Perhaps he's hurt. He wants to come home and talk to either his father or mother, but they are out. He can't even get in the house to use the lavatory, so they do what they have to do in the halls.

Children and young people who grow up in a community in which a large proportion of families have no father in the home, a community in which 40 per cent of the men and 47 per cent of the women aged 14 or over are unmarried,[12] find it difficult, if not almost impossible, to know what an "adequate" family is like. The cycle of family instability continues uninterrupted.

Broken families and poverty also usually mean reliance upon public assistance. In 1961, 226.5 per 1,000 Harlem youth under eighteen years of age—nearly one in four—were supported, in part, by aid-to-dependent-children (ADC) funds, three times as many as in the city as a whole (72 per 1,000). In that same year in Cleveland's Hough area, three times as many families received General Assistance and about four times as many received ADC help as for the city as a whole. Similar trends could doubtless be discovered in the other urban ghettos.

Therefore, the Negro's despair at his racial rejection is reinforced by the knowledge that he is often a heavy financial burden to himself and to the community. Fear of the poor, in turn, reinforces the white's prejudice against the Negro. Many white people have come to fear the "influx" of Negroes, from the South into Northern cities and from the large urban ghettos into smaller cities and suburbs, as a threat of social and economic dimension—the threat of higher taxes to care for the

[12] This statistic for Harlem is roughly the same proportion of unattached adults as obtains for the city as a whole, but in New York, especially Manhattan, a large number of single young people congregate at the start of their careers and a large number of elderly persons find living convenient —conditions not true of Harlem.

dependent, lowered property values, and the like. Few look at the causes of the vicious cycle, which lie in the white community —the low-paying menial jobs unskilled Negroes are compelled to take; the chronic rising Negro unemployment rate, the poor education of Negro children; the compulsive bargain selling of property, encouraged by "block-busters," i.e., unscrupulous real estate agents (Negro as well as white); and many other factors.

The white society which has to deal with massive social problems of poverty and despair tends to rely on the temporary expedients of counseling and emergency help rather than on direct social change. The poor, and especially the Negro poor, often seem ungrateful and resist what help is offered.

The poor, thought of as being ignorant, illiterate, and unimaginative, have developed a variety of ways of coping with the welfare worker; evasion is frequent as recipients become "welfare wise."

And so we have a typical situation of a great deal of police and control efforts on one side and a considerable amount of matching efforts at evasion on the other. The stalemate that is reached is one where frequently there is repugnance on the part of the authorities and a lack of respect on the part of the recipients.[13]

One family service agency director observed that the energy of "multiproblem" families of the lower socio-economic class seems directed almost entirely to giving social workers the "run-around." She felt the explanation lay in the fact that such persons are not "geared to talking," and do not know how to "make good use" of social agencies.

A young man who has, for months, sought work in vain would be expected to be pleased by the offer of a decent job or training in a desired skill. But the alienation of the Negro poor is such that the "hustler" or "bop" or unwed ADC mother, the members of the "deviant subculture," often respond with an attitude of "include me out," which reflects the cynical desire to "cash in" on a less demanding mode of adjustment. In the ghetto to "cash in" means to earn a livelihood for imaginary services, or for an outright disservice, and it means that one must establish a mutually exploitative relation with others—one must have a "hustle." "Cashing in" and the "hustle" reflect the belief that one cannot make a living through socially acceptable vocations

[13] S. M. Miller, *Poverty, Race and Politics,* Syracuse University Youth Development Center, 1963.

in a complex and rejecting racist society. "Cashing in" tends to be seen as the way the world is.

Agencies that encourage their clients to accept dependency or to accept transparent "make-work" contribute to the perpetuation of the pathology of the ghetto communities. It is reasonable to assume that people who have not already been severely damaged want wholesome work. When the client cannot find such work, the professional cannot have wholesome work of his own either. This necessarily leads to a mutually protective estrangement of client and worker, to the "flight from the client" illustrated by the exodus of most of the family service agencies out of Harlem. It may also increase the contempt of the "client" for all who claim to be willing to help him.

For social service and social agencies to be relevant to the pressing problems of the ghetto, those who are in control of this part of our society must have the courage to re-examine ruthlessly their present assumptions, methods, and programs and prune those postures and pretenses which reflect only traditional and bureaucratic lags or fund-raising gimmicks. To be relevant, social service agencies must above all accept and respect the humanity of those in need of help—and express this acceptance and respect through courtesy and the warmth, cleanliness, and beauty of the physical surroundings in which the help is offered. Social service cannot be relevant to the pathology of the ghetto, except to reinforce it, if it encourages even subtly the dependency of the people of the ghetto—because to encourage dependency is to rob the individual of the sense of his own dignity and to strengthen his feelings of inferiority. Relevant and human social services must dare to run the risks of being a part of a real and comprehensive program of social action and social change.

Realistic Intervention

The Haryou program was based upon the above rationale and the finding that piecemeal, isolated, and peripheral social agency programs neither helped individuals nor stemmed the tide of ghetto pathology.

To build a new culture designed to enable the ghetto to service itself would cost far less in the long run than the present list of human casualties. The ghetto needs to replace hostility and alienation with a creative, constructive culture.

Who are the most effective workers in such programs? As catalysts in this enterprise, Haryou found during its planning explorations that it could make use of artists and ex-delinquents as well as trained social workers. The advisability of recruiting large numbers of professionally trained social workers and teachers has been seriously questioned. Often it appears that professional training itself enhances the "flight from the client." Furthermore, large numbers of trained personnel are not available. The best recruits for these jobs may be residents of the community themselves who stand to benefit not only financially but also by gaining status, self-esteem and the new satisfaction of "meaningful" work. With such workers there is less of a possibility, also, that the communication barrier will be a factor, since they are literally part of the world of their clients. They will probably be more willing to endure the long hours which some of the programs require, since they have not developed a working tradition which shies away from sustained relationship with clients, from week-end and night work. They have not yet developed professional ennui.

Many of the ghetto's working mothers who now work outside the community, taking care of other people's children, could be paid instead to work within their own community as aides in preschool academies. Other potential recruits would be young mothers who have recently left school, many of whom are just beginning the aid-to-dependent-children treadmill to apathy. This plan seems more economical than the family-by-family casework approach, particularly in view of the tragic fact that many ghetto parents may be "too far gone" to be reclaimed as a wholesome influence in the lives of their children. For those persons in the community who are not yet too far gone, but who lack the personal and social skills for sound influence over their children, training may serve as a substitute for "treatment." It may be that many lower-class persons who now refuse the role of client will accept the same therapeutic help if it is offered in a course of training as part of a position as paid or volunteer trainee.

It may also prove more feasible to train sensitive lower-class persons in the necessary skills to overcome the demoralizing impact of cultural shock in middle-class workers. Most social workers and teachers are themselves middle class, some far enough removed in time and circumstance to cause an inevitable sense of strangeness between themselves and the client; others too close themselves in time and circumstance to accept without anxiety the reminders of a rejected past. The problems are not merely ones of psychological alienation between the two groups but more concrete ones of speaking different languages and responding to different standards of behavior.

In training schools and community centers in which deviant peer group codes dominate, the would-be influentials, the professionals, are often stymied by a communication barrier. The point cannot be overstressed that in Harlem, and probably elsewhere, there are people in the helping services, probation and parole officers, group workers, caseworkers, and others in presumably influential roles who have abandoned any meaningful attempt to help the people who are in need. When they show any insight into this fact, these professionals almost always explain it by pointing to some lack or deficiency in the clients whom they cannot reach or cannot help. These clients are commonly called "unreachables" or those "hard to reach." Whatever the label, it means that the professionals have abandoned hope.

Yet many of these new recruits may later decide to complete their education and qualify for professional training, and it would be one of the risks of a program of encouraging such endeavor that the workers would quickly become middle class themselves.

The problem of class and race alienation is more difficult to solve than to understand. Bureaucratic organization is such that promotion and status are related to moving up the ladder to administration, and administration in social work, in education, as in many other professions, means supervising the work of other staff personnel. It is ironic that the further "up" one goes, the further one moves from the persons for whose service the profession exists—the client in the social casework agency, the child in the classroom. Yet this movement up the ladder to status, title, and higher pay is hard to resist. Perhaps it would be important for all administrators of programs dealing with human beings to keep in touch by some degree of direct involvement—the supervisor keeping a few clients, the school principal teaching an occasional class. Yet this, too, may be impractical, for the stance of authority upon which administrative success depends is itself related to a certain distance between the "top" and "bottom" levels in the hierarchy. In any event, one must be conscious of the danger of the flight from the client and insure that personal advancement does not rest on escape from the essential service.

To insure that the ghetto gets its share of social and community services, a large group of citizens of the ghetto, both youth and adult, who are disciplined and politically sensitive, would need to be organized. Otherwise, these vast and wide-ranging programs of reform would only amount to a benevolence from outside the community, vulnerable to control and abuse, and tending to encourage further dependency.

Given a community climate of indifference and apathy, even simple services like those of the Department of Sanitation will not be efficiently performed, as Harlem's many dirty streets make obvious. That the Department of Sanitation neglects to clean Harlem's streets as frequently as it cleans the streets in other communities may be seen as a simple sin of omission. On the other hand, genuine exploitation may be at work in such neglect as when building inspectors fail to inspect, or accept bribes from landlords to overlook violations. The ghetto community fails to get necessary public services and yet, through taxation, it is also involved in subsidizing its own deterioration.

The Haryou Associates Leadership Training Workshop in the summer of 1963 combined a paid job in social service with an unpaid training period in community action projects that helped to teach Harlem youth how to insist upon and get public services their taxes had already paid for. Unfortunately, these workers often lose the very qualities for which they were recruited from the community once they are placed on the payroll and brought into contact with professional colleagues whose style they sought to imitate.

Local neighborhood boards of adults and youth who live or

work in the neighborhood could help change the patterns of community immobility and impotence by defining problems and by accepting responsibility for evaluating public and private services to the community. Such neighborhood boards would have powers of patronage from the outset—recruiting staff, providing service—but if they are to become a potent voice in the local neighborhood, patronage is not enough. They must have imagination and daring, and they must assume the risk of demanding real social change.

It may well turn out that a major role in insuring that the local boards do not begin to "play it safe" could be assumed by an organization run by the youth themselves. Since young people have less to lose by a radical stance and have fewer vested interests in "the system" than most adults, hopefully they could lend the clear and fresh vision, enthusiasm, and courage of youth to the adult members of the local boards and the adult staff alongside whom they would work.

Without such grass-roots activity in the neighborhoods, no comprehensive program, no matter how imaginative, will be safe from bureaucratic dry rot and exploitation. Neighbor would be responsible for neighbor. Individuals would come to have confidence in their ability to assess conflict, incompetence, and stagnation, and their right to do so. If the youth and adults of a neighborhood cannot be brought into the actual operation of reform programs, the programs themselves, no matter how elaborately and thoroughly planned, will merely contribute to the proliferation of irrelevance.

"The resentment of the weak," writes Eric Hoffer in *The Ordeal of Change*,[14] "does not spring from any injustice done to them, but from the sense of their inadequacy and impotence. Our healing gift to the weak is the capacity for self-help. We must learn to impart to them the technical, social and political skills which would enable them to get bread, human dignity, freedom and strength by their own efforts."

There is harnessable power to effect profound social change in the generally repressed rage of the alienated. There is much energy and imagination in the deviant subcultural forms in

[14] New York, Harper & Row, 1963.

which this rage presently finds expression. Initially operating as close to the marginal world as is possible, a successful program of social rehabilitation must help the poor and the delinquent rehabilitate others like themselves and, in the process, effect their own salvation. This is one of the hopes for the ghetto. But if it is to work, the people of the ghetto must be respected and must learn to respect themselves through evidence of actual success in attempts at improving their condition. They cannot have this opportunity without serious risks and the many forms of turbulence inevitably associated with genuine social change.

Black Social Mobility

In response to white society's criticism of Negro family instability and the patterns of poverty, many middle-class Negroes have tended to accept the judgment of many whites that they are responsible for their own troubles, that economic dependency is related directly to immorality. As one Negro woman put it:

Whenever a woman has a child of course she will do anything to provide for it, even to accepting welfare, but family breakdown and the moral state that we find ourselves in as a people has accounted for this development of the welfare programs.

Now we could develop ourselves morally, perhaps, and this can only come about through an economic development. If we had some of the better things in life, that is, if we had the necessary leisure to develop ourselves intellectually, or if we had enough money to provide for ourselves and enjoy life, and to be happy, then the family would become stronger, and the moral development of the people would increase, and these welfare programs would be done away with.

The middle-class prisoners of the ghetto are ashamed of these elements in the community which bring disgrace to that community. They view themselves as an example of respectability and are viewed by others in the same way. After the summer revolts of 1964, it was they who called for counter-rallies of religious commitment to show the world "the other Harlem." They often preach that if the lower class would work hard and clean up their homes and not litter their streets and show more interest in their children, the Negro predicament would be solved.

One such rather influential woman leader, in a talk to a Negro church in Harlem, urged Negro women to organize for community reform. On every block in Harlem, she said, a committee should be rallied to buy brooms; squads of women and children would be recruited to sweep the streets. She argued that people who live on dirty streets could not hope to gain the respect of others. Negro children, she said, should be taught to respect cleanliness and this would in turn give them pride in their parents and in themselves.

She did not understand that it is not the job of the people to sweep the streets; it is the job of the Department of Sanitation. It had not occurred to her to advise these women to organize to gain these services to which they were entitled. In a middle-class neighborhood, the people see to it that government does provide services. To lecture the miserable inhabitants of the ghetto to sweep their own streets is to urge them to accept the fact that the government is not expected to serve them. But to force the government to provide sanitation and care is an effort beyond their capacity for, in such ghettos, people are so defeated that their sense of powerlessness becomes a reality. They are immobilized against action even in their own behalf.

Most disturbing of the implications of her advice was that Negroes are responsible for their own condition, that dirt reflects defects in the inhabitants. She was buying the position of many middle-class whites that social victims are responsible for their plight. She was in error, but even more important was the fact that she was, in effect, presenting an apology for oppression.

Ghetto residents, particularly members of the middle class, are often obsessed with what they feel to be a lack of initiative and moral fiber on the part of other Negroes. In a ghetto each member identifies, to some degree, with the other, and feels shame at the other's plight as though a member of the family had gone wrong. Often he resents the troublesome lower-class Negro, and then responds to this dislike by a pervasive sense of guilt—particularly when he finds there is no escape, after all. Although in the days of extensive European immigration, the second generation often felt guilt at its wish to escape the language and habits of their parents' "old country," a white person who moves into the middle class or upper class today can afford to forget his origins; he no longer needs to identify with those he has left behind. But in a society where wealth, aristocratic bearing, and talent are insufficient to overcome the stigma of the color of one's skin, there is no such escape for any generation. While this sense of relatedness may have its points, it also imposes a heavy psychological burden upon people whose own lives are hard enough to bear without the additional shame they feel the white community asks them to feel for their neighbors. Shame and despair, unlike anger, seldom lead to effective social or personal reform.

There are few middle-class sections in the central urban ghetto of Harlem. One of them is the Riverton Development and its residents are proud of the fact that it is an oasis in the slums in an area that was once one of the worst slum neighborhoods in the city. The middle-class Negro points with pride to the fact that the grounds are well kept, that the halls are scrupulously clean, that the elevators are in working order. Neighbor vies with neighbor in Riverton for the most luxuriously furnished apartment. As a consequence, James Baldwin's article in *Esquire* about Riverton outraged most of Harlem's middle-class residents.[15] Actually Riverton is not a slum, but James Baldwin was right that in an important sense it *is*. It is a spiritual slum, a paradoxical symbol of the phenomenon it seeks to deny, a symbol of Jim Crow. Riverton exists because at one time the Metropolitan Life Insurance Company's policy excluded Negroes from Stuyvesant Town on Manhattan's East Side, containing them in the ghetto. Today there are only a token number of Negroes in Stuyvesant Town, and there are no white families in Riverton. Thus, residents of Riverton are as much prisoners of the ghetto as their neighbors in rat-infested tenements across the street or in the low-income public housing on the other side. Their very attempt to exist in isolated defiance inevitably involves them in the total system of the ghetto. They constantly fight the slum but can never be victorious. The ghetto is all-encompassing, a psychological as well as a physical reality. It consumes all its residents.

Yet the struggle of the middle-class Negro against the ghetto

[15] "Fifth Avenue Uptown," *Esquire*, 1960, Vol. 54, p. 70.

cannot be cynically dismissed. It is from this group of upwardly mobile Negroes that outstanding Negroes come. These are the young people who are stimulated by the desire and determination for personal success in spite of or because of the handicaps of rejected racial status. If they succeed, many whites nod approvingly: "I said so all along; American racial oppression is not unbearable; it can be overcome." The masses of lower-class Negroes regard this movement up the ladder with mixed feelings, both proud and resentful of the success of "one of their own."

Such middle-class Negro youth spend a considerable amount of their human energy seeking to mold their lives in rigid conformity to the prevailing middle-class values and standards. They are clean, they dress well, they speak well, they strive very hard to make good grades in school and to get a good education. They dedicate their lives to the task of becoming walking refutations of negative racial stereotypes. They are the opposite of the flamboyantly rebellious ghetto youth, more likely to withdraw passively and seek to repress any sign of hostility. Many express a subtle form of self and group hatred by denying awareness of any racial problems, or even by interpreting racial discrimination as an understandable response to the uncouth "lower-class" street Negro.

One poignant example was reflected in the response of a Negro undergraduate at Columbia College. An interview in the college magazine described and quoted him, as follows:

A sophomore who was raised in Harlem, Henry graduated third in his class of 400 ("beaten by two girls, as you might suspect") from Benjamin Franklin High School, which is 90 per cent Negro and Puerto Rican. His parents migrated from South Carolina; his father is a power press operator. Although his high school had no football team, he is out for the lightweight football squad. He lives in a single room in John Jay. Henry shuns demonstrative protests, preferring to participate in such projects as SEER, a Columbia College-initiated national program to help prepare Negro students for college during the summers. He likes social studies, but is toying with the idea of becoming a physician.

"Most people in Harlem, and, I suspect, other Negroes, feel very discouraged and are full of resentment against whites—too much so,

I think. Negroes have to stop feeling so sorry for themselves and start trying to help themselves. Harlem could actually be a nice place to live. My parents have taught me not to expect to have things handed to me, but to work hard and get what I wanted. My teachers have encouraged me in the same way. But maybe if I had different parents and teachers I would feel trapped and bitter too. I really like Columbia, but I sometimes wish it had a lake."[16]

As adults they embark on the competitive cycle of conspicuous consumption and seek to share the good life of American middle-class suburbia. Some struggle to break through into non-segregated communities in order to escape the ghetto, prepared to run the risks of overt hostility or even of violence. Others accept the easier escape to one of the middle-class suburban Negro ghettos. On the surface, the ghetto population in New York—unlike that in other cities—seems to be declining. (Harlem's population has decreased by 27,000 between 1950 and 1960, roughly a 10 per cent loss despite the high birth rate.) But the fact is that Harlem's Negroes are merely shifting to other ghetto pockets in the city—Brooklyn's Bedford-Stuyvesant, the Lower Bronx, or Queens, or to suburban ghettos, such as those in Englewood, New Rochelle, Mount Vernon, and elsewhere. Many of those who move away from the central city are young couples—another drain on the ghetto's sources of energy and leadership.

Middle-class Negroes do not generally react with the overt, active hostility prevalent in many members of the "working class," but they, too, are often hostile, in ways similar to the larger pattern of white middle-class competitiveness, yet complicated by the persistent problems of racial anxiety, hypersensitivity, and defensiveness.

Negroes who do not succeed in reaching the point of real competition with whites and who are rewarded with high-status jobs do not find that they have thereby resolved the problem of being Negro in a white society. Negroes brought into high-status jobs must be significantly above the norm, but feel they must adopt a style of compensatory gentility, allowing the whites to feel less threatened and even causing many to assume a protec-

[16] Negroes and the College. *Columbia College Today.* New York: Columbia College, Columbia University, Vol. 12, No. 1, Fall 1964, p. 32.

tive role toward them. Negroes who do take this precautionary step must be certain that it is appropriate to the nature of the job itself, for a "show Negro" cannot afford to play, in an executive management job, a comic or subservient role. He needs an air of authority or he will lose status. If he adopts a stance or role of subtle deference, he will also be successful in protecting himself by assuaging the fears of whites. He must be constantly careful not to make his white colleagues uncomfortable, either by apparent arrogance or inappropriate obsequiousness.

Other Negroes in status jobs choose to protect themselves by keeping a careful distance between themselves and others, by neither asking for nor granting favors, by remaining aloof so that no one can be effectively patronizing. This pattern of over-compensation often leads to great productivity and intense concentration on the job. Less time and energy are available for socializing with others. Both closeness and acceptance are feared. Cliques are avoided as risky involvement. Friendship—with its danger of rejection—is not sought. When solicitousness is offered, it is regarded with disdain. The reputation sought is one of remoteness, single-minded dedication to the job, unremitting self-respect. If the Negro seems also to be cold and to lack concern for persons, he will accept this as evidence that his stance of invulnerability is effective. Colleagues are expected to be sophisticated enough not to intrude beyond the limits the Negro has set. If one sets the boundaries oneself, excluding others, one cannot oneself be excluded.

These protective devices to which high-status Negroes often resort are evidence of the depth of damage which racism has done. Such defenses must be seen for what they are—a response to fear of rejection and the anticipation of pain.

The middle-class Negro is demanding the right to share in the status symbols of personal success—quality education for his children; white-collar, managerial, or executive jobs; a fine home in one of the better neighborhoods. Having accepted the same value system which the middle-class whites live by, middle-class Negroes are forced to compete with them even at the risk of conflict. The demand for nonsegregated public schools comes largely from upwardly mobile middle-class Negroes; the demands for better white-collar, managerial, and executive jobs

and for better nonsegregated housing come from the more successful and stable middle-class Negroes. If whites respond without mere grudging tokenism—"We already have a Negro in our
firm (in our block) (in our school) (in our church)"—the
masses of workingclass and lower middle-class Negroes will
benefit. Other Negroes, too, will come to believe that the average Negro can win rewards through persistence, hard work,
thrift, and character.

The competitive demands of the growing Negro middle class,
if successful, would open more doors for all Negroes. A Negro in
a managerial or executive position tends, also, to reduce the
novelty of a Negro foreman or Negro salesman. A Negro professor might increase the employment chances for Negro secretaries on a college payroll. The tendency of white Americans to
lump all Negroes together could lead ironically to major social
advances, as Negroes in high-status jobs prepare the way for
gradual acceptance of all Negroes. Still, whites who otherwise
generalize about Negro racial traits ("All Negroes look alike to
me") are often inconsistent when confronted with a Negro in a
high-status post, viewing him as an exception to the rule.

To leave the heart of the ghetto is the goal of the average
young educated Negro. The retreat of young professional Negro
men and women—doctors, nurses, lawyers, engineers, teachers—
from the central ghetto to the opening suburbs imposes a burden of decay of leadership upon the central city; yet the psychological stability of these families often seems to depend upon
just such flight. The reminders of the ghetto, however, are never
far away, for as Negroes—educated, clean, dignified, self-respect-
ing families, the elite of Negro society—come to a formerly
white community where whites had earlier retreated, white
families often flee before them as though they were carriers of a
dread disease. The only contagion they carry is freedom, but
what could be more dangerous than freedom to those who themselves live insecure, unhappy lives bound to frequently abhorred
routines of family duty, unfulfilling job, and status-seeking? The
insecure try to enhance their own personal status by denying
others the very security and status they seek for themselves.

This flight of the middle-class white to suburban, presently
all-white, communities is a temporary stopgap only, unrealistic

in view of the constant pressure of middle-class minority group members to escape the ghetto's deterioration and distress. Suburban communities can only be temporary havens for whites who desire racial homogeneity. The pressure for open occupancy in the suburbs will increase in the next decade with rising momentum. The pressure for integrated suburban schools will follow, as the struggle to abolish *de facto* school segregation in Orange, Englewood, and Teaneck, New Jersey, and in New Rochelle, White Plains, Manhasset, and Malverne, in New York, already demonstrate. It would indeed be a pathetic repetition of social, economic, and political folly if whites respond by techniques of exclusion that "worked" in the past, by developing suburban ghettos. But such a routine, unimaginative, and fearful response is all too likely—people tend to follow familiar patterns of behavior unless interrupted. An immediate systematic plan is needed to introduce minority group members into the suburbs without, at the same time, building new suburban ghetto substitutes. Such a plan could "interrupt" accustomed patterns of response to anxiety and break the cycle.

But though many middle-class residents of the ghetto do have a constant wish for physical and psychological escape, the ghetto has a devouring quality and to leave provokes a curious struggle. In an important sense no one can ever leave. Those who do not try feel that those who *do* try should have some feeling of guilt and a sense of betrayal. They demand allegiance to the pathology of the ghetto. The ghetto develops the sinister power to perpetuate its own pathology, to demand conformity to its norms; it ridicules, drives out, or isolates those who seek to resist those norms or even to transform them. This is an almost irresistible social Gresham's Law that none is allowed to escape with impunity.

That Negroes continue to seek to imitate the patterns of middle-class whites is a compliment, not the threat it may seem, but a compliment in large part undeserved, and the scars inflicted upon Negroes who are constantly confronted by the flight of those they encounter are deep and permanent. The wounded appear to eschew bitterness and hatred, but not far below the often genial, courteous surface lies a contempt that cannot easily be disguised.

FOR FURTHER READING

The literature on the poverty of Negroes is increasing steadily, attesting to the recognition of this problem as central to the whole question of poverty. The classic work is Gunnar Myrdal's *An American Dilemma* (New York: Harper Bros., 1944). The Fall 1965 issue of *Daedalus* contained several interesting articles. An important background study is Eric E. Williams, *Capitalism and Slavery* (New York: Russell & Russell, 1964). On the problem of mental health, a good source is Frank Riessman, Jerome Cohen, and Arthur Pearl, eds., *The Mental Health of the Poor* (New York: Free Press, 1964). On family problems, E. Franklin Frazier, *The Negro Family in the United States* (Chicago: University of Chicago Press, 1966) is a standard source. An excellent overall view of the current situation is Charles E. Silberman, *Crisis in Black and White* (New York: Random House, 1964).

HUMAN

OBSOLESCENCE

Jules Henry

When nearly half the population is under twenty-five years of age, when younger people—for a variety of reasons—have little regard for those over the age of thirty, it is not likely that our society will be very concerned about the aged. Consequently, the final stages of life turn into a painful period of obsolescence. The aged may be among us, but they are not part of us. They are generally poor because their income is severely limited. Poverty often comes with age.

Our system of social security and social welfare has not been much help, for the benefits are too meager to sustain two old people decently. Hence, an elderly couple must depend on relatives, hoard their resources, or simply enter a home for the aged. For those without additional sources of income, there is often poverty. The fact is that a third of all poor families are headed by older persons.

It is the quality and character of their existence that is most oppressive for the aged poor. Nowhere is this more clearly demonstrated than in Jules Henry's *Culture Against Man*, from which the following selection has been taken. Professor of Anthropology and Sociology at Washington University in St. Louis, Dr. Henry poses a disturbing question: What has 150 years of an acquisitive

Source: Jules Henry, *Culture Against Man*, pp. 406–441. © Copyright 1963 by Random House, Inc. Reprinted by permission.

society done to the American character? The portrait he sketches is not a pleasant one. The impact of the Cold War, advertising, the conflict of generations, schools, and institutions for the aged —he feels these have all served to undermine human values rather than enhance them.

Melvin Tumin, a Princeton sociologist, has described *Culture Against Man* as "so cogently conceived and so brilliantly executed as to command that any future work . . . take this book seriously into account or be diminished by the failure to do so." Dr. Henry's book presents an unsettling view of American culture. It is an impassioned work; any intelligent response to American culture cannot help but be impassioned.

Rosemont: Hell's Vestibule

Steaming from the pit, a vapour rose
  over the banks, crusting them with slime
  that sickened my eyes and hammered at my nose.

Once there, I peered down; and I saw long lines
  of people in a river of excrement
  that seemed the overflow of the world's latrines.

I saw among the felons of that pit
  one wraith who might or might not have been tonsured—
  one could not tell, he was so smeared with shit.

. . do you see that one
  scratching herself with dungy nails. . . ?[1]

I have described a ward in Muni San (Municipal Sanitarium). It is bad, but not the worst place I have seen for obsolete paupers. In Muni San there is a sense of responsibility: somewhere among its vast reaches there are doctors who, though never encountered by our researchers, must exist, for patients have seen them, and doctors prescribe for them. Muni San furnishes medicines and dresses injuries; it provides diets for diabetics, and if they become gangrenous they receive surgery. Linens are dingy at Muni San, but they are changed and washed regularly, and the sheets of incontinent patients are removed as

[1] From *The Inferno*. Canto XVIII.

soon as the overworked staff can get to it, sometimes even in the dead of night. There is plenty of food, and water is always handy for the thirsty. The help is often busily about, and patients who make requests receive a response. Bedpans and urinals are provided, and the beds are not smeared with excrement. Patients are never beaten by the staff and staff must not let a patient fall. But each of these conditions could be reversed: there might be just one doctor for hundreds of patients just to meet "regulations"—and he might breeze through the establishment in an hour one day a week. There might be no diets; linens might be smeared with feces and washed only when the Health Department threatened; baths might be a rarity and given with dirty water. Patients might be half starved and made to beg for a drink. Urinals might be mere tin cans, and immobilized patients might have to beg to be taken to the toilet or else be considered incontinent. "Troublesome" patients might be beaten. None of this occurs at Muni San. Rather what the patients suffer most from there, perhaps, is the sense of being dumped and lost; the emptiness of the life, the vacant routine, the awareness of being considered a nuisance and of being inferior to the most insensitive employee.

But in Rosemont all the indecencies and filth that do not occur in Muni San are piled on top of an empty life. Rosemont[2] is the Vestibule of Hell.

Overview[3]

Rosemont is a private institution run for profit by Mrs. Dis. She is genial, cooperative, and always one legal step ahead of

[2] The ward described here has about a score of patients. The building holds around a hundred. For these there is a registered nurse and somewhat less than a score of other employees including licensed practical nurses (LPN's) and attendants. All of Rosemont contains about twice the number contained in the building we studied, and there is one physician, who comes once or twice a week and "sees everybody real fast," as the researcher put it, in about an hour. No researcher saw him, except one day when one happened to be in the main office. It should be added that nothing in Rosemont is very clear because of the great difficulty in getting anything straight from the Office.

[3] My discussion of Rosemont is based on 35 observation periods on each of two wards. Observations were made 'round the clock for one hour each day between the hours of 9 A.M. and 7 P.M.; and thereafter for half an hour.

the Health Department. This report starts with an overview of a typical ward.

As I entered the ward a few of the men turned their heads in my direction. Others paid no attention or were asleep. Most of them were dressed in street clothes. A few were in pajamas and robes. The clothing looked old and poorly fitting and some of it was torn at the elbows. The ward smelled strongly of urine even though the windows were open. The beds were so close together that often there was room only for a chair between them. All walls were lined with beds and there were some in the center of the room. The mattresses were thin, the beds sagged in the middle, the sheets were dingy and some of them were smeared with dried feces. The beds with no assigned occupants were covered by a thin grayish cover; others had a faded blue, red, green, or brown blanket folded at the foot or spread over the bed. The upper half of the windows had dark curtains. On the walls were a picture of George Washington, one of Jesus, another of the Madonna and Child, and a religious calendar. A couple of men had clocks at the head of their beds. The dark floor was dotted with wet spots, and I noticed several men spitting on it. Most of them were staring into space and they did not talk to one another.

I could not but notice the contrast between the attractive flooring and the drabness of the rest. The floor is tiled in colored squares and at one place there is a crest set in tile bearing the letter R. The floor is clean and waxed but two walls are dingy and have soil spots. A third has unpainted areas where remodeling has been done. The fourth wall is a flimsy partition between the two sides of the division. A picture of George Washington hangs askew on the wall above the Negro patients, and there are two other pictures.

There was an odor of urine. My general impression of the patients was one of apathy and depression. Most of them were sitting slumped over, heads bowed, hands folded. The few who were moving did so slowly and without animation. . . . While I was standing near the center of the ward Mr. Nathan, a large man in a dirty green shirt, walked slowly over to me. . . . He talked about how hungry he was, saying that this was true of all the patients. He had never had a large appetite, he said, but even he was hungry on the food they got here. While he was talking several patients walked over and looked at a clock on the south wall. Mr. Nathan explained, "You see, it's getting near lunch time and they're all hungry. That's what everyone does from eleven o'clock until lunch time—they look at the clock."

There was some activity at the east end of the division, so I walked over. Mr. Quilby and Mr. Segram, two dirty, thin, gray-haired little men, were in the same bed. One was talking loudly and the other was paying no attention. The bed had no linens, and the mattress, which was slit from end to end, had several wet spots. A second bed was empty and it too had no linens. The empty bed had a large wet spot in the center. In the third bed Mr. Quert, a patient who seemed more oriented, was sitting on the side of his bed apparently keeping the two patients from getting into his bed. He explained that someone had to watch or they would hurt themselves. Mr. Quert seemed to be keeping the two men in the bed by putting a bedside table in front of them whenever they tried to get out. I noticed that Mr. Quert had a puddle of urine under his bed too. . . . The two men were the most depressing sight I have ever seen. They were only partially dressed and neither of them had shoes on. They bumped into each other as they constantly moved back and forth in the bed. One of them was kicking or scratching the other. One tried constantly to get out of the bed, first on one side and then on the other, but was always prevented by the table. As he turned from side to side he would bump into the other man in the bed and would lift his legs high to avoid bumping him. Horrified, I stood watching for some time. I tried to speak to the men but they seemed not to hear. Mr. Ansmot (a patient) shouted at one to get into his own bed, but got no results. . . . From the way he moved, one of the men must have been blind, for he always felt around with his feet or hands before he moved in any direction.

When I had seen enough of this I walked out. As I went through the north division I saw a white and a colored aide sitting in chairs, and a white aide was calling loudly and sternly to a patient who had had an incontinent stool and had feces smeared all over himself and his bed, "Sam, you get that sheet up over you."

I watched the patient in the second bed in the center for a few moments. He had feces all over himself and the bed. I failed to find out what his name was. He did not reply when I spoke to him. I left the division feeling completely depressed and contaminated.

I noticed that Mr. Link and Mr. Scope were both incontinent and that the odor was especially bad on this side of the division. As I walked down this aisle I looked down and noticed I was standing in a puddle of urine about an inch deep. I jumped over it and looking back saw that the urine had collected in the center aisle and ran almost all the way from the east to the west end of the division. It started from the beds of four patients, Link, Scope, Yankton and Merchant. I walked down the aisle carefully avoiding the stream of urine.

The Irony of God and Salvation

Hell's Vestibule is a Place of Many Ironies. Let us start with the Irony of God and Salvation.

The religious theme is expressed strongly in an interview with Mrs. Dis' Second in Command.[4]

Second in Command put on the pained expression of a martyr and said, "I guess the good Lord intended for me to do this kind of work. I just love these old people—you never know what's going to happen when you get old, and, if the Lord intended for me to do this work, I certainly will be as good to them as I can. . . ." (The researcher says) "I thought it might be hard to get help out here, it's so far out. . . . Maybe Mrs. Dis pays better than other places?" "Well, I don't know exactly, but she does pay well. I never ask what the pay is. I guess the good Lord wouldn't want us to do it for the money." . . . "What would you say would be the qualities of a good person to do this kind of work?" "Kindness," she whined, "and practice of the Golden Rule, just like the good Lord intended. We all must be kind to these old people; Mrs. Dis just wouldn't tolerate anything else." "Sometimes these older patients get upset; what do you do then?" "Oh," said Second in Command, "they're just like children. I feed them good. Why, they can have almost anything they want to eat; there's always things in the refrigerator. Mrs. Dis always keeps it well-stocked. I talk with them and just be kind to them and they just calm right down. . . . Oh, I just love the patients; I just love to be around them—just anything at all. (Second in Command was never seen on the wards.) The only thing that bothers me is when they die and you have to take that scum out of their mouth," and she drew up her face in disgust. "I always tell the aides it has to be done for the poor dears; we never know when we'll be like that, and it's a part of the Lord's work." She asked if I'd like a soda or 7-Up. I thought I'd better

[4] The interview with Mrs. Dis is not given because every question simply touched off a long digression, which, though giving insight into her personality, did not bear on the subject. Aside from this Mrs. Dis' interview contained protestations of affection for the patients and slightly veiled invitations to the interviewer to enter some questionable deals.

take something out of the machine. They might bring me coffee, and I didn't want to drink anything out of that filthy kitchen.

The Bible also is present in Rosemont. A very nice looking copy is owned by Ed Alvin, a cruel old man, who earns his keep by helping out with the work. Ed always keeps the Bible on his bed.

Mr. Benton said to Ed, "Junior, you better take care of that," and handed Ed a nice looking Bible. An aide was feeding Mr. Quilby, and said to him, "Oh, shut up, will you? Wait a minute, I'm not ready to give it to you yet, you silly thing." Then the aide handed Mr. Quilby two pieces of white bread, but since she didn't look as she put them toward his hand they fell on the floor. She fussed about this and told him to watch what he was doing as she picked up the bread and gave it to him. He began to eat it. Mr. Quilby is blind.

It can be seen that advertising is not the only place where values are burlesqued. The following is from observations of blind Mr. Benjamin:

Mr. Harlow came up to Mr. Benjamin and spoke to him and sat down on his bed. I could not understand all that Mr. Benjamin was saying but it had something to do with his paying money and not having anyone to care for him. As he was talking Mr. Harlow left without saying anything and Mr. Benjamin continued to talk. Mr. Harlow came back to Mr. Benjamin and Mr. Benjamin again spoke about no one's caring for him and about someone who was supposed to take care of him but did not. Mr. Harlow said something to him softly and Mr. Benjamin said, "I've been baptized," and started to cry. He said, "They shouldn't treat me this way. I hope to goodness you aren't treated this way. I'll pray for you." Mr. Harlow said, "I ain't got nothing in the world, John," and Mr. Benjamin said that he didn't have anything either and no money to buy anything either. He talked about his things having been stolen last night and how terrible it was that people should steal from a blind man. He continued in this vein for a long time and Mr. Harlow answered very sympathetically.

Mr. Benjamin entertains two illusions: the illusion of the power of the sacred in this world, and illusory expectations. Since all his life Mr. Benjamin was taught how to be woolly-minded and uncritical—beginning with a school system that never taught him to think—now a blind old man, he still believes that baptism and blindness can deliver him from the evils of this world when he does not have the money.

The Benediction of the Bath

Since bathing is a secular, not a sacred, ritual in our culture, the bathing of Mr. Benjamin does not quite belong here. On the other hand, since it is associated so much with purification, relaxation, and surcease even in our culture, it seems a veritable lay benediction. Besides, in Rosemont, where we saw only two bathings in thirty-three days—both of Mr. Benjamin—bathing gives us a chance to witness, for the first time, one of the dominant traits of a hell—the union of opposites. In this case it is the conjunction of filth and cleanliness.

An aide came to Mr. Benjamin and said "Come with me Mr. Benjamin" but Mr. Benjamin said, "I don't want to go anywhere." When she said, "You come with me," he said, "I ain't got no breeches on; I don't want to go around naked." She said, "That's all right." As he started to get up she helped him and was going to guide him out, but he said, "I can't get through; there's something in the way," but she said, "There's nothing, come on." As he started to move she began to help him walk out. A patient came in and said, "The water's getting pretty dirty," but the aide said, "I've only got two more."

Hunger

Since social security checks are notoriously small; since the men in Rosemont, not being residents of The City, are not eligible for admission to Muni San; and since they either have no families or have families that will not take them in, there is nobody to receive them but Mrs. Dis. Meanwhile Mrs. Dis has to make a decent living. In what follows, therefore, one should guard against judging her too harshly. After all, what would happen to obsolete people if not for the Mrs. Dises?

Mr. Hill tells the researcher of a very serious accident. He was hit by a car driven by a maniac who then turned and drove over him. At County Hospital he had many operations and a complete surgical reconstitution of his legs. He had dried feces under his fingernails and there is a bedpan almost completely full of urine setting on his bedside table. He had been told he had to get up and start using his legs. He said also that the doctors had told him that he must eat a good diet, with lots of protein for tissue repair and he expressed concern about the diet he was receiving here. He said he was constantly hungry and that everybody here is constantly hungry. He said that for breakfast they had a small bowl half full of oatmeal without cream, sugar or butter, two slices of toast and coffee. Lunch wasn't bad, but not all that it should be. Supper was a small bowl of very thin soup and two slices of toast. I could not but wonder how beneficial this major surgical repair is if the patient is not given adequate diet and care. He said that here nobody cares about the patients.

Before discussing Mr. Hill I shall give one more example of the union of excrement and food.

As I entered the kitchen several women, apparently patients, were scraping and stacking dishes, and the smell of urine greeted me. This is indeed a shock to the nervous system—to see food, hear the clatter of dishes, and to smell urine.

Hell has its logic, just like any other culture, and a fundamental postulate of it is that *Hell is the meeting place of opposites,* for while The World is relatively ordered so that opposites are kept apart, Hell is chaos, so they come together. For this reason Hell contains many incongruities that seem ironical from our point of view. The first incongruity we noticed was the religious and patriotic pictures on the walls; now we see people eating with excreta on them and all around them.

The decline of the disgust function, so that a person can bring himself to eat amid filth, is an ultimate stage in dehumanization. So closely linked is the *disgust function* to humanness that there is no culture known to anthropology where people do not have it. My friends the Pilagá Indians believe they were expelled from heaven because Asien, their high-god, could not stand the smell of their feces.

Another irony is the discrepancy between the good medical attention Mr. Hill received at Muni Clinic and the bad feeding he gets at Rosemont, so that the latter destroys the value of the former.

I now present a selection of observations on hunger.

Mr. Edwards was lying down, and asked what time it was, and I told him it was about ten after twelve. He said, "That's good. I'm hungry and it should be time to eat soon." I said, "Yes, it should be. What time do you have breakfast?" He said, "I don't know. We had that a long time ago." I asked, "What did you have this morning?" and he said, "Oh, we had toast and oats. I saved some of my bread and I ate that just a little while ago. You have to have something to tide you over until the next meal." As I started to leave he put out his hand to me to shake my hand. I shook his. He said, "I've been here a long time—it's almost 12 years now. I had to come because I was paralyzed from my waist down. I could move my arms OK but not my legs." He continued with this and also talked about his hernia operation and other ills, even telling me about his being burned on the leg when he was a child. I listened a while longer and then went on to the next bed.

Mr. Nathan walked up to me, eating a slice of toast. He smiled smugly and explained, "They gave me two breakfasts by mistake this morning, so I ate all the cereal and saved the toast. This should tide me over until lunch; I wish this would happen every morning."

Mr. Triste was eating. Occasionally he would lick his plate, bending his head to the plate and drawing the food to his mouth.

Mr. Nathan saw Mr. Edwards licking his plate, and said to me, "See him lick his plate? They get so damn hungry here. I was too. I usually buy something from the bread man when he comes, but I must have been asleep today."

Mr. Inkle was at the kitchen door asking for bread, but they would not give him any, and said, "Go on; get back to your bed." Some of the patients who were sitting in the solarium kept telling him to leave, to go back to his bed, and he finally did. Mike, who works for his keep, said several times, "I don't want no bread."

He went to the women's side room to get their trays. When he came out with them he stopped by Mr. Jacks' bed and offered him some bread that one of the patients had left and Mr. Jacks took it eagerly and put it in his bedside table. Then Mike stopped by Mr. Roberts' bed and offered him the coffee a patient had not drunk. Mr. Roberts thanked him, took it, and quickly drank it so that Mike could take the cup out with the rest of the dishes.

Mike stopped by Mr. Jacks' bedside and held out a partially eaten tray of food. He smiled and asked Mr. Jacks if he wanted the bread from the tray. Mr. Jacks said something, took the bread and placed it on the shelf of his bedside table.

Mr. Edwards had been asking for food again. Lilly, an aide, said, "Ed, get up and make Edwards leave Tom's tray alone."

For supper the patients had mush, coffee or milk, chocolate pudding, bread, and a graham cracker. The men ate rapidly, hungrily, and silently, and scraped their bowls.

Mr. Benjamin, who is blind, was talking as I approached. He said good morning to me when I spoke and went on talking. I did not get the impression that he was talking to me. He said, "We don't have anything to eat. Oh, we have lots of food around here, but we don't get anything to eat."

THE CANINE METAMORPHOSIS / Dogs eat hungrily and silently, beg for food, eat leavings, and lick their bowls. Inasmuch as books on dog raising recommend that they not be fed to capacity, the canine transformation of the inmates of Rosemont is almost complete in this respect. Perhaps this is an exaggeration, for not all the inmates lick their plates, beg for food, or get a chance at leavings. Leavings go only to the favorites of Ed and Mike, two patient-workers, who get their keep in exchange for the reluctant and often punitive services they render the inmates. Thus one could say that canine traits are only sprinkled among the population. Other canine traits are bone-burying, which emerges in Rosemont as setting something aside to tide one over, and being told to get back out of the kitchen, etc., when one begs for food.

All pathological environments must metamorphose the creatures in it. Franz Kafka, transformed by his humiliating father, saw himself as cockroach, various animals, and "hunger artist." Pathogenic families change their children into bugs, horses, dogs, garbage pails, phantoms, and so on. Many psychiatric institutions transform patients into simple "animals" or, at a more benign level, into retarded children. Pathogenic institutions simply cannot handle a human being, for humanness is a threat. For a cruel institution to function within its cruelties, it has to redefine its inmates—hence the pathogenic, lethal metamorphosis. In a pathogenic society, Negroes become animals; Jews become monsters and murderers; Chinese become evil, yellow, little men, and so on. This redefinition of a human being into a persecutable category I have called *pathogenic metamorphosis*. Of course, the transformation cannot be perfect unless the subject acquiesces, but obsolete paupers with no place to go have no choice. Let us look at further examples.

With that silly grin on his face, Mr. Reach was watching as I talked to Mr. Heard. He motioned for me to come over, so I walked over and said hello. Still grinning, he said, "I'm hungry. Get me something to eat. Take me home with you." I told Mr. Reach that he had just finished lunch and that he shouldn't be hungry and that I couldn't take him home with me because I didn't know where he lived. He immediately supplied the address for me, and told me that he owned his own home. I walked over to say hello to Mr. Edwards.

I walked over to Mr. Ansmot and asked, "Is it good?" He was eating very rapidly, but said, "It's all right." The soup looked mostly like liquid, with very little vegetable or meat in it. Most of the men ate very rapidly and when finished just sat and stared.

If I define a person in a particular way, it follows that I must define his entire perceptual apparatus in accordance with that definition. If I define him as "child," I talk to him as to a child, i.e., misrepresent reality to him because children cannot comprehend much. If I define him as "dog," it must follow that I talk to him as if he did not understand a great deal aside from, let us say, "go away," "come here," "lie down," "stand up," "bone," "food," and a few other simple signals—unless, of course, he is a highly trained dog. *Every institution thus establishes a culture in terms of definitions of its inmates as special kinds of entities*, and in terms of its conceptions of the inmate's capacities for seeing, hearing, and understanding. Everyone entering the institution must act accordingly: the staff must behave towards the inmates according to the definitions, and the inmates must defer to the staff's formulation. This process is at work between the researcher and Mr. Reach: the researcher assumes that Mr. Reach is some mixture of child and dog, so she tells him that he cannot be hungry because he has just had a meal, and instead of telling him simply that she cannot take him home because that is forbidden, she lies. Thus she *challenges Mr. Reach's capacity to perceive correctly* his own hunger and his ability to understand. We therefore say that the researcher *has taken on the culture* of the institution—she acts and thinks like one of the personnel in terms of their definitions of the patients. A lethal component of pathogenic institutions is that *they challenge the soundness of the perceptual apparatus of the inmates,* thus forcing them to lose confidence in their own judgment and to become as they are defined.

Continuing, we find a different researcher functioning in much the same way, for perceiving that the lunch is miserable she yet asks Mr. Ansmot, "Is it good?" How does one account for this paradox except in terms of the theory, and in terms of the total detachment of inmate from staff engendered by the metamorphosis? The worlds of staff and inmate have become totally separate, so that the former does not enter into the world of the latter. It is obvious that if the staff at Rosemont *did* enter the world of the patient, the staff would quit.

Now we can state a *law of pathogenic metamorphosis: pathogenic institutions metamorphose the inmates into specific types and treat the perceptual apparatus of the inmates as if it belonged to the metamorphosis*—dog, cockroach, child, et cetera.

SOME IRONIES OF HUNGER / Hungry men may have obsessive phantasies of succulent fruits.

I stopped to talk to a little man on the east end of the north row of beds. I think his name was Yankton. He smiled at me brightly and immediately told me, "I always work hard but I have a good appetite." I asked him about his work and he told me he was a produce man. He said, "You know, I sold, oh, apples, oranges, melons, and bananas. Oh, those bananas, um-m-m." He shook his head and smiled as he talked about bananas. Then he said, "I work hard but I love my mother." His eyes became moist as he spoke of his mother, and he told me how dearly he loved her. He said, "Whenever there would be a little argument . . . you know how it goes, I'd give my dad the devil. I always stuck up for my mother."

Mr. Yankton tries to escape the reality of chronic hunger by transmuting it into "good appetite." Then good appetite reminds him of the arch-feeder, his mother. Thus, in an effort to avoid the reality of hunger he reminisces, only to collide with the most poignant symbol of food.

Mr. Benton, on the other hand, escaped from hunger by

thinking that it was not lack of food but rather poor cooking and the specialized character of the food that bothered him.

Mr. Benton asked, "Do you eat here?" and I said, no. He said, "You're lucky you don't," but immediately added, "Oh, I don't mean to be sarcastic, it's just that they have diet food here and it's not as good as ordinary food would be." I said, "Home cooked food always seems better," and he said, "Yes, it does."

Mr. Benton and Mr. Yankton both have *delusions of extrication*. Mr. Benton evades the full impact of chronic hunger by telling himself that he is merely taking the consequences of "diet foods" and bad cooking, and Mr. Yankton escapes it by converting hunger into a robust "appetite."

The final example of hunger's irony deals with Mr. Fenn, an inmate who, like Ed, receives his bed and board for helping with the incapacitated inmates. Like Ed and many other patients, he is callous and harsh to the weak and disoriented; but like them, he is hungry.

Mr. Fenn was looking very tired, and when I said hello to him he said, "I certainly wish I could eat early. Since I have to do so much heavy work I get hungrier than if I just laid around all day. That's really hard work, getting some of those fellows up for their baths. That one weighs 230 pounds—you know, that colored fellow we were talking to." (Time is now between 12 and 1 P.M.) I asked him more about the kind of work he did and he said that he helped with everything that needed to be done if heavy lifting was involved. He said, "I don't get enough to eat for that kind of work."

Here the irony resides in Mr. Fenn's failure to understand that the profit drive in Rosemont leaves little room for consideration of even his strength, and that the staff does not care very much whether the work assigned to him is performed. If the inmates he is supposed to take to the toilet are incontinent because he is too tired and irritable to get them out of bed to the lavatory, and back again, the regular staff simply lets them lie in their urine and feces until they get around to wiping off the bed and the inmate. Then he learns to sleep on a rubber sheet or a plastic covered mattress.

WHOEVER DOES NOT WORK SHALL NOT EAT / The next example contains a précis of almost everything that has been discussed in this section on hunger.

Mr. Ansmot asked the aide, "Why didn't we have meat for dinner?" and the aide said, "We work, you don't," and Mr. Ansmot said, "Don't meat help make you strong?" and the aide replied, "You ask the cook." And Mr. Ansmot said, "You live here, you ought to know." Mr. Quert walked to the cart full of dirty dishes and took a spoon out of a dirty cup to eat the rest of his lunch with. Ed handed Mr. Stone a partially drunk cup of coffee from another inmate's tray, and he drank it.

Meat appeared in Rosemont only twice during our study, though we observed eleven midday and evening meals; yet even minimal expectation was enough to keep alive in Mr. Ansmot the hope of getting it. Apparently, however, the staff did not get too much meat either.

Mr. Ansmot had not eaten his meat and Lilly said, "You going to eat that meat?" And when he said no, she said, "Ed, get that meat from him." Ed handed her Mr. Ansmot's tray and she said, "I'm not going to give it to him, I'm going to eat it myself," and she pointed to herself.

A hell where keepers envy victims is ironical. Perhaps this envy of people who eat but do not work makes the keepers good ones: since their food is unsatisfying too and they have to work, they may dislike the inmates enough to treat them like dogs. Since the aides' work is drudgery, all *they* may be able to see is that the inmates live a lazy life. In such a context Mr. Ansmot's question, "Don't meat help make you strong?" could only have seemed ridiculous to the aide—if she thought about it at all—especially in view of the fact that not strength but acquiescence and profit is what Rosemont wants. Mr. Ansmot's failure to understand this shows that he is afflicted with false hope.

Before going on let us review what we have found out so far. We have seen that Rosemont, besides being dirty and run-down, is staffed by callous personnel and underfeeds the inmates. Rosemont is characterized by what I have called *pathogenic ironies*, paradoxes, or incongruities, which can be either material objects (like pictures of saviors) or attitudes (like the belief that one should be taken care of) which are out of place there. It was seen that such paradoxes occur because the institution is indifferent to values and because some of the inmates have *false hopes* and *delusions of extrication*. Because it is a pathogenic environment Rosemont transforms its inmates and then *defines their perceptual capacities in terms of the transformation*, thus dehumanizing them and undermining their ability to make correct judgments. Culturally imposed *definitions of persons* and culture-bound *delineations of perception* are universal human tendencies, but deviant, pathogenic environments impose pathogenic definitions of persons and perception. The difference between an Australian tribal definition of members as kangaroos, wallabies, witchetty grubs, and so on, and the definitions imposed by Rosemont and similar institutions, is that in an Australian tribe everybody is defined as an animal in accordance with his totemic status, whereas in Rosemont *the imposed definition grinds status and dignity to powder*.

The Functions of Reminiscence

Among people in a home for the aged one finds much reminiscing, for through reminiscing the old and the obsolete become aware that they exist. They seem to be saying, "I reminisce, therefore I exist." [Earlier] it was said:

Since memories are a family's folk-lore, reminiscences about the happier moments of life affirm and stabilize the family, for the recollection of pleasure actualizes past solidarities and mutes whatever threatens the present. When a family is miserable, happy reminiscing becomes an idyllic quasi-life, narcotizing pain and lending the appearance of validity to real life. . . . the past "was another way of existing" and "each event, when it had played its part, put itself meekly into a box and became an honorary event."

Even in Hell's Vestibule memory can serve similar functions; and sociable reminiscing creates transient social solidarities also. Meanwhile, one cannot escape the pervading ironies. We have observed some reminiscing in Mr. Yankton's conversation with the researcher about his former occupation as fruit vendor, and viewed this as ironical because Mr. Yankton was remembering succulent fruits where he was chronically hungry. The following is another example of a reminiscence of consumption:

Hilda (an aide) was saying to Mr. Ansmot (Mr. Reeves was also included in the conversation), "Scotch, you've got to develop a taste for that. The scotch and gin family are nasty." Mr. Ansmot said, "Stag was my favorite beer." Ethel (an aide) replied, "I used to drink Stag. I like that Old Forrester hundred proof whiskey. Don't give me none of that eighty or ninety-two. I always wake up with a headache with those others; but with that I come to work, work all day, and nobody ever knows the difference." Mr. Reeves broke into the conversation, saying, "That's the dark beer. I like that."

Here Mr. Ansmot reminisces about alcoholic beverages, although in Rosemont it is difficult to get even a drink of water. At the same time he gains a transient solidarity with Hilda, imbibing from her a kind of phantom selfhood; by talking to an active person he somehow gains the impression that he is like her. For a moment a kind of fleeting contagion passes from her to him; it is this *contagion of life* toward which the socially dead yearn with clinging minds and hands.

The next example shows more clearly the development of transient sociability.

Mr. Edwards and Mr. Ruben were still talking. Mr. Gregory was sitting on his bed looking in his bedside stand. Mr. Benton came in from the porch and said to Mr. Karst, "Well how'd you like to be back on the road there, junior?" Mr. Karst replied, "It'd be all right." Mr. Benton said, "You worked for Boyle, didn't you?" Mr. Karst nodded and said, "And I worked for Acme twice but I quit both times." Mr. Benton said, "I helped when he sold out to Boyle —that wasn't here, that was in New York. I worked in Los Angeles and New York both." Then Mr. Karst said, "I was in La Jolla, California." Mr. Benton replied, "That's one of the most beautiful spots in the United States. How far did you say it was from San Diego to La Jolla?" Mr. Karst replied, "Sixteen to eighteen miles." Mr. Benton said, "You're right," and Mr. Karst said, very indignantly, "Certainly I'm right, I lived there." Mr. Benton was quiet for a little while and then said, "I used to work for Marshall Fields in Chicago." Mr. Karst did not respond.

Men who are obsolete cannot talk about the present for they have nothing to do; they can discuss past roles only, and since they end by boring each other they drift apart. Past lives devoted to doing what they had to do rather than what they wanted to do; to jobs requiring neither study, thought, nor speculation, do not prepare them for old age where there is nothing to do. So there is the all-pervading irony: this time it is talk of roles by men who have no role left but that of *acquiescent inmate,* and talk of the pleasure of travel by men who will travel no more. The cream of the irony is the pathetic little quarrel between Mr. Benton and Mr. Karst over the distance between San Diego and La Jolla. Yet for a little while these men are drawn together and are able, perhaps, to forget the miserable present.

Not all the reminiscing heard at Rosemont had this directly *narcotizing quality,* for some of it was sorrowful. Yet the recollection of suffering in the past might conceivably be less painful than looking the present in the eye. Mr. Link's memories seem to be an example of this.

Mr. Link was sitting in a chair beside his bed, and he expectorated from time to time into an old tin can on the floor. He talked about his daughter, saying something about her being very happy. I did not understand most of what Mr. Link said, nor did he answer questions or repeat statements when I asked him to. He asked me, "Are you happy? Are you married? Do you have children?" He talked about some business and financial problems of the past but again I understood only a little of what he said. I caught phrases like "big shot," "election," and "I had lots of money." Apparently he was telling me about some man who took his money away from him, but I didn't understand all of it. He alternated between a happy and a sad expression and at one time I was smiling because I thought he was talking about something happy. He said what had happened to him was a terrible shame—that he could be rich and happy now had this not occurred. He repeated something about "happy" and then lowered his head as if he was about to cry; but he pulled himself together and began to talk about his daughter again.

On the verge of tears, alternating between thinking of his daughter and his money, Mr. Link sits incontinent of urine in Hell's Vestibule. In his case the union of the past and present is so close that beyond the thoughts of his daughter, memory can give him no comfort. Why is he compelled to remember, then? Surely the *recollection of past misfortune must serve some biological function*, some adaptive, preservative goal. Perhaps, sunk deep in an unhappy past, Mr. Link still blots out the unthinkable present. On the other hand, it may be that regardless of circumstances the corrective (cybernetic) function of memory drives on, constantly presenting us with our past mistakes so that we will not make them again. Memory too is a function of hope, for tormenting memories mean only that memory "hopes" things will be better next time. The adaptive functions of the brain do not die even in Hell's Vestibule because basic, indissoluble properties of the *cell* are hope and memory.

A Note on Acquiescence

The dictionary definitions for *acquiesce* include the meanings "to assent tacitly, comply quietly without protesting," and since the outstanding characteristic of the inmates is acquiescence, it is necessary to say a few words in general about it. First, a few examples:

Mrs. Luna said to Mr. Ansmot in a very irritated way, "I told you you had to get in bed!" And with that Mr. Ansmot very quickly got into bed. Mr. Gregory asked Daisy something, and she said, "You don't need that. Go and sit down. Which is your bed?" When he pointed to his bed she said, in a very irritated voice, "Well, it ain't made yet. You go and sit down right back where you came from." He sat down on his own bed. Daisy said to Mr. Gregory, "Get off your bed. Go out there somewhere and sit down." She was even more irritated than before.

With Mr. Holz in it, Ed dragged Mr. Holz' chair over to Mr. Holz' bed, jerked him out of the chair, dumped him into the bed, and said, very harshly, "Sit, sit, sit." An aide said, "Quit aggravating him, Ed; he ain't ate." Ed was lying on his bed making funny noises like "meow, meow." Mr. Holz was calling, "Granma, granma, ask her if she's coming." Then Ed went, "Arf, arf," imitating a dog. I had the feeling he was making fun of Mr. Holz. An aide came in with a tray, put it on Mr. Holz' bed, and said, "You know you're a nuisance." She sat down in a chair, and as she started to feed him, she said harshly, "Keep the hand down. Here, take that bread. Here, open your mouth. Here, here."

Mr. Heard was awakened by Miss Luna's pulling the pillow from under his head without saying anything to him. She left the ward with it. Mr. Heard immediately went back to sleep.

Human beings everywhere are required to acquiesce in their material conditions of life and in the way they are socially de- fined (as free men, as servants of the state, as slaves, as members of the kangaroo totem, and so on), and the social definition of a person always imposes an attitude toward him by those who define his position in society. But acquiescence in material con- ditions and in one's social position always require one to take up an attitude toward one's Self, for it is obvious that if I am de- fined as slave my attitude toward my Self will be very different than if I am defined as a free man. The problem of acquiescence is more critical for modern than for primitive man, because the social structure in which the latter lives usually has been rela- tively stable for centuries, and all who live in it have traditional roles which they learn to desire very early and with which there is little tampering thereafter. In contemporary society, however, though men are taught they are free, they are constantly being compelled to accept material conditions and social positions they reject with their hearts and souls yet find that circumstances compel them to acquiesce. Thus it comes about that acqui- escence runs a gamut from quiet social conformity to terror- stricken appeasement. Actually, in our culture, the problem of acquiescence is the problem of masochism, for the masochistic approach to life is merely an assent to life. The problem then arises, why are the men in Rosemont acquiescent? In the first place they are members of a relatively docile population. It is many generations since Americans fought anything but external enemies, and they have entered the armed forces mostly on pain of imprisonment. Controversy, the flare of political passions, righteous anger about or rebellion against anything is not much part of the American scene. But equally important are the following:

POWERLESSNESS / All the men in Rosemont have to their names is their preposterous social security checks. As Mrs. Dis put it, they have been dumped in Rosemont by their relatives and for- gotten. So they have neither money enough nor friends to extricate them. This breeds hopelessness, and hopelessness is the parent of acquiescence. The feeling of powerlessness compels them to accept the treatment they receive.

THE SOCIAL DEFINITION / The social definition of the inmates is that of near-paupers who are a mixture of dog, child, and lunatic; and the social definition makes it possible for the help to treat them like creatures without personality. On the other hand the powerlessness of the inmates makes it necessary for them to accept the definition and the treatment that goes along with it.

PSYCHIC MECHANISMS / Delusions of extrication, reminiscence, and resignation—an aspect of hopelessness—make it possible for the inmates to accept. With their delusions of extrication they can imagine themselves in different circumstances; and reminiscence can preoccupy them while carrying them back to a former life. Finally, hopelessness itself assuages some pain, because hope presents images of better possibilities and so stirs discontent.

TERROR / Behind the arbitrariness, the anger, and the contempt of the help (and also of the inmates) loom the ultimate threats of restraint or expulsion for those who object too much, for since a "hospital" has enormous powers, it can "restrain" the troublesome inmate by tieing him to his bed or by expelling him.

There is only one important ingredient missing from Rosemont, and that is *reward*, or the hope of it, for in Rosemont, contrary to most other acquiescent situations outside of prisons, there are no rewards for acquiescence. The adolescent who conforms (acquiesces) to group behavior can have good times with his friends; the advertising man on Madison Avenue receives raises and promotions in exchange for his organizational acquiescences; and the child who gives the school teacher the answer she wants gets a smile, a pat on the head, and a good grade.

Distorted People

An intact human being is sound in mind and body. This includes sight, sanity, hearing, and continence. But a distorted one is insane, or blind, or deaf, or incontinent, and so on. Some peo-

ple are distorted in several ways. The more distorted a person,
the greater the tendency of others to withdraw from him. Some
distortions like incontinence, for example, are more repulsive
than others. Of course, not everyone withdraws from distorted
people; and it is probable that the more degraded an intact
person is, the greater his tendency to withdraw from those who
are distorted. It is hard to imagine that a person who has had
love and good fortune would be as quick to withdraw from a distorted person as one whose life was a series of deprivations and
humiliations. Thus the tendency of sound people to withdraw
from distorted ones is related to the experience of the former
with deprivation and degradation in their own lives. But withdrawal must somehow be related also to one's fear of the distorted person; if people are afraid of a distorted person, they
will be more likely to turn away than if he is safe. Finally we
may surmise that if a distorted person—let us say, a hunchback
—has something to give, like human warmth or gifts, people
will be less inclined to reject him. All of this can be summarized
by what seems to be a kind of law of distortion and withdrawal:
*the tendency of sound people to withdraw from distorted ones
is determined by the extent and nature of the distortion, by the
degree of degradation of the sound individuals and their fear of
the distorted person*, and *by the distorted person's own resources*,
e.g., human warmth, property, etc. The ability of the distorted
person to "get around" plays an important part in the withdrawal of others also. For example, a blind incontinent patient
can be terrifying in a crowded place like Rosemont because
those around him are always afraid that, groping his way to their
bed, instead of to his own, he might dirty it.

I have chosen what is, perhaps, a harsh word to refer to all
those who suffer among us because they differ in extreme ways
from the more fortunate who are well-formed and have all their
faculties. But the word "distorted" seems to me to convey better
than any other the inner meaning to us of such misfortunes. For
what most people in our culture experience in contact with distorted people is not compassion or annoyance at some anticipated burden, but the cold sweat of revulsion.

Mr. Quilby, the little blind man with the bad toe, whom one
of the researchers saw rolling around in bed with another man
on the first day of her research, is a good illustration of the oper-

ation of the *law of distortion and withdrawal,* for not only is he blind, but he is psychotic, incontinent, and highly mobile. On the other hand, he has no resources at all. It is interesting that Mr. Benjamin, who is also blind and mobile, but has a little personal cache of aspirin, hot water bottles, and so forth that he is willing to make available, and who is not incontinent or psychotic, is not treated as badly as Mr. Quilby. But let us follow the natural history of Mr. Quilby for a month; this will tell us much about the law and provide further knowledge of Rosemont.

Mr. Quilby hallucinating and talking loudly. Chased from Mr. Ansmot's bed: "You get off my bed—get away from here." Mr. Quilby walks smack with his head into a wall but simply reverses. Yvonne was sweeping the floor on this side and she said to Mr. Quilby, "You get in your bed now or sit down in your chair, or you'll hurt your toe again." On Yvonne's instruction the researcher took him by the arm and directed him to his chair and he sat down with no resistance.

Human beings, like most other warm-blooded animals, appropriate and defend territory. In Rosemont we have the culturally determined expression of this territoriality emerging as *defense of the bed.* Yvonne is hard to explain—she was a decent human being with a real feeling for the inmates.

The aide feeding Mr. Quilby replied, "I'm going to give him a whole loaf of bread some day," and Daisy said, "You think he'll eat it?" and the aide replied, "Sure he will." Daisy said, "Yeh, I guess he will." Then the aide who was feeding Mr. Quilby said, "I'm not talking to you. Keep your mouth shut." Then she immediately said, "Open your mouth." Mr. Quilby said something about being fed too fast and the aide said, "Don't tell me I'm feeding you too fast." Ed said, "He's for the birds."

Here the sarcasm and contempt of the aides is echoed by Ed, who works for his keep. The pig metamorphosis ("I'm going to give him a whole loaf of bread some day") is an institutional irony: men who are underfed are likened to pigs because they are hungry. We can see that Mr. Quilby is a nuisance, yet he has to be fed because if he feeds himself he will make too big a mess.

The aide was finished feeding Mr. Quilby. His tray was empty and she said to the other aide, as she got up to leave, "Watch him holler for water." The aide replied, "No, you've had enough for now" and left. The other aide continued to sit on Mr. Triste's bed. Mr. Ansmot said, "He's been hollering for water for a long time." Mr. Ansmot and the aide were talking very softly and I couldn't hear what they were saying. . . . Mr. Quilby said, "Guess there ain't no water in that jug." Then he began calling, "Alice, Alice, Big Alice will be down next week." He repeated this several times. When Daisy came back into the ward she looked as if she was eating either an orange section or a piece of orange candy. She went to Mr. Quilby's bed and gave him a piece of it, saying to him, "Don't bite my hand now."

The bit of orange is pseudo-expiation—a gesture to the conscience that guarantees that, since the feeble conscience has been satisfied by a sop, the behavior will be repeated.

Mr. Quilby got up and started walking toward Mr. Ansmot, who yelled, "Get away!" but Mr. Quilby kept going toward him. Ed, who was lying on his bed at that end of the hall, got up, slapped Mr. Quilby, dragged him back to his bed, and laid him down. During this Mr. Quilby was saying, "I've got to wash myself; let me go, I've got to wash myself." Ed said, "Shut up!" several times; and then "Stay in bed; them guys don't want to be bothered with you." When Ed lay down, Mr. Quilby got right up, and Ed said, "All right girls, he's all yours now." Daisy came in from the other side and put Mr. Quilby back in bed, saying, "Get on that bed." When he started pulling the sheets off and then taking his pants off, Daisy called to Ed and said, "Look what he's doing, Ed. Help me." But Ed ignored her and Daisy said in a louder voice, "Come on, Ed, and help me. Don't you see what he wants?" Ed got up and took Mr. Quilby to the lavatory and Daisy straightened his bed while he was gone. Ed turned Mr. Quilby loose at the door of the lavatory and he wandered rudderless. Ed returned and handled Mr. Quilby roughly. He got him to his bed and set him down in it quite roughly, saying, "You stay there; I'm sick of you," and lay down in his own bed. Daisy was sitting there, and when Ed kept saying over and over again how sick he was of looking at Mr. Quilby she said, "Maybe some people are sick of you too."

Ed had a Bible lying on the top corner of his bed. Mr. Charles seemed concerned that it might fall and started moving it over toward the center of the bed. Ed said, in a very nice tone of voice, "That's okay, I want it there."

Over and over again blind, psychotic inmates try to excrete but get into trouble either because they cannot find their urinals or because no one will take them to the toilet. "Incontinence" is related to inability to excrete decently because the patient cannot get to the lavatory or cannot find his urinal. Mr. Benjamin who is blind but not psychotic puts it concisely:

Mr. Benjamin began feeling around where he was sitting, and as he did so he reached out further and further until he was no longer sitting on his bed. Mr. Ansmot, who was at the opposite end of the ward, yelled, "Get on your bed." Mr. Benjamin moved over to the next bed, which is Mr. Nathan's, and Mr. Ansmot called out in a very loud voice, "Get on your own bed before they tie you in!" Mr. Benjamin paid no attention but kept moving around. Ed came in carrying a long, narrow cabinet. He had to pass through the aisle in which Mr. Benjamin was, and said, "Get out of my way, Benjamin. Come on, move." Mr. Benjamin did, and Ed went on. Then Mr. Benjamin started to walk around again and groped around as if he were trying to find something. I thought he was trying to find the can he uses as a urinal. He said, "I can't see." Mr. Nathan came in and stood close to me, and said, "He doesn't know what he's doing. He's out of his place," and walked on past Mr. Benjamin to the lavatory. . . . Mr. Benjamin finally sat on Mr. Ruffe's bed, and Mr. Ruffe looked kind of upset by this and got up out of his chair, pulling the blanket at the foot of the bed away so that Mr. Benjamin could not touch it. . . . Mr. Benjamin, sitting on Mr. Ruffe's bed, kept reaching out and asking at intervals for "my pee-bottle." At last he said, "If you don't give me my pee-bottle I'm going to go on the floor." . . . Mr. Fenn came in and said to Mr. Benjamin, "What's wrong?" and took Mr. Benjamin to the lavatory.

During this time three members of the staff were in and out of the ward and several patients were looking on.

Mr. Quilby, because he is blind and disoriented, and because no one wants to help him, is pushed to incontinence and then penalized. This can only disorient him further, increase his anxiety, and make him even more likely to be incontinent. The *provocation–punishment* cycle is present in feeding too: Mr. Quilby has to be fed, but since he is unable to see and is disoriented, he does not eat as the aide wants him to, so she curses him, which makes him inept, which brings further scolding, and so on.

Mr. Quilby was bouncing on Mr. Segram's bed and Mr. Segram was sitting on the end of it. Mr. Segram was hitting at Mr. Quilby. Ed came in pushing a mop bucket of steaming water. He went to Mr. Quilby's bedside, grabbed him by the arms and bounced him down on his own bed. Turning to Mr. Segram, he said harshly, "And you get on this chair." Yvonne came into the ward carrying a tray which she took to Mr. Quilby's bedside. She said to him, "Come over this way, Mr. Quilby, I've got your supper. That's it. come over; that's good." She said this softly, not roughly as many of the aides and attendants do. Yvonne smiled and laughed frequently and appeared to be talking with Mr. Quilby as she fed him.

Ed is at least as cruel as any of the regular help; to him the inmates are merely a burden, and since they remind him of his own degradation he vents his spleen on them. The researcher's observation is particularly striking because it throws Ed's harshness into relief against Yvonne's kindness.

What follows now is a long extract from the nineteenth study day. Mixed in with observations of Mr. Quilby is much of the life of the ward.

Mr. Quilby had just urinated into a urinal and then poured the urine on the floor under his bed. Mr. Fenn (an inmate working for his keep) came in from the northeast entrance pushing Mr. Ansmot in a wheel chair. He helped Mr. Ansmot into bed, talking to him. Mr. Ansmot asked, "Get my spout (urinal) before someone else gets it." Mr. Fenn replied, "Right away?" and then went out to the north ward. Mr. Ansmot said, "Yes, right away." A bell clanged three times. Mr. Quilby was saying, "I want this door opened so I can get in." He was crawling around on his bed as if he was looking for something. Mr. Ansmot turned to Mr. Triste and said, "How are you feeling today?" I couldn't hear Mr. Triste's response. Mr. Quilby said, "Oh shit." Mr. Fenn brought the urinal to Mr. Ansmot. He saw Mr. Quilby crawling and stumbling about his bed, shrugged his shoulders and left the ward. Mr. Fenn went to Mr. Quilby, and said, quite harshly, "Wait a minute." Mr. Quilby was pushing and pulling chairs about that were at his bedside. There were three in the direct vicinity of his bed. Mr. Fenn said, "Put it down; now sit it down." Then he said, "Oh, the hell with you," and left the ward. Mr. Quilby then turned one chair over, another one and another one upside down, stacking them one on top of the other until there was a maze of chairs. He was mumbling all the time, and the only thing I could understand was, "Where is that good rocking chair?" Mr. Ansmot and Mr. Triste were watching. Mr. Quert said to Mr. Stone, "He's crazy." Mr. Quert replied, "Yeh." Mr. Ansmot said to Mr. Quilby, "That's a chair you're turning over."

At the same time at the other end of the ward Mr. Benjamin (also blind) was talking aloud. No one was paying much attention to him. He was saying, "Now you'd better bring my shoes now. I told you last time you'd better bring my shoes." The floor was wet under Mr. Quert's bed and chair too. Mr. Edwards was also yelling at this time, "Bring my supper. Damn you, bring it, you slowpokes. I'll dynamite you, you bitch." Mr. Benjamin was continuing to call out that someone had stolen his shoes. Mr. Ansmot said to Mr. Quilby as Mr. Quilby approached Mr. Ansmot's bed, "Leave my bed alone. Get away from here." Then Mr. Stone went into the north ward. Mr. Benjamin was still talking about his shoes, "Bring those shoes back and put them where you got them from." Mr. Edwards was damning the staff about supper. Mr. Quilby was saying something about, "I can't get over" and Mr. Ansmot was slapping at Mr. Quilby with a towel, telling him to get away, "Get out of my bed, get!" Mr. Quilby was sitting on Mr. Ansmot's bed, and Mr. Ansmot said, again, "Get back. Don't wet on my bed." Meanwhile the TV was blaring though no one was watching it. Mr. Benjamin continued to talk for quite some time. Suddenly Mr. Ansmot yelled for Ed. Mr. Nathan came into the ward and looked at the clock above Mr. Roberts' bed. Mr. Triste stood up by his bed and watched Mr. Quilby. Mr. Ansmot was still trying to get Mr. Quilby to go away from his bedside, saying, "Get away from there. Leave that bed alone." Then Mr. Quilby went to the chairs he had stacked and scattered about on the floor. He sat on the floor and crawled about, over towards Mr. Harlow's and Mr. Benton's beds. Mr. Edwards left the ward yelling, "Dynamite." Mr. Ansmot yelled for Ed again and Mr. Quilby said, "Now I can't pee at all." Mr. Harlow yelled at Mr. Quilby, "Get out of here," four times, and then said, "Turn around," but Mr. Quilby said, "I can't," and Mr. Harlow slapped him. Then Mr. Harlow and Mr. Quilby seemed to be struggling with Mr. Harlow's chair. . . . Mr. Benton slapped Mr. Quilby's face, and Mr. Quilby said, "Quit slapping me on the face," and sat down on Mr. Benton's bed. Mr. Benton pushed him rather gently with his foot, saying, "Get over to your own bed. . . ." Mr.

Quilby and Mr. Harlow are now struggling with each other and Mr. Harlow is trying to push Mr. Quilby toward the latter's bed. When Mr. Quilby got on Mr. Reeves' bed Mr. Benton got up, went to Mr. Quilby and slapped his buttocks, pulled him over to his rightful bed, hit him hard again on the buttocks, and bounced him onto his bed. Then he straightened the overturned chairs and said to Mr. Quilby, "Damn you," and went to his own bed, saying, "He'd drive a man crazy." Mr. Quilby continued to mumble to himself. . . . Many of the patients did not seem to be aware of the scuffling going on. . . . Mr. Quilby was up again, groping about his bed. He moved it to and fro, as he talked to himself. He bounced his mattress, crawled across his bed, stepped into urine and then toward Mr. Segram's bed. As he moved Mr. Segram's chair he patted his foot in the urine on the floor. "Door" was the theme of his mumbling. When he pulled Mr. Segram's bed about two feet toward his own Mr. Segram said, "Oh, get the hell out of here." . . . Mr. Benton said to Mr. Charles, "He hasn't got any mind to cope with. No other method works except to be rough with him."

A consequence of the operation of the processes of distortion and withdrawal is to drive a badly distorted person to ever more extreme expressions of distortion, as extreme withdrawal increases his inability to cope with the environment. This increases his distortion, and society responds by withdrawing further. Mr. Quilby walks in urine and pats his foot in it, making himself more disgusting and accentuating tendencies to withdraw. When a person is distorted an ideology develops about how to deal with him. Mr. Benton says, for example, that since Mr. Quilby "hasn't got any mind to cope with, no other method works on him except to be rough with him." This is part of the ideology of hostile withdrawal.

During the researcher's hour of observation no regular staff appeared, so that the "handling" of Mr. Quilby was left entirely to the inmates, including Mr. Fenn and Ed. Though this "handling" was more of a crushing, the law of distortion helps us to understand the process: this highly mobile, disoriented, and incontinent old man threatens the only integrity left to the degraded inmates—their *bed-territories*. Whoever's bed he alights on and dirties on is blasted. Hence a massive though transient solidarity is mobilized to defeat him. It is the excremental patriotism of the degraded and the lost.

Daisy (an aide) brought in another tray and went to feed Mr. Quilby. She tugged at his shirt and said very harshly, "Sit up, sit up." Mr. Quilby sat on the side of the bed and Daisy poked food into his mouth. Supper was soup, coffee or milk, two slices of bread, two medium cookies, and a dish of apricot-colored pudding or something of similar consistency.

Daisy had given Mr. Quilby seven pieces of bread and he was eating the last two now. As Mr. Quilby went toward Mr. Jacks he picked up his cane and hit and poked Mr. Quilby, saying, "Get out of here." Mr. Twine, who had been trying to overtake Mr. Quilby, at last caught up with him and taking his arm, led him to bed, and he left. Mr. Quilby was up walking around again and climbed up on Ed's bed. Ed came into the ward and jerked him off his bed and Mr. Quilby screamed, "Oh, oh!" Mr. Edwards laughed as he watched. Mr. Quilby began to yell, "Hey, Mary (his sister)." Mr. Edwards muttered to himself, "Him and Mary." Mr. Quilby was saying, "I want to see my sister, Mary." He yelled particularly loudly, "Mary!" and Mr. Ruben said, "Oh, shut up." Mr. Segram talked to Mr. Quilby and I could hear Mr. Quilby say, "Somebody's going to get hung in here tonight. They're going to hang me and then get a needle and thread and sew me up." Someone else yelled, "Oh, shut up." Mr. Twine went to Mr. Quilby and Mr. Quilby yelled, "Go away, go away!" Ed went to Mr. Roberts' bedside, picked up his bedside table, put it on his head, wiggled his hips and sang. Mr. Roberts looked disgusted. Mr. Quilby was still yelling and Mr. Twine was holding him down in bed.

Mr. Quilby continued to talk and soon began to cry loudly. As Mr. Fenn passed him he bent down to Mr. Quilby's ear and yelled, "Ow!" and left the ward. On his way back into the ward he went over to Mr. Quilby and said in his ear, "Arr, arr, ow!"

It will have been observed that the law of distortion and withdrawal does not state what becomes of the distorted person, but simply that others withdraw from him. I have pointed out, however, that the withdrawal of others increases his anxiety and disorientation and thus further increases withdrawal. Mr. Quilby's anxiety has reached such a pitch that he expects to be hanged and sewn into a shroud. The unimpeded working out of the law would thus lead ultimately to a pervading sense of doom and finally, perhaps, to suicide. Before this, however, the distorted person will engage in ever-widening swings of disorientation until he becomes totally intolerable and is beaten, tied up, or killed. We have already seen Mr. Quilby beaten.

Mr. Quilby is restrained, flat in his bed, with leather straps on his wrists and ankles. Ropes are attached to the straps and tied to the legs of the bed. A sheet is over his head and he appears to be asleep. He appears to be tied tightly.

Everything was quiet except for Mr. Quilby. He seemed to be moaning softly. He was restrained and lying on a bare mattress and was partially covered by a sheet.

Everything on the division is quiet: there is no activity and no noise. Suddenly Mr. Quilby sat upright in bed and said, "Well, who passed away this time?" After a few minutes of silence he said, "It looks like we're all here again this morning—well, thank God for that."

Thus the law suggests increasing rejection of the distorted person by the environment leading to more and more punitive measures and the development in him of a *pervading sense of doom*. Obviously all of this can occur only in the presence of degraded fellow inmates and in an absence of controls. We have seen just this in Rosemont, a private home for obsolete paupers.

Something about the Help

Before bringing this section to a close I will present some more of the rather scant materials on the staff. From the observations and from the interview with the Second in Command, the reader will already have formed some opinion of their general indifference and callousness. The data I present now are intended to give insight into the poor self-conception of the staff, for it is important to restate the idea that unless a person feels degraded himself he will not be able to degrade others. It does not follow, of course, that all degraded people will try to degrade others; I suggest rather that a person with strong self-respect has no need to degrade his fellows.

Our first piece of data derives from an interview with Josephine Pike, an aide.

A huge woman in a dark print cotton dress entered the room. "Do you wanna see me?" she asked. "Yes, I do." I introduced myself, and since she didn't say anything but, "Howdy," I asked her name. "Pike," she said. Her dress was torn in a couple of places and her body odor was terrific; however, it was the hottest night of the year. Her tongue seemed too large for her mouth, and she was difficult to understand. Occasionally she drooled, and I wondered if she'd had a stroke. I didn't smell any liquor. She sort of sprawled down into a chair and draped the upper part of her body across the table, laying her head on one arm so as to face me. "Man," she said, "it's hot," and turned to brush a cockroach away. The cockroach kept inching up and she would nonchalantly throw out her arm to make him move. A couple of times she tried to swat him. This went on during most of the interview. . . . I first asked her the question about the qualities of a good aide, and she listed kindness, conscientiousness, and understanding the patient. . . . When I asked her, "What do you do when a patient gets upset," she brightened and sat up and said, "Well, I talk with 'em. I'm a Christian woman and I'm kind. I go and fix 'em a glass of milk or a jelly sandwich, because those men are hungry. You know, men: just love 'em and feed 'em and they're happy."

Perhaps not the dirt and the rags but the nonchalant familiarity with roaches is the symbol of degradation here. The reader's attention should be called to the fact that both Josephine and the Second in Command responded to the question, "What do you do when a patient gets upset?" by saying that they feed them, thus certifying to the fact that hunger is a chronic problem.

In the next example the researcher gets into a conversation with Lilly, an aide.

Lilly was feeding Mr. Quilby, and I heard her say to him sternly, "Shut up. Eat this. I said eat it." She told me that Mr. Quilby could feed himself but that she didn't like to see him do it—"The poor thing can't see and he makes such a mess." She put the cup to his mouth and he drank a big swallow of milk. Lilly said, "Oh, he likes his bread and milk. You'd live on it, practically, wouldn't you?" She said she would like to do more for all the patients but that it was impossible for her to do it all alone. She said there are 88 patients and that most of them would rather have her take care of them than anyone else, but that she isn't able to do it all.

Lilly said, "I'm a nurse, you know—or I could be if I would just go ahead and finish." She sounded proud and a little defensive. I said something noncommittal and she went on, "I could finish without half trying, and I'm sure I will some day; I think I should. I wouldn't have to do anything. Mrs. Dis said she could get it for me, and I'm sure she could. I could just get it from working under her. Then I could be a licensed practical nurse." The aide who always wears the black velvet hat came up to Lilly and me. Lilly said to me, "This is my helper." I said, "Well, that's nice." Lilly said, "Well, I have to have some help around here; I can't do it all myself."

The aide in the black cap then proceeded to give Lilly, her "superior," orders, including telling her to wipe up the puddles of milk on Mr. Quilby's bed, and Lilly obeyed.

It would be a misunderstanding of Josephine, Lilly, and Second in Command to interpret their misrepresentations as defense of the institution only. They may be far more interested in defending themselves—not against outer, but rather against inner criticism. When they talk as they do to the researchers they seem to be addressing their own consciences, saying, "I am really a human being; and you, my conscience, and I, are really one; you are not buried and alienated at all."

Summary and Conclusions

Every institution establishes a "national character" of inmates and staff in accordance with the remorseless requirements of the institution and in relation to the characteristics brought to it by inmates and staff. Given the commitment of Rosemont to profit, the laughable social security checks of the inmates, and the cost of food, comfort, and a high standard of living, certain consequences have to follow. In order for Mrs. Dis to be comfortable and make a good profit, according to her lights, she has no choice but to extract as much as she can from the pensions of the inmates and the salaries of her help and to limit the standard of living of both. That of the inmates is cut to a level just above starvation but below that of a good prison. In order to do this a fundamental transformation has to be brought in the mode of life and the self-conception of the inmates and in the staff's way of perceiving them. In short, Mrs. Dis makes it necessary for her institution, as personified in her staff, to conceptualize the inmates as child-animals, and to treat them accordingly. This in turn is made possible because in our culture personality exists to the extent of ability to pay, and in terms of performance of the culturally necessary tasks of production, reproduction, and consumption.

But the transformations are possible in Rosemont only because of the acquiescence of the inmates; and this is obtained not only because the inmates are old and powerless, having been abandoned by their relatives and a miserly Government, but because, with one or two exceptions, they recognize that being obsolete they have no rights; because they understand that having nothing they are not going to get anything. Meanwhile their degradation is intensified by the fact that while economically poor they are intellectually poor too; for the schooling they received, and the culture in which they have lived, provide no resources for making life in a filthy hole more bearable. They can neither read nor carry on conversations of interest to one another; nor, having lost faith, do they have the culture of worship. Rather they spend their time staring into space, defending their beds against the gropings of the blind, the incontinent, and the disoriented, or watching the behavior of their blind and psychotic fellows, while they wait obsessively for the next meager meal.

Thus the "national character" of all the inmates becomes reduced to several simple components under the tyranny of the institution. These components are apathy, obsessive preoccupation with food and excreta, the adoption of the role of child-animal, and defense of the bed. To this may be added general acquiescence in everything the institution does, decline of the disgust function, and preoccupation with reminiscence.

FOR FURTHER READING

A useful work on aging is *Aging in Today's Society* (Englewood Cliffs: Prentice-Hall, 1960) by Clark Tibbitts, a leading authority on the subject. Interesting material will be found in the compendium issued by the U.S. Senate Committee on Aging, *Developments in Aging: 1959 to 1963* (Washington: Government Printing Office, 1963). Most readable is the short essay by Harold L. Sheppard, "The Poverty of Aging," in Ben B. Seligman, ed., *Poverty as a Public Issue* (New York: Free Press, 1965). There are numerous standard texts on social and economic security. For an incisive analysis, the student should consult Margaret S. Gordon, *The Economics of Welfare Policies* (New York: Columbia University Press, 1963); a critical view is offered by Gilbert Y. Steiner, *Social Insecurity: The Politics of Welfare* (Chicago: Rand McNally, 1966).

CRISIS IN
THE SCHOOLS

Jeremy Larner

Children in the slums have little chance of reaping the harvest promised by education. They do badly in school because the school expects a poor performance. Many a ghetto child comes to school with as much motivation as a middle-class child but discovers, within a few years, that he is expected to fall behind; and fall behind he does. He becomes withdrawn, a slow reader, uninterested in school, a drop-out, a delinquent. In referring to their charges as "them," the teachers confess their expectation of failure. The slum child comes to believe that the teachers and school officials are in collusion against him, and the teacher-pupil conflict becomes intense. The school then concludes the slum child is uneducable and hangs on the label of "psychological unreadiness."

Slum children show no achievement because they are greatly oppressed by school, street, and slum. The synergistic impact that results corrupts the environment and the child as well. The larger society offers few meaningful goals to the slum child; it is not surprising that he spends his time doing nothing. As difficulties develop, the school decides for the child—and often against him —by forcing him into vocational courses, the usual dumping

Source: Jeremy Larner, "The New York School Crisis," *Dissent* (Spring, 1964), pp. 243–269. Reprinted with permission.

place for slower students. The drop-out becomes a "push-out" who lacks a marketable skill that would help him climb above poverty.

How these conditions develop is detailed by Jeremy Larner in a special report originally prepared for *Dissent* magazine. Mr. Larner visited numerous schools in New York City, spoke to teachers, parents, and students, and his prognosis is bleak indeed. The crisis in the schools is deeply rooted; it will take more than an occasional special program or teachers' conference to rectify matters. Mr. Larner teaches at the State University of New York at Stony Brook. An editor of *Dissent,* he is the author of a novel, *Drive, He Said,* and a study of drug addiction.

I. THE CIRCUMSTANCES

UFT Official: *Why is it we can get young people to volunteer for the Peace Corps to teach in Ghana, yet we can't get them to teach in public schools in Harlem? Answer: Because in Ghana, there's hope.*

Let me start with some statistics. There are 132 elementary schools and 31 junior high schools in New York City whose students are almost entirely (over 90% in the elementary schools; over 85% in the junior highs) Negro and Puerto Rican. In the past six years, while Negro and Puerto Rican enrollment has gone up 53%, white enrollment has fallen 8%, and the number of predominantly Negro and Puerto Rican schools has doubled. Of New York's one million schoolchildren, roughly 40% are Negro and Puerto Rican, 60% "other." Efforts of the Board of Education in the past six years to eliminate blatant gerrymandering and allow some voluntary transfers have reduced by a third the number of schools where Negroes and Puerto Ricans are less than 10% of enrollment. But the problem gets more difficult all the time, as is indicated by the fact that 52%—an outright majority—of the city's 1st graders are Negro or Puerto Rican.

The increase in segregated schools is due to three factors. First, rural minority groups are moving into the city and middle-class urban whites are heading for the suburbs. Second, discrimination, economic pressures, and lack of effective planning confine the newcomers to ghettos. Third, cautious whites send their children to private or parochial schools rather than "risk" a neighborhood school where minorities predominate. Over 450,000 New York children attend private or parochial schools, a figure that would represent a staggering percentage even for an exclusive suburb.

Thus New York City suffers from an educational problem which it has come to describe as *de facto* segregation. The Board of Education says the facts are essentially beyond its control; the civil rights groups say they are the facts of a racist society, and must in all justice be eliminated by whatever means possible.

Segregation in ghetto schools is more than racial; there is segregation by economic class as well. Wherever Negro parents reach the middle class, at least some of them send their kids to private schools. Lower-class Negro kids find themselves isolated in schools which are understaffed, underequipped, overcrowded, demoralized, and conspicuously lacking in the mixture of cultural backgrounds which can make life in New York such an educational experience. Many of them are children of parents who are in effect first-generation immigrants from southern and rural areas; for of New York's 1,100,000 Negroes, 340,000 have arrived in the last ten years, 630,000 in the last twenty years. Most of the 600,000 Puerto Ricans have come in the past decade, while the white population has dwindled by 500,000.

Teaching middle-class children the ins and outs of a culture made for them is obviously easier than struggling with ghetto children, most of whom are members of a racial group which has never been allowed to recover from the effects of slavery. Some minority schools have annual teacher turnover rates of over 60%. Some teachers flatly refuse to take assignments in such schools; others drop out as the school year proceeds. Not only is one out of every two teachers a substitute, but some classes may stay without a regularly assigned teacher all year, defeating one temporary substitute after another. One can see that the atmosphere in minority schools is hardly conducive to learning. It is estimated that 85% of the 8th-grade students in Harlem are "functional illiterates," which means that their reading is not above 5th-grade level—in many cases it is much below.

Though some authorities, e.g., Kenneth Clark, disagree, it is hard to believe that the social conditions under which most New York Negroes live are not responsible for some of the difficulty. According to the Harlem Youth survey, whose figures many observers regard as conservative, only one-half of Harlem children under 18 are living with both parents, more than one-quarter of Harlem youth receives welfare assistance, and the rate of narcotics addiction in the area is ten times that for the rest of the city.

By the time they reach junior high school, ghetto children are well aware of their social situation, and it does not exactly give them a feeling of unlimited possibilities. Let me quote from two batches of essays which were gathered at different Harlem elementary schools from a 6th-grade class of "slow" readers (S) and a 6th-grade class of "fast" readers (F). I think the language shows as much about the children—their educational retardation and yet their straightforwardness and toughness—as about the conditions they describe.

6th-grade boy (F): This story is about a boy namely me, who lives in a apartment in and around the slum area. I feel that other people should be interested in what I have to say and just like me, *try* to do something about it, either by literal or diatribe means. This book is only to be read by men and women boys and girls who feel deeply serious about segrigation and feel that this is no joke.

6th-grade girl (S): I am not satifeyed with the dope addictes around our block. They take dope in our hallway every night. Another is they break in stores and bars. I am desatifed with the lady that live under us. she set fire to Doris's door. Some dope backs live under us. The lady under us robbed Teddy's aunt for $17.00's. One night a dope addict went cazey in our hally way. They are so many bums in our block. Please help to get and keep them out.

6th-grade girl (S): I don't like people going around youing bad Lanugwsh around litter Kide a bearking in Store and fighting and youing dop. And Killing people. And drunk in hallwall. They should stop drink They are teacher the Kide how to Steel I see it alot of tim but I dont pay it no mind I am surrounded by them.

6th-grade boy (S): Im not happy about the people who dink. wiskey and go to sleep And I not happy about the peole who come in my hallway and go up stairs and take a neals and. stick there themselve in the arm. I not happy about the people who buy wine and wiskey and broke the bottle in the hallway

6th-grade girl (S): the be out there in the hall taking dope and I be freighten.

6th-grade boy (S): I deslike the peple being hit by cars, the car crashes, peple fighting, the peple jumping of roofes, stelling paper from the stores, peple picking pocketes, the peple with out thir cubs on dogs and stop peple from taking dop in this naborhood.

6th-grade girl (F): (True) *What a Block!* (true)

My block is the most terrible block I've ever seen. There are at lease 25 or 30 narcartic peple in my block. The cops come around there and tries to act bad but I bet inside of them they are as scared as can be. They even had in the papers that this block is the worst block, not in Manhattan but in New York City. In the summer they don't do nothing except shooting, stabing, and fighting. They hang all over the stoops and when you say excuse me to them they hear you but they just don't feel like moving. Some times they make me so mad that I feel like slaping them and stuffing bag of garbage down their throats.

The fact that these kids have been encouraged to describe their surroundings is the first sign of hope that they will be able to change them. The school should represent that possibility; it should be a fortress of security in which the children are respected, accepted and developed. Otherwise they are surrounded, as the little girl says; drug addiction, for example, will begin to appear in their ranks while they are still in junior high school—and addiction is only the most dramatic form of withdrawal and defeat.

Looking around him, the young Negro boy will find few "father figures" to imitate; for the men of his world have not been accorded the honorable work men need to earn self-respect. Bitter, confused, withdrawn, violent against one another, lower-class Negro men do not usually last long with their women. The families are matriarchal, the children remaining with their mothers while a succession of "uncles" come and go. There is small hope of that masculine self-respect which is the traditional basis of family pride. The little boy is regarded as inferior to the little girl, and has less chance of survival—by which I mean simply less chance of getting through life without cracking up, without sliding into some form of self-obliteration.

Dismal to tell, the schools in many ways duplicate the situation of the homes. The classroom confronts the child with the same old arrangement: a woman with too many kids. Far too few of the elementary schoolteachers are men, let alone Negro men. The size of classes, usually around 30 pupils per class, makes individual attention—and thus the development of positive identity and incentive—as unlikely at school as it is at home.

When lower-class Negro children enter elementary school, they are already "behind" in several important respects. In crowded tenement apartments children are in the way from the moment they are born. While the adults of the matriarchal clan unit work or wander, children are brought up by older children, who have reasons of their own to feel impatient or harassed. According to the teacher whose "fast" 6th-grade pupils I quoted above,

. . . middle-class Negro kids need integration. But what the lower-class kids need right now is that somehow we conquer the chaos they live in. They have no stability whatever—no family, no home, no one to talk with them. They live in a world without space or time. I mean that literally. Even by the time these kids reach the 6th grade, most of them can't tell time. You can't talk to them about the future—say, about jobs—because they won't know what you're talking about. And when you refer to concepts of space, why you can't talk about "somewhere else," tell how far away another city is, how long a river is, or simple facts of geography. Though they're fantastically sophisticated, more sophisticated than maybe they ought to be, about how adults behave, their mental orientation is almost utterly without abstract concepts. Look: they don't even know who pays the welfare! They don't even know what checks are!

Of course this particular teacher will get his kids talking and thinking about time and space and jobs and where the money comes from. But there aren't enough like him, and one year of a good teacher can dispel the chaos for very few. The class he has taken such pains with finds itself a year later without an assigned teacher, and the boy who last year wrote a brilliant autobiography is in danger this year of flunking at junior high, breaking down, and spending his high school years in and out of institutions.

Why don't teachers make more progress with these children? Because they are woefully short of books and materials, especially good readers based on the facts of urban life. Because they have to spend so much time on discipline.[1] Because they get poor support from their principals and from the rest of the top-heavy school bureaucracy. But the truth is that most of New York's teachers are too middle-class, too insensitive or too fragile to teach ghetto children successfully. Not that they are worse than teachers in other places, they are simply less suited to their jobs. Not all of them are bothered by their failure; some stay in slum schools because apparently it gives them a sense of security to blame the kids for what they fail to teach them. Others, with the best will in the world, are baffled by children who literally speak a different language. One young white teacher, extremely hard-working and perhaps more honest than most, told me after a grueling day,

I hate these kids. They're impossible. How did they get this way? I never thought I'd become so authoritarian.

Most of the teachers are conscientious: that's one of the hallmarks of the professional person. But the manner in which teachers are trained and chosen—which I will discuss below—is practically guaranteed to eliminate those possessing the imagination and flexibility to get through to slum children.

As for the curriculum, it is hopelessly inappropriate. The readers still current in practically every school are those insipid productions featuring Sally, Dick and Jane, the golden-haired cardboard tots from Sterilityville. One could go on by describing a series of tests and achievement-levels, but tests and levels are irrelevant to children who mostly do not pass or reach them. Let me quote Martin Mayer (from his book, *The Schools*) on what our young tenement-dwellers are supposed to be learning by the time they get to high school:

[1] Discipline as opposed to socialization. The 6th-grade teacher quoted above reports that with a "slow" class he begins with checkers, and that it takes weeks to get the children to play together without turning over the board and having at each other. Then he brings out the readers.

In New York . . . the major Theme Center for tenth-grade "Language Arts" is "Learning to Live with the Family." . . . The curriculum guide suggests "round-table, panel, and forum discussions" on "questions relating to allowances, dating, working after school, selecting and entertaining friends, choosing a career, minding younger brothers and sisters, helping with household chores, contributing earnings to the family, decorating one's own room, choosing family vacation places, using the family car."

But what difference does high school make? The battle is lost long before then. Perhaps it's already lost by the time 1st graders move to the 2nd grade, when only 10% of them are on reading level.

Yet, when all is said and done, are not these conditions surmountable by individual effort? Is it not possible for the majority of these youngsters to pull themselves up by their own bootstraps, as so many of their 2nd-generation American teachers say that they or their parents did? Or is this problem unique somehow, does it have to do with the unprecedented oppression and separation of a group that has never in the history of this country been free? Is it really true, as the 1954 Supreme Court decision contends, that "Segregation of white and colored children in public schools has a detrimental effect upon the colored children. . . . A sense of inferiority affects the motivation of the child to learn"?

In the opinion of this observer, no one could sit for long in Harlem classes without seeing overwhelming evidence of the demoralizing effects of segregation. These children are treated as inferior, just as their parents and grandparents and great-grandparents were—and there is no sense of any possibility that such treatment is ending! In the classroom of a 1st-grade teacher who was a militant supporter of the boycott, I was surprised to find cut-out pictures of white children used almost exclusively as bulletin board illustrations. Later I found the purified faces of Sally, Dick and Jane beaming out at me in ghetto classrooms of teachers Negro or white, liberal or not: as if to say, these are what good children are like.

5th-grade Lower East Side boy (F): I have a problem that I am colored. I would like to be handsom but I cant because other people have strait blond hair and they are handsom.

In a 2nd-grade Harlem classroom the teacher, a lively, intelligent Negro woman, has her kids acting out a nursery tale. In front of the class stands a shy, finger-sucking little girl, her hair in pigtails, absolutely adorable and black. From her neck hangs a large square of cardboard, on which an adult has painted the head of a white girl with abundantly flowing golden hair. Caption: "GOLDILOCKS."

In another 2nd-grade classroom, where well-cared-for Negro children are industriously and quietly working under the direction of a Negro teacher, I glance up and see a row of self-portraits above the front blackboard. I count: of 23 portraits, 1 red, 1 green, only 2 brown, and 19 white as the paper they're drawn on.

The sense of inferiority runs deeper than skin-deep. I remember a junior-high-school social-studies teacher trying to discuss the school boycott with his 9th-grade "slow" pupils. Most of them are long since lost; they look as though they have drawn curtains across the inside of their eyeballs. It develops that they do not know the words "boycott" or "civil rights," and to them "discrimination" is something that happens down South. And oh the tortured embarrassment with which they answer questions! From beneath the embarrassment there slinks a kind of arrogance, thriving it seems on the mere fact that the teacher is trying to teach them—as if to say, imagine this fool, asking *me* a question! Whereupon they laugh. They have to. And we are all relieved.

Whether they know the word "discrimination" or not, these kids know they are not worth much to the world they live in. Some of them, all too many, are not worth much to themselves, and lash out in self-hating violence at the nearest target, usually someone who reminds them of themselves. Already the white people of America are beginning to dread the day when these children, as some day they surely must, will recognize their real enemies. As they are at last beginning to . . .

West Harlem 6th-grade boy (F): Teacher! In the caveman days, if there were Negro cavemen, did the white cavemen use them as slaves?

II. THE FRYING PAN

Almost never has the New York Board of Education voluntarily taken steps for greater integration. The highly-touted Open Enrollment program was initiated in the fall of 1960 only after neighborhood school strikes and the threat of further strikes led by Rev. Milton Galamison and Paul Zuber. Open Enrollment is a voluntary transfer program designed ostensibly to relieve overcrowding as well as to integrate. In Open Enrollment overcrowded schools (mostly minority schools) are designated as "sending" schools, whose pupils may apply—on an individual basis—for transfer to "receiving" schools in other neighborhoods. The responsibility is on the parents of each child, and the response to Open Enrollment has indicated no desire on the part of ghetto Negroes to rush their children to schools in "better" neighborhoods. To date Open Enrollment busses at city expense only 15,000 children each day. Surely, many of these are middle-class Negroes . . . and whites. A teacher on the Lower East Side whose school is over 95% Negro and Puerto Rican reports that the only ones who left her school in Open Enrollment were ten of the remaining white kids, who bussed daily all the way to Queens.

Even since the 1954 Supreme Court decision, the Board of Ed has never done much to relieve *de facto* segregation unless pushed. The emphasis has usually been on adding "cultural enrichment" to the minority schools rather than on breaking them up. The missionary approach is well articulated by a writer in *Commentary* (January, 1964):

> The draining away of the white middle classes from the public schools could probably be slowed down by the addition of more cultural opportunities to the curriculum. This, in turn, would still the fears of Negro leaders about racial imbalance.

Easier said than done. The best-publicized program along these lines so far is the Higher Horizons program (since 1959), which grew from the Demonstration Guidance program (1956). Demonstration Guidance provided extra reading and math teachers, guidance counsellors, materials, and trips to symphonies, museums, etc., for the more intelligent members of a certain junior high school, with the result that their achievement levels went up considerably, many fewer of them dropped out of high school, and more went to college. But this was only a pilot program which did not reach every child even in the school where it took place. And now that the project is over, that school is depressing to visit: performance seems as low as ever and white children in the neighborhood look for excuses to transfer elsewhere for junior high.

As for the Higher Horizons program, most of the better teachers in the system regard it as a farce. An occasional movie or trip to the museum does not effectively change a child's view of himself or help him learn what he is not learning. And why assume that the official "culture" is truly educational? A Negro teacher told me that the last Higher Horizons film he had taken his class to see was about Jamaica, and every scene depicted Negro servants smilingly waiting on whites. The class didn't like it, though not all of them could say why.

Another enrichment concept is the designation of minority schools as "Special Service" schools. This program involves beefing up school staffs with extra *non-classroom* personnel: psychologists, guidance specialists, and teacher coordinators. The coordinators supposedly gather special materials, brief teachers on the problems of teaching certain subjects, keep records of individual cases, etc. As a rule the Special Service personnel are resented by other teachers. It's hard to believe that they do a lot of good. Students tend to mistrust the motives of guidance interviewers from class backgrounds different from their own, and to put them on. The NE (non-English) coordinators, who are supposed to help teachers teach Puerto Rican kids English, are not required to know Spanish, and many will explain to you that it's *better* they don't.

It is true, however, that New York has done more for school integration than other cities of comparable size. In Chicago, for example, the Negro sections lie in two long narrow strips, so that it would be easy to pair off overcrowded Negro schools with adjoining white schools. Instead, the school board, as in St. Louis and other cities, prefers to attach portable classrooms to the Negro schools, and this has led to rioting and great bitterness.

Last June, when New York State Commissioner of Education, Dr. James Allen, called for all local Boards of Education to submit plans to end "racial imbalance" in the public schools, the Board of Ed was not unresponsive. On August 23, Superintendent Gross submitted a plan calling for a free transfer program —wherein *any* pupil in a school with a high percentage of minority enrollment might transfer to *any* school with an empty seat for him, transportation supplied by the city. Beyond that Gross announced the pairing of two junior high schools, some limited rezoning, and a number of studies, advisory groups, and community cooperation gimmicks.

The civil rights groups were up in arms. They pointed out that at this rate the school system would never be desegregated. Banding together as the Citywide Committee for Integration, they threatened a school boycott unless greater use were made of the techniques for massive rezoning. These included the pairing of elementary schools (the Princeton Plan), the reorganization of junior high feeding patterns, and the building of "educational parks," i.e., clusters of schools either in central locations or on the fringes of the city, to which thousands of children of all ages would be brought by special transportation. Also, the civil rights groups demanded a "timetable," a guarantee that in a given number of years desegregation would be complete. Otherwise, any plan might amount to lip service.

At this point Dr. Gross evidently felt that his professional competence was being challenged. He was not anxious to confer with laymen or let them have a voice in the planning. Correspondingly, the rights groups were anxious to make the Board assume full responsibility. But as the boycott loomed nearer, public pressure brought the city administration into the act, and the main combatants were brought together in the office of the City Commission on Human Rights, where they signed an agreement on September 5. The boycott was called off, and in turn the Board of Ed agreed to have a tentative plan for integration by December, 1963, and a final plan by February, 1964. Both plans were to "include provisions for a substantial, realistic and working program of integration in every school district in September, 1964."

In essence the December 3 plan was identical with the August plan: its basic approach was the free transfer program and a study of the Princeton Plan with a view to applying it at some unspecified date to only sixteen schools. There was great stress on beefing up minority schools through special "crash" programs: as a starter, the Board initiated an after-school study center program, to begin immediately, under which some teachers would receive extra pay to help pupils who stayed to do homework or receive extra instruction. As for the timetable, Gross disposed of that with a masterpiece of white liberal rhetoric:

Like other cherished aspirations and ideals of humanity, [the timetable] represents a direction rather than a fixed point, and a general movement upward.

In other words, no timetable.

From that point on, quiet hatred changed to open warfare. Said June Shagaloff, education director of the NAACP,

The Board of Education has simply proceeded as if a commitment did not exist—as if the civil rights movement did not exist—as if the Negro community did not exist.

And Milton Galamison:

Gross's interim plan is like saying we're gonna have you and your wife for dinner but not saying *when*.

The Citywide Committee, led by Galamison, went ahead with boycott plans. In the middle of December and again on December 31, Galamison led picketing and sit-ins at Gross's office which resulted in the arrest of 62 demonstrators. Gross's office—manned by an extremely able public relations staff—made a big show of conferring with "responsible" parent groups, and staged several open meetings to collect "constructive" opinions from civic groups that had already published their opinions. Meanwhile press and public worked themselves into a frenzy about "bussing," and the notion was widespread that the leaders of the boycott were fanatics who did not really speak for the civil rights organizations.

To open the Free Transfer program, 65,000 questionnaires were sent out to eligible families and only 5,500 applications were returned. Which proved to the Board that Negro parents are interested in improving their neighborhood schools rather than in integration, and to the Committee that it is asking too much to expect individual parents to make exceptions of their kids.

Most teachers feel that the after-school study centers have been a total flop. Both the principals' association and the UFT came out against them. As one Harlem teacher involved in the program told me:

It's bull. It was conceived as a political device to seem to be doing something for integration. But after a month have we received any materials? And those kids who most need to stay don't. Let's face it: what we're running is a baby-sitting service. I suspect that when the warm weather comes, the after-school centers will be empty.

Meanwhile, on January 5 Gross announced to the press—in language worthy of the Pentagon—a "saturation program" for minority schools, involving "task forces" of "hand-picked" teachers, who with the cooperation of universities and teachers' colleges would carry out a program of "reading mobilization." Despite the fact that the announcement carried not a word as to finance, training, methods, probable limitations or starting date, *The Times* and *The Post* flipped over it.

NY *Times* editorial, Jan. 6: The saturation program combines imagination with good sense. In contrast to the political publicity stunts of the school system's critics, it offers a realistic and at the same time dramatic road to improved education for slum children. Such demagogic devices as the projected school boycott and the Public Education Association's "March on Albany" create divisions in the community that impede integration, rather than advance it.

Alas for the PEA! They weren't for the boycott; all they wanted for the schools was money.

III. The Boycotters

The structure of the boycott organization is interesting as a sign of the new forms the Negro movement is taking. The charge that the boycott leadership was not the true Negro leadership was essentially a red herring. The original Committee was formed by the local chapters of the NAACP and CORE, plus the Harlem Parents Committee and Parents Workshop for Equality (from Brooklyn). The local Urban League went along as a supporting member and later the Committee was joined by Puerto Rican groups also. If the opposition—or the reluctant approval—of national leaders like Roy Wilkins was recorded on the front pages, local leaders could legitimately claim the stronger grass-roots contacts. Besides, men like Philip Randolph and James Farmer supported the boycott from the beginning, as did most other Negro leaders from Jackie Robinson to Martin Luther King. That the national NAACP did not participate as strongly as it might have is an old complaint of local-action projects.

Whether or not the boycott represented the Negro people as a whole is another question. But who does represent the Negro people? Who could? Not necessarily the national civil rights organizations, which for years have been run by small cadres of dedicated people, some of them white, who struggle to collect dues from their rosters of mostly inactive members. Yet to read the papers, and to hear the president of the Board of Education, one would think that the Negro could not be "responsibly" represented unless Booker T. Washington dropped down from heaven for a cup of tea.

Not that the leadership didn't have its weaknesses, which stemmed from oversimplification both in the boycott's demands and in the way demands were pressed. Perhaps the most serious lapse was the failure to establish liaisons with liberal or labor groups and to publicize those liaisons. Not until Bayard Rustin joined the Committee just before the February 3 boycott were there any great efforts in this direction. Before then, Galamison specialized in statements like the following:

White people just don't understand the problem. You hear all this talk about our losing friends, but what friends do we lose? The friends who are only friends as long as things stay the way they are. But I think the white liberal has had to do a lot of thinking in the past year—answer a lot of questions—and when he answers those questions he finds he's not a liberal after all.

Though there was some truth in this sort of statement, it was not the most useful kind to make. Losing false friends was one thing, but the boycott did not do enough to make positive supporters. As a result, many whites and Negroes alike remained puzzled and gave only passive support.

Of all groups involved the most bewildered and uncertain were the teachers. The boycott leadership made only token efforts to reach them, and up to a week before the boycott they were hopelessly confused and uninformed.

Schoolteachers are especially prone to what used to be called bourgeois individualism—which is the greatest virtue of the best and the most exasperating failure of the mediocre. And so many teachers are mediocrities in the world of adults—timid, stubborn, and prissy. An individualism of petty crankiness is perhaps most pronounced in the Negro teachers, some of whom struggle mightily *not* to think of themselves as Negroes.

Young Negro man teaching kindergarten in Harlem: The unfortunate thing about the black teachers is that they are threatened by these kids—because the teachers themselves have swallowed the middle-class dogma hook, line and sinker.

The UFT was caught in a difficult position. Those of its officers who were sympathetic to the boycott felt they were way ahead of the membership, so far ahead that open support could lead to mutiny and collapse of the union. Besides, relations with the Board of Ed were tenuous, and the UFT leaders wanted to improve them; for they envision a day when the UFT will be an important voice in making educational policy. As indeed it should be, but the effect of such ambition is to pull the teachers away from political action. Consequently, the union straddled the issue, passed a vague motion in favor of integration, and vowed it would defend any teacher penalized beyond loss of a day's pay for his absence on a matter of individual conscience. This stand drew the fire of both sides. The press generally counted the union with the forces of evil, while a group of boycott-minded teachers which tried to force UFT into a position of outright support, was easily outmaneuvered on the floor of the delegate assembly by UFT president Charles Cogen. Afterwards one of the rebel teachers said to me,

Yes, I know the union might be destroyed. So what? What good is this union if it can't take a stand on the most important issue in our whole damn society? Is there anything that could be more relevant to teaching or schools or education? That's the trouble with unions in this country; they can't look beyond the ends of their noses.

By the morning of the boycott, most teachers were sincerely trying to look beyond their noses but not at all sure that the issues were clear to see. Most of those who stayed out did so in observance of the picket line. Many who went in felt a kind of wretchedness they had never before been forced to feel.

IV. THE FIZZLE

As the crisis developed, Dr. Gross became ill and flew to California. The pre-boycott warfare tended to concentrate on Milton Galamison and the president of the Board of Education, James Donovan. Donovan soon emerged as a self-righteous type. "This is a Board of Education, not a Board of Transportation or a Board of Integration," he blurted out to reporters. Later he wrote a letter saying he was misquoted and sent it to the leaders of national, not local, organizations.

Galamison for his part took strong moral positions, but remained fuzzy as to details. It was up to the experts to work out the details, he said: the advice of his group had been consistently rejected anyway. His positions on the two most frequent objections to the boycott were candid and sharp and right as far as they went, but they didn't go far enough to lift debate out of the circular tail-chasing it soon settled into.

Galamison on bussing: Anyone who says he's in favor of integration *and* the neighborhood school is a liar—he's in favor of segregation. This whole subject of bussing has been caricatured and exaggerated by these same anti-Negro values that created segregation in the first place. We bus blind kids, retarded kids, handicapped kids, 15,000 Open Enrollment kids, and thousands of private and parochial school kids. We're not against bussing, we're against the Negro.

Galamison in answer to the objection that segregated schools can't change until housing is desegregated: If you're gonna say you need housing first, well—to get comparable housing, you gotta have comparable income; to get comparable income, you gotta have comparable training; to get comparable training, you gotta have comparable *education*—and here the schools are turning out thousands of retarded Negro children each year! So you can't start with housing.

There is obviously something rhetorical about these statements. They are not necessarily the words of a man who wants to bus every Negro child, but the words of a leader fighting an enemy who he knows from experience will not even admit he's under attack, let alone move an inch, until he's hit with every weapon one can command.

While the February plan was being drawn up, a sincere if belated effort might have been made to give the civil rights groups representation among those responsible for the planning of school integration. Instead Donovan chose to confirm their opinion of him.

Donovan on TV: The grave danger here has been that the responsible leaders . . . are having their leadership threatened by some irresponsible publicity seekers.

Donovan to press: [The Board of Ed] is doing more than those who are advocating freedom now and integration now. [Civil rights leaders are] dealing in jingles [instead of] constructive, practical plans.

The more Donovan insisted that the boycott leaders were irresponsible, the more he convinced them that only the most extreme demands could bring worthwhile results. The only positive event in the final stages of preboycott hostilities was the entrance of Bayard Rustin, Coordinator of the March on Washington, who evidently decided that if this boycott was going to occur, it would be better off with him than without him. He gave the boycott exactly what it lacked: an organizational efficiency which got signs made, statements issued, propaganda mimeographed, volunteers directed. Also Rustin's attitude toward the boycott itself was different from Galamison's, as we shall see.

The Board's final plan was supposed to be announced on February 1, and if it were unacceptable the boycott was scheduled for February 3, the first day of the new semester. Galamison, in order to keep the various member groups of the boycott organizations together, had reluctantly agreed that the boycott would last one day only—would be, in effect, a demonstration rather than a reprisal. Only if the boycott failed to produce significant changes would it be repeated. Donovan, meanwhile, staunchly resisted all attempts to bring the disputing parties together again. Jumping the gun on the February deadline, he took the whole Board on TV January 29 to explain the new plan directly to the people.

The essence of the new "first plan" (as it was mysteriously called) was that 10 out of 31 segregated junior highs and 20 out of 134 segregated elementary schools would be Princeton-planned, and a definite and quick timetable was announced for this. Also, specific efforts would be made to eliminate double-sessions, overcrowding, and school construction in segregated neighborhoods.

This plan drew attack from both sides. The boycotters pointed out that it would leave the bulk of the ghetto schools untouched. The American Jewish Congress—which has been offering "constructive" integration plans since 1957—stated that at least 83 segregated elementary schools could be paired immediately. On the other side, an organization called Parents and Taxpayers prepared to go to court to save neighborhood schools and the purity of their children. Some newspapers criticized Donovan and the Board for going beyond Gross; anonymous board members were quoted to the effect that it would be impossible to carry out this new plan, that there was no money to finance it, and that when the paired schools were announced in March there would be hell to pay.

And the boycott was on. "Even if you don't understand the situation," Galamison appealed, "give us the benefit of the doubt." Few people, black or white, fully understood the aims of the boycott.

No one knew what to expect; boycott leaders were predicting 50,000 absences and were ready to call that a victory. In a bit of brilliant improvisation, Galamison when interviewed on TV pledged that his demonstrators would remain nonviolent, but warned that nonviolent action often attracts "sociopaths" to the scene. The only remedy was for parents to keep their children home. Donovan played right into his hands. Instead of responding with a guarantee of safety for all children attending school, he ranted that he would hold Galamison "personally and criminally responsible" if any child, Negro or white, were injured during the boycott.

On boycott day, whether from principle, fear of injury, or a natural desire to take the day off, 364,000 pupils stayed home. Donovan, missing no opportunity to put his foot in his mouth, was quick to announce that the boycott had been "a fizzle." While the newspapers began deciding he was "not the right man for the job," Donovan was announcing that the boycott would make absolutely no difference in the Board's program or policy. And the civil rights groups began to argue among themselves about just when and how they would take further action.

V. The Aftereffects

What effects did the boycott have? In terms of Negro self-respect, undoubtedly positive. In terms of its own objectives, too, it was successful, forcing a more definite integration plan than the Board of Ed would ever have volunteered. But in other areas the effects were moot.

The Schools

Anyone who knows anything about the New York schools cannot help but be uneasy about the gap between the strategy of the boycott and the situation it attacks. The issue is by no means so simple as Galamison often made it out to be:

We feel that if we desegregate the public schools, these other problems—like overcrowding, low curriculum, etc.—will go away. Like when you have an injection, and you take a shot of penicillin.

One problem that will not go away is that of money. In the 1964–65 state budget, New York City, which has 34% of the state's schoolchildren, is slated to receive only 25% of total state aid to schools. Due in part to the machinations of a rurally-dominated state legislature, the City and its residents pay 49.7% of all state taxes and get back only 37.3% in benefits. The rationale for low school aid is that New York has an abundance of taxable property with which to finance its schools; the catch is that the City also has stupendous upkeep expenses.

To be specific, the value of taxable property per pupil in New York City is $31,878, far above the state average of $26,600; and it is this ratio on which state aid is based. But whereas City taxes amount to $54.27 per $1000 of property valuation, the City spends $39.39 of that money for municipal purposes and only $14.88 for schools—which compares poorly with what is spent by surrounding districts. Even though the City tax rate is high, moreover, funds collected are minimized by the gross undervaluation of property holdings. Real estate in New York's five boroughs is currently valued at the bargain total of $35 billion; theoretically Manhattan is worth only $13.5 billion—but don't try to buy it if that's all you can raise. Furthermore, much of the non-school bite on New York's property taxes goes to pay for problems that only large cities have—such as the costs of tearing up streets and assigning extra police to direct traffic when property owners decide to pull down or put up new buildings for their private profit. And since current property taxes don't entirely cover the costs of municipal overburden, the City shifts the load to the public in regressive taxes such as the 4% city sales tax.

Financial shortages drastically affect the operation of the schools. According to a study of the New York schools sponsored jointly by the PEA and the UFT, "30% of the daily instructional staff is made up of substitutes and other persons on similar temporary or emergency status." The schools are short by 27,500 permanent staff members, including 12,500 "professionals," who would be required to bring the City up to the *average only* of the school districts among which it once enjoyed leadership. That leadership position was held in the early 1940's, before suburban flight began in earnest, when the City spent more per child than its suburbs did. Now it spends $200 per child less, which amounts to about $200,000 per school and a total of $200 million per year simply to bring the system up to par in staff, materials, textbooks and upkeep. The $200 million does not include extra funds urgently needed for new construction.

At present, there is not enough room, time, or personnel to take care of all the children. A major classroom problem is that one or two children can disrupt an entire class and dissipate most of the teacher's energy; and as one might expect, difficult children are more prevalent in slum schools. According to one assistant principal,

It's the 2–3% who are unteachable and uncontrollable—the ones with very deep emotional disturbances—who take so much time and trouble in the lower neighborhood schools. There's no place to put them. We can't even assign them to a "600" [special problems] school without their parents' permission. The "600" schools have no more room anyway. Sooner or later these kids are caught committing a serious crime: you send them to a judge and he sends them right back to school.

There are also curriculum problems which integration will not necessarily solve. One of the most controversial is the practice of grouping the children according to reading level, and later, IQ test, so that fast, "achieving" children are in a homogeneous group entirely separate from the classrooms of the slow, "non-achieving" youngsters. One of the effects of such grouping is that in schools where a small population of whites remains, it is in effect segregated vertically in the advanced classrooms. So transporting kids from their neighborhoods will not by itself guarantee them an integrated classroom experience; in fact, since most Negro children lag in classroom skills, it might not do them much good to be thrown in with white children of their own grade level—at least not without drastic changes in the present set-up. Most experts now agree, however, that homogeneous grouping leads to stereotyping of individuals and is not desirable on the grade school level. To quote Martin Mayer, "in New York, Wrightstone's study of comparative performance showed no significant advantage for bright kids grouped with their fellows over bright kids scattered through the school at random." But experts also agree that heterogeneous groupings cannot effectively be taught unless class size is reduced to no more than 15 children, a procedure which would require twice as many classrooms and teachers. For the present, boycotters might take some satisfaction in a provision of the February integration plan, wherein the Board agreed to eliminate IQ tests.

Also beyond the reach of the boycott is the teacher herself, who is often unaware of her middle-class attitudes and the damage they do her ability to teach. I remember one young teacher with an all-Negro "slow" 1st grade, extremely conscientious and worried that she is not more successful, yet unaware that her tone of voice is superior and humorless. At any given moment, only about five of her children are paying attention, and at least three-quarters of the words she utters are devoted to discipline. Let me give some flavor of her monologue:

. . . well, why did you raise your hand if you had a pencil? I asked for only those who didn't have pencils to raise hands! That's not funny, Wilma! That's not funny! Boys and girls, we're not getting our work done and if we don't settle down we won't be able to have recess today. NOW I WON'T HAVE ANY MORE TALKING IN THIS ROOM! I'll start over again . . . we draw two lines across and that's the big A. Now I see that Freddy didn't hear me, Becky didn't hear me, Nicholas didn't hear me, Roger didn't hear me. And you're not looking! You can't learn to make the big A unless you're looking! Now can you make a big A? Let's see if you can. Raise hands if you need help. You don't have paper? Deborah, where is your paper? All right, I'll give you more . . .

After twenty minutes, a majority of the children are making big A's. As the teacher starts on the little *a*, I do what most of the kids want desperately to join me in: escape.

To give you an idea of these kids six years later, here is the teacher of a 7th-grade English class.

Now take a sheet of lined paper and write at the top "English notes." I want all of you to copy down right this second the facts I'm going to give you. Norma, would you be so kind as to put your hand down. Now your assignment is going to deal with this, so get these facts accurately. Hurry up, I haven't got too much time.

The Whites

Naturally the boycott did nothing to ease the growing anxiety of white middle-class parents. If many more of them withdraw their children, there will be no question of integration.

At an open meeting of a district school board, a white mother stood up and shouted hysterically,

What are you going to give me to keep my child in the public school system? I've worked for the NAACP for years, but I don't want 300 years of wrong to weigh upon the shoulders of *my 5-year-old!*

The woman went on screaming while her listeners applauded her. It was some time before she could be quieted. Whereupon Mrs. Thelma Johnson, who was onstage as a representative of the Harlem Parents Committee, made the following reply:

I offer you your child's future. Because your child's future and my child's future are bound up together. You cannot accept the privilege of being superior because you're white any damn more than I can accept the stigma of being inferior because I'm Negro. How much longer must I prove to be your superior in order to be accepted as an equal? Bussing is worth it for me because I'm on the lower end. You have to decide if it's worth it for you.

Mrs. Johnson, too, was applauded.

The Negroes

Neither did the boycott clear up the confusion among those Negroes who had, as requested, given the civil rights organizations "the benefit of the doubt." Among the children of a certain Harlem school that was empty on boycott day, there was great fear of "integration," for rumor had it that white kids were coming to fight the black kids.

Negro parents, for their part, might well wonder what changes a boycott might make in the depressing economic conditions they face. It would seem, too, that for some the boycott only reinforced doubts as to the value of nonviolent protest in general. Though the Negro in the United States has been historically nonviolent in relations with his white oppressors, nonviolence is by no means the lesson he learns from the life around him.

6th-grade Harlem boy (F): Fable

Once a boy was standing on a huge metal flattening machine. The flattener was coming down slowly. Now this boy was a boy who loved insects and bugs. The boy could have stoped the machine from coming down but there were two ladie bugs on the button and in order to push the button he would kill the two ladie bugs. The flattener was about a half inch over his head now he made a decision he would have to kill the ladie bugs he quickly pressed the button. The machine stoped he was saved and the ladie bugs were dead.

MORAL: smash or be smashed.

Or, as one of the fable-teller's female classmates puts it:

I think the white people should stop taking advantage of the color people before they get punched in the face.

The boycott was a punch thrown off-balance: it brought on all the reaction to a punch in the face without gaining enough of its satisfaction.

VI. BOYCOTT AND POLITICS

6th-grade West Harlem boy (F): How come we don't have no Negro president! We have to strike for president! We ain't gonna pay no more taxes!

His teacher: We've got to keep these kids from exploding ten years from now when they grow up and can't get jobs.

One of the conspicuous failings of the boycott was its lack of political content. It was a beautiful example of what Tom Kahn . . . calls "project-centered provincialism" based on "a middle-class integrationist ideology." It made no attempts to connect itself with the Rent Strike that was gaining headway in Harlem at the time, nor did it seek identification with efforts to end job discrimination.

When Bayard Rustin made his last-minute entrance into the boycott organization, he tried to broaden the perspective. Speaking at a rally January 31, he reminded his listeners that the Negro is at the center of all America's problems; for if America is to solve them, "the lowest must come first."

In a country with 50 million poor, only the black people are in movement. But we black people cannot by ourselves solve the problems of housing, unemployment and schools. The only solution is for the working classes to forge a *political* movement.

The trouble with demonstrations for limited ends is that the "power structure" can easily afford a compromise which will soon be absorbed in the shifting sands of our profit-controlled economy, without much damage to the status quo. No matter how firmly demonstrators insist that they will not compromise within their area of attack, complete change of one institution is not possible unless other institutions are also transformed.

The unemployment crisis indicates a natural alliance between the Negro and the labor movement: they must jointly demand full-scale public works programs to construct race- and class-integrated schools and housing, even whole new decentralized cities. Also, the Negro has a natural basis for alliance with those liberals who fear the military-industrial complex: they must jointly demand that a substantial portion of the annual multi-billion defense budget be diverted for education and social reconstruction. Until the problem is understood and attacked on this scale, the local projects of the Negro movement cannot achieve their full objectives.

And yet there was a "revolutionary" ardor to the boycott that went beyond political programs. I say "revolutionary" because at times the driving figures behind the boycott spoke with that appetite for pure destruction which far exceeds the reasoned desire for social reform. It comes from the feeling that the society one lives in is so hopelessly corrupt that one's only recourse is to tear the whole thing down. Let me quote the girl who warned of "a punch in the face":

If I could change my block I would stand on Madison Ave and throw nothing but Teargas in it. I would have all the people I liked to get out of the block and then I would become very tall and have big hands and with my big hands I would take all of the narcartic people and pick them up with my hand and throw them in the nearest river and Oceans. I would go to some of those old smart alic cops and throw them in the Oceans and Rivers too. I would let the people I like move into the projects so they could tell their friends that they live in a decent block. If I could do this you would never see 117 st again.

At times Galamison, the Presbyterian minister who sends his own son to a private school and drives an expensive car, made statements that would have done justice to Cromwell or Lenin. The most quoted of these was inspired by the radio interviewer who asked him if there was a chance that the integration conflict might destroy the public school system. Replied the Reverend,

I would rather see it destroyed. Maybe it has run its course anyway, the public school system.

By contrast, Bayard Rustin knows what he wants, and hopes against hope it will come about peacefully.

I think we are on the threshold of a new political movement—and I do not mean it in the party sense—that is going to change the face of New York in housing, in jobs and in schools.

After the success of the boycott, however, the only "new political movement" in the offing was a national group coordinating school boycotts in big cities across the nation. If such a development gains further momentum, the civil rights movement will continue divided against itself, exhausting itself in desperate forays.

VII. SOCIETY AND THE CLASSROOM

The subject of New York's schools and what's wrong with them cannot entirely be discussed in terms of more cash, more teaching and more integration. What is needed for the classroom above all else is a free and democratic, truly revolutionary society based on human value instead of compulsive striving, competition and accumulation. I doubt, for instance, that there is a single public school in this country where children are given a chance to learn at their individual rates of speed and without grading. Even at best our schools educate our young to fit into a world where ability is measured by quantity only. Concepts of art, science, knowledge, creativity *for their own sake* survive at kindergarten level only; the purpose of an American education is to replace these values with symbols of measure. What can be said of a society which reduces its culture to True-False and multiple-choice tests even on the college level? Among other things, that this society rewards cheating, and that the more advanced the competitors the more extensive and complex the cheating will become, until the cheaters finally cheat themselves of the knowledge of what they are doing.

Our ideal should be schools in which each child can develop as an individual, according to his capacities and desires. A good teacher is someone with a talent for getting through to children and letting them get through to him. If a teacher doesn't in some way enjoy being alive he has nothing to teach. What we need is to replace the authoritarian teacher who has traditionally plagued and scourged the children, whether black or white, achievers, nonachievers, or underachievers. We need a teacher who will nourish talent and individuality rather than crush it.

Unfortunately, teaching attracts types who enjoy relations where they have undisputed superiority. Thus the effort to "understand the disadvantaged child" turns out in practice to be the science of patronizing the slum-child without feeling guilty about it. For the disadvantaged child, of course, is really not that at all, no matter what it helps one to know about his background: he is a person, and as such something splendid in his own right even before a teacher gets to him.

In every ghetto school I visited, teachers recommended a book called *The Culturally Deprived Child* by Frank Riessman. Reading this book, they told me, had helped them to understand the nature of the children they had to deal with. Sure enough, I found Riessman's book preaching "a sympathetic, noncondescending, understanding of the culture of the underprivileged." But neither Riessman nor the average teacher realizes how un-noncondescending sympathy delivered from the top can be:

Moreover, self-expression and self-actualization, other aims of education, particularly modern education, are equally alien to the more pragmatic, traditional, underprivileged person.

No! You just can't talk that way about a child entering elementary school. Kids from "underprivileged" homes want to express themselves and realize themselves just as much as anyone else. Maybe the most important thing for them is to have a teacher who will *expect* something from them, let them know there is some authority who cares. The best teacher I met in Harlem had taken a class of bright 6th graders who up to that time were demoralized and undisciplined. Fortunately he did not assume they weren't interested in self-expression. He assumed that they had something to express, the fruits of their own experience, which is in so many ways deeper and more demanding than that of middle-class children. It was a long haul, after eleven years of neglect, but eventually he got them writing and writing well. He read them French translations and they wrote him parables and fables; it seems Negro children are natural-born fable-writers, for—as we have seen—they are not likely to pull their punches when it comes to the moral. He read them Greek myths and stories, and they wrote him back their own myths, classic transformations, and one boy even wrote an illustrated history of the Trojan War. (One of the transformations begins, "I was transformed from a poor little infant into a nice boy, and as I grew I was transformed into a magnificent extraordinary deceiving nuisance to the world.") Most of the children wrote novels, and one 11-year-old boy, without having read a single modern novel, began a remarkable autobiography with the sentence, "I am dreaming and crying in my sleep."

This was an ordinary 6th-grade Harlem class; there were some high IQ's, but it was not an "SP" (specially gifted) class and had attracted no special attention to itself. The teacher disciplined them, yes, kept them in order, but did it not to triumph but to show them he cared. He respected them, which is something you can't learn from books. He visited their homes, which is absolutely unheard-of. He worked patiently with each child, and got them to work with each other.

Now it is a year later, the kids are dispersed into a notoriously depressing junior high, and most of them have lost what they gained. Some are flunking; their former teacher bitterly wonders how the life in them can survive. But for that one year they produced a body of work uniquely theirs.

VIII. THE GROUPING OF GROUPINGS

If conditions within the classroom are bad enough, to look beyond them is to find oneself in a jungle of stumbling and makeshift, where stentorian voices boom from the tops of trees, and clusters of officious missionaries rush about distributing memoranda on the cannibal problem.

First of all, there is the school bureaucracy. According to Martin Mayer, "New York City employs more people in educational administration than all of France." I believe I have alluded to the public relations men on the Board of Ed staff, but I have perhaps failed to mention the endless associations, commissions, sub-commissions, advisory committees, deputy directors, associate supervisors, district superintendents, coordinators, directors, foundations and independent consultants who must be involved in every policy decision. The trouble with such a set-up is that the basic concern on every level points up, toward impressing the higher-ups, rather than down, toward serving the classroom teacher. Would it be heresy to suggest equal salary for every school position? With the present system, the class-room teacher can be in a panic for materials she ordered three years ago, while the assistant superintendent is sincerely assuring the area superintendent that everything is all right in his sub-sector. In such a bureaucracy, the people who move toward the top are the yes-men, the round pegs, whom the public pays to rise away from the children. They have a priority on operating funds, too; if they could not get their paperwork properly sub-mitted and filed, the system would collapse. In fact, despite the teacher shortage, there are a number of employees listed on the Board of Ed budget as classroom teachers who never report to their assigned schools; they are clerks and typists working in the central offices. Ironically, the policy directives they type, like great portions of our public school funds, may never filter down to the classroom; but they do reach the publicity department, from which they are carefully distributed to the newspapers, which in turn describe to us a school system that doesn't really quite exist. Nevertheless, its paper achievements will be proudly recounted by the functionary flown to a conference of "edu-cators" at public expense. Life in the big city goes on somehow, though where it goes no one knows.

The gap between theory and practice is nowhere more striking than among the school principals. Many of them know little of what goes on in their own schools and make no effort to learn. The job of the principal is to spend his time in educational con-ferences, or addressing committees, or preparing reports for higher-ups who never come to check. At the Harlem school where the 6th-grade "slow" letters I have quoted were written, the principal assured me,

I don't notice any demoralization on this level. The children are happy, well-behaved and eager to learn.

Small wonder that one of the best teachers at this school could not get enthusiastic about the boycott:

What if the boycotters are successful and get the Board to come up with a plan? Who has to implement it but these same shits!

Then there is the problem of the teachers themselves and their organization, the UFT. It would be unkind to expect too much of an organization so urgently needed and besieged with such difficulties as is the UFT. But it must be said that an excessive concern of teachers black and white is their own respectability. The most pressing practical issues are submerged in the desire to preserve their "professional image." For instance, a teacher's license in New York City cannot be obtained unless the applicant has passed the expensive and utterly idiotic education courses offered at teachers' colleges. I never talked to a single good teacher who claimed to have learned anything of value in these courses. Furthermore, they discourage many of the specially talented people gathered in New York City from seeking employment as public school teachers. Bright, educated people who want to try their hands at teaching children can't, not in New York, not even if they have PhD's, unless they are willing to go back to school for their "education credits."[2] Yet the union, although ambitious to work out a joint recruiting program with the Board aimed at attracting Negro teachers from the South, shows little interest in this question. The current teachers' pay scale is based on these pointless credits, and to upset it would invalidate years of useless course-taking.

Finally, there is the conglomeration of civil rights groups, divided and sub-divided within itself, spreading out towards too many separate targets with only the most general slogans to hold itself together. The structure of the rights organizations is chaotic beyond description. Let me say simply that the end effect is too often the mirror image of the bureaucracy they are arrayed against. And the boycott offered no program for the Negro children to realize their own particular talents, no social-action program with which to unite the Negro community in self-respect. Was not the boycott in some sense one more appeal to the great white father to do right by his poor black children?

[2] Education courses are not the only obstacles in the paths of potentially valuable teachers. Teachers from the South or from Puerto Rico with advanced academic degrees may find themselves disqualified on the interview section of the teachers' license exam for "speaking English with an accent."

IX. No Ending

Have I captured the confusion? Here is New York City with a
mass of black people, most of whom have never been allowed to
partake of our civilization. Now they must be allowed that
dubious privilege; for there is no other place for them. In previous eras of American life, there was some room for a variegated
lower class, which took care of the dirty work and was not permitted entrance into the cultural mainstream. Little by little
most groups surfaced into the middle class, leaving behind
among unlucky remnants of themselves a permanent body of
American Negroes, who, handicapped by years of slavery and
oppression, remained what a Negro teacher describes to me as
"a colonial people encapsulated *within* the colonial country."
But now automation is chopping away at the colony; we see the
natives in the street, shaking their fists. We must open the door
and let them in.

The big question is, will they come in having truly changed
and purified and reformed our social structure, as some say they
must? Will we have to chip away at our stone walls to let them
in, as the Trojans did for the Greek horse? Or will the Negro
scrape through bloody, bitter and confused, ready to perpetuate
the authoritarian ethic he has so far, to his unique credit, managed to evade?

The answer to this question depends in part on our schools.
But all school systems are—and have always been—failures.
Even Leo Tolstoy, with all his genius, his wealth, his command,
and with not a single bureaucrat to hamper him, could not educate his peasants into free men. His failure, our failure . . . the
failure is always the same: the failure to educate each man—not
for a prestigious "function" or "role"—but to fulfill his own
capacities for living, for being alive, for finding and making his
own kind of beauty, for respecting the diversity of life without,
in his frustration, turning to violence, self-suppression, and the
worship of authority.

So what the boycotters are demanding, ultimately (and more
power to them!), is a change in the nature of the lives we lead.

6th-grade Harlem girl (S): I wish that the hold city can chage,
and that the governor make new laws, that there to be no dirt on

streets and no gobech top off and wish that my name can chage and I wish that whether can trun to summer.

6th-grade Harlem boy (F) : *Fable*

Once upon a time there was two men who were always fighting so one day a wise man came along and said fighting will never get you anywhere they didn't pay him no attention and they got in quarrels over and over again. So one day they went to church and the preacher said you should not fight and they got mad and knock the preacher out

Can't find no ending.

FOR FURTHER READING

The consequences of poor education are outlined in a startling factual analysis by Patricia C. Sexton, *Education and Income* (New York: Viking Press, 1964). Sympathetic insight into the plight of poor young people in an affluent society may be found in Paul Goodman's *Growing Up Absurd* (New York: Random House, 1960), and a concise account of these youths is given by Harold L. Sheppard, "The Young Who Are Poor," in Ben B. Seligman, ed., *Poverty as a Public Issue* (New York: Free Press, 1965). On rural youth, the report by Robert K. Merton and Robert A. Nisbit, *Contemporary Rural Youth in Crisis* (Washington: Government Printing Office, 1964), is most useful. Martin Mayer's *The Schools* (New York: Harper & Row, 1962) is reportorial but worth consulting. Kenneth Clark's *Dark Ghetto* (New York: Harper & Row, 1965) includes a powerful analysis of school segregation in New York City. And what teachers in a slum school can do to misshape their young charges is detailed with stark reality in Jonathan Kozol's *Death at an Early Age: The Destruction of the Hearts and Minds of Negro Children in the Boston Public Schools* (Boston: Houghton Mifflin Company, 1967).

HOUSING
AND WELFARE

Charles Abrams

Richard M. Elman

The riots in the slums of our cities in recent summers have been rebellions against rat-infested tenements—as much as rebellions set off by joblessness and the bitter feeling that society has turned its back. Walking through the streets of any slum in the United States, Harlem or Watts, one wonders how an affluent society can possibly tolerate such physical degradation within its midst. For despite low-cost housing projects, our slums continue to spawn delinquency, disease, filth, and crime. Is it possible that the high-rise apartment buildings, which appear so aseptic from a distance, really aggravate rather than alleviate community decay?

Decay is also reflected in the welfare system that the slum inhabitants are subjected to. It is Richard Elman's thesis that our welfare programs perpetuate the very conditions they set out to alleviate. He finds these programs inadequate, grudging, and finally degrading for the people they are supposed to help. Mr. Elman has served as a research assistant at the Columbia University School of Social Work and as a writer for National Educational Television. His selection is taken from his book *The Poorhouse State*. The other selection, by Charles Abrams, one of the nation's leading authorities on housing, originally appeared in a special issue of *Daedalus* on the Negro American.

The Housing Problem and the Negro
by Charles Abrams

When Hell broke loose in the Watts area of Los Angeles last August taking 36 lives and injuring close to 1,000 people, reporters were astonished and reformers shocked to find that the area which was the scene of the most expensive riot in United States history was hardly a slum in the usual sense. Instead of rat-infested crumbling tenements on littered streets, the section was made up of small homes mostly about twenty-five years old, many of them surrounded by lawns, and only 20 per cent of them actually dilapidated. In the public mind, the Negro housing problem was therefore discounted as one of the causes of the eruption in favor of hoodlumism, anti-white emotionalism, and poverty.

The rioting in Los Angeles highlighted one of the five fictions that surround the Negro housing problem and still condition federal housing policy. One reason these fictions persist is that officials are not eager to probe too thoroughly into the Negro housing issue, while the vocal Negro leadership has relegated the issue to a low priority in the fight for Negro rights. Yet, until these fictions are put to rest, the Negro's housing problem will remain one of the conspicuous failures in the nation's effort to elevate his status in American life.

The fiction which the Watts area exposed is that the primary aspect of the Negro's housing problem is the slum, that is, insanitary or structurally deficient housing. The fact is that many Negroes do live in slums and some do not. The accelerated movement of whites to the suburbs has been providing Negroes with a wider choice among the leavings, while improved income has enabled others to venture into neighborhoods once inhabited by middle-class whites; thus the houses Negroes occupy are no longer all on the other side of the tracks but are now part of a mixed inventory. Despite this, the housing problem persists for most Negro families, and in many places it is becoming worse. About half the nonwhite renters in California, for ex-

Source: *Daedalus* (Winter, 1964), pp. 64–76. Reprinted by permission of *Daedalus*, published by the American Academy of Arts and Sciences, Boston, Mass.

ample, and two-fifths of the nonwhite home owners live in sub-standard houses in contrast to only one-fifth of white renters and one-tenth of white homeowners. The physical condition of the Negro's homes, however, is only one aspect of the Negro's housing conditions. The neighborhoods are run-down; official-dom is less concerned with their maintenance, and their general atmosphere is demoralizing; the schools are segregated and in-ferior, and so are the recreational, hospital, and social facilities; there are also fewer new buildings erected in Negro areas, even for those who can afford them. Above all, the Negro is discrimi-nated against in almost every aspect of housing and neighbor-hood life, and he feels it. Urbanization and suburbanization have recast the American scene and redistributed the population into areas inhabited by a new white "élite" and a black un-wanted. If poor housing was not the mainspring that touched off the rioting, it certainly has not been a force for advancing interracial harmony—in California or elsewhere.

The 1961 report on "Housing" by the United States Com-mission on Civil Rights is punctuated by references to housing discrimination in California. Builders refuse to sell Federal Housing Administration and Veterans Administration homes to Negroes, and lenders are chary of lending them money on mort-gages. Negroes have been refused access to houses repossessed by the VA, and the Los Angeles Realty Board has consistently rejected Negro applications for membership. The California Advisory Committee of the U.S. Commission on Civil Rights said it was "almost impossible" for minorities to buy homes in new subdivisions. In Northern California, fewer than 100 non-whites have been able to buy houses in unsegregated tracts in a period during which 350,000 new homes were built. In a check on 117 advertisements for apartment rentals in Northern Cali-fornia, only two were available to Negroes and both were in Negro areas.

Far more serious, however, are the overcrowding within the buildings the Negro occupies and the high proportion of income he pays for rent. A sixth of Los Angeles Negroes, for example, were crowded into the Watts area in conditions four times as congested as those in the rest of the city. A U.S. census survey in March 1965 in the renewal areas of 132 cities showed 36 per cent of the Negroes paying 35 per cent or more of their incomes for their shelter. Moreover, the isolation of the Negro from the main stream of community life keeps resentment well-kindled and gives Negro mischief-makers little trouble in churning up hate of the white man on the ghetto fringe.

Because official policy still views the slum as a building instead of a condition, a second fiction has worked its way into official housing policy, that the best way to solve the Negro's housing problem is to tear down his slums. Because many of the houses are deteriorated, they have been the primary targets for slum clearance. In the United States, from 60 to 72 per cent of those who have been displaced from their homes by urban renewal projects have been Negroes, while only a tiny fraction of the new houses built on the sites have been open to them. Through May 1962, 5,105 Negro families were evicted by renewal projects in California and 58 per cent of those displaced were nonwhite. In the Western Addition redevelopment area in San Francisco, which had a population of 13,000, about 90 per cent of the children among the evicted families were nonwhite.

The renewal program is not the only or even the main culprit, for code enforcement and displacement for public works have taken an even greater toll of Negro homes. Whatever the motivation, these evictions have been disrupting neighborhood life before it has had a chance to mature. In Stockton, California, a renewal project not only leveled a whole Negro neighborhood but destroyed 32 Negro churches in the process. Negro displacement cannot always be avoided, and renewal of central sections is often necessary to salvage the economies of the beleaguered central cities; but as M. Justin Herman, Executive Director of San Francisco's Redevelopment Agency, told the U.S. Commission on Civil Rights: "Much of the problem is a matter of economics—the inability of families to afford such housing as can be made available in the market today. The biggest problem is the discrimination that exists with respect to non-white persons." Thus, low income, coupled with high housing costs and anti-Negro bias, has been at the root of the Negro's housing problem not only in California but throughout the nation. In 1963, the median Negro income was $3,465, compared with

$6,548 for white families, and the Negro unemployment rate was twice as high; as a result, many Negro families have found it difficult to secure decent housing even if builders were ready to offer it to them.

Instead of expanding the number of houses available to the Negro, demolitions have been shrinking the housing supply in sections in which he has established footholds, thereby intensifying his overcrowding. The Negro, crowded into his shelter and paying more than he can afford or facing eviction, continuously eyes the white areas on the borders of his ghetto. This does little to enhance his popularity with his white neighbors—which brings us to a third fiction, that Negroes and whites do not mix and that Negroes will spoil any neighborhood and destroy its social status. This fiction is usually supplemented by claims that, once the Negro establishes a beachhead, more Negroes will follow—which is often the case—causing real estate to topple— which may or may not be the case.

As long as the Negro had been a small and docile minority in the North, the feeling that Negroes always destroy social status and market values never gained widespread acceptance. "Where the Negro pitches his tent," wrote Jacob Riis in 1902, "he pays more rent than his white neighbor next door and is a better tenant." In Washington, D.C., Baltimore, and Philadelphia, Negroes lived in small clusters near the better white dwellings, and, before 1915, they lived in almost every section in Chicago— a third of the city's Negroes living in areas that were less than 10 per cent Negro-occupied. The Negro's presence in cities rarely caused a white exodus; it would in fact have disturbed the equanimity of the whites in those days if their maids and butlers moved too far from the town houses.

The situation changed in the thirty years following 1910 when 1,750,000 Negroes moved northward. By 1960 the central cities of the twelve largest metropolitan areas accounted for 24 per cent of all United States Negroes. They were then 29 per cent of Detroit's population; 35 per cent of Baltimore's; a quarter of Cleveland's and Philadelphia's; 34 per cent of Newark's; and 55 per cent of Washington, D.C.'s. As the Negroes moved to the cities, they accelerated the white movement to the burgeoning suburbs so that by 1960 less than a third of the urban and suburban whites were living in the central cities. Though they constituted only a ninth of the national population, 78 per cent of all Negroes in the nation's 212 metropolitan areas lived in the central cities compared to only 52 per cent of the whites. Only in the South do more whites still live in the central cities than in the suburbs.

As the Negro's numbers increased and as he moved into the adjoining sections or made inroads into white sections, the whites moved out in droves. Homes were often offered at bargain prices. Since cause was confused with effect, the Negroes were always blamed for declines in values.[1]

As opposition crystallized, racial zoning became the main device to keep the Negro in his place and, when the courts struck it down as unconstitutional, the restrictive covenant was thereafter written into deeds in the effort to maintain white supremacy in neighborhoods. About 80 per cent of the vacant land in Los Angeles was at one time covered by such covenants. When the courts held racial covenants unenforceable, subtler devices were ushered in, including overrigid zoning ordinances sternly enforced against Negroes but relaxed for whites. Condemnation for incinerator dumps or other public works is another current device, while building inspectors and other petty officials are always on hand to harass the Negro who ventures where he is not wanted. When, for example, a private builder announced he would sell a few of his houses to Negroes in Deerfield, Illinois, his site was promptly condemned for a park. When the Ford

---

[1] There is no single price reaction to minority infiltrations. Prices may remain constant, fall, or rise and depend on a complex of factors, including the social and economic status of a particular minority at a particular time; its numbers in relation to the numbers in the majority group; the latter's social and cultural level; the minority's capacity for social improvement and assimilation; the size of the city and the physical condition of its neighborhoods; the particular pattern of minority distribution; the nature of the then current minority stereotype; the type of social and educational leadership and maturity in the community; and the relationship between the groups in employment. Shortages may intensify competiton for dwellings and increase values. Whether values rise or fall may also depend upon the ability of the newcomers to bid up prices. Nor do values automatically collapse because the minority happens to be of a lower economic status. A minority family may be of lower economic but higher social status, and vice versa. See Charles Abrams, *Forbidden Neighbors* (New York, 1955), pp. 285 ff.

Motor Company moved its plant from Richmond, California, to Milpitas, and when the union tried to build houses for its Negro workers, the area was promptly rezoned for industrial use. Thereafter came a sudden strengthening of building regulations, followed by a hike of sewer connection costs to a ransom figure. It is not surprising, therefore, that discrimination in housing also reduces the chances of Negro employment; many suburban firms refuse to hire Negroes either for fear of offending the local community or because they know the Negroes will have trouble finding housing.

The big city has thus been performing its historic role as a refuge for minorities, while the Northern and Western suburbs have become the new Mason-Dixon lines of America; of the total suburban population of metropolitan areas with a population of half a million or more, barely 4 per cent are Negroes and a substantial number of these live either in the South or in little fringe ghettos that have precariously survived suburban engulfment.

A fourth fiction is that the federal government is and always has been the prime protagonist of equal rights in housing. One gathers this impression from hearing so often of the law of 1886 which supposedly guarantees the Negro the right to own and lease real property, or the protections of the 14th Amendment, or the recent liberal rulings of the Supreme Court. But the law of 1886 was soon a dead letter and still is; the 14th Amendment, enacted to protect Negroes, was long used primarily to protect corporations; as for the Supreme Court, up to 1948 it supported the use of the racial restrictive covenant as a private prerogative, and so did the highest courts of twelve states. Although the Supreme Court after 1948 became the spearhead in the drive for expanding the Negro's civil rights, and although general economic improvement has helped raise the Negro's sights, he has made little gain in housing.

One of the reasons is that the federal government, during the New Deal period, not only sanctioned racial discrimination in housing but vigorously exhorted it.[2] From 1935 to 1950, dis-

[2] "If a neighborhood is to retain stability," said the FHA manual, "it is necessary that properties shall be continued to be occupied by the same social and racial classes." (Section 937) Among "adverse influences" was

crimination against Negroes was a condition of federal assistance. More than 11 million homes were built during this period, and this federal policy did more to entrench housing bias in American neighborhoods than any court could undo by a ruling. It established a federally sponsored mores for discrimination in the suburban communities in which 80 per cent of all new housing is being built and fixed the social and racial patterns in thousands of new neighborhoods.

In 1962, two years after he had made the promise to do so, President Kennedy signed an executive order outlawing discrimination in federally aided housing. By that time, seventeen states and fifty-six cities had passed laws or resolutions against housing discrimination. This movement at the state and local levels originated in New York in the 1940's and spread elsewhere partly as a liberal protest against discrimination in publicly assisted undertakings and partly because the minority numbers were beginning to become more politically significant. But the Executive Order was hardly a prophylactic against the virus that now afflicted American neighborhoods. In the first place, it embraced only about 23 per cent of all new housing construction and only 13 per cent of the housing not already covered by state or local action. In the second place, it explicitly excluded the federally regulated and federally assisted savings and loan associations which are the principal mortgage lenders in the

---

infiltration of inharmonious racial or nationality groups." Protection against "adverse influences" included "prevention of inharmonious racial groups." (Section 229) "Presence of incompatible racial elements" (Section 225) and "the social class of the parents of children at the school will in many instances have a vital bearing" on whether the neighborhood is "stable." The neighborhood will be less desirable if there is "a lower level of society or an incompatible racial element . . . in such instance it might well be that for the payment of a fee children of this area could attend another school with pupils of their same social class." (1936 Manual, Section 266; 1938 Manual, Section 951) FHA advocated not only deed restrictions but zoning to bar the wrong kind of people, and it included stables and pig pens in the same categories as sections occupied by the wrong kind of race. (1936, Section 284 (3f)) It advocated the use of hills, ravines, and high-speed traffic arteries to discourage the wrong kinds of parents and children (1936, Section 229; 1938, Section 935), and even prescribed and urged the use of a racial covenant form in which it left the space blank for the group excluded to be inserted.

nation. It was hardly surprising, therefore, that the order could
not crack the vitrified prejudices and fears that had become im-
pacted during the sixteen years of concerted federal anti-Negro
policy. Nor has the enforcement of the order done much to
secure equal rights to housing in American suburbs. At best, the
order manifests a shift from officially sponsored prejudice to an
invertebrate morality.

The rising tide of state and local anti-bias laws in housing has
insinuated a fifth fiction into the housing issue, that such state
and local anti-bias laws provide the means for ending discrimination. These laws have had educational value, have helped
create a better moral climate in some areas, have secured housing for a few upper-income Negro families, and have demonstrated that such laws do not adversely affect property values.
But they have brought no solution to the Negro's housing
troubles. City anti-bias laws cannot affect the suburbs where
most of the exclusionary practices exist. As for state-wide laws,
it is all but impossible to buck the concerted power of the suburbs to which the political balance has shifted. Proceedings
before anti-discrimination commissions are protracted and costly,
and, when a Negro complainant wins a favorable ruling, he must
be ready after the long delays to brave the pressures of his hostile
landlord, neighbors, and local officials. He must be willing to
have his child be the lone Negro child in an all-white school.
Most important, he must be financially poised to pay the suburban rents or, if he buys a house, to get a mortgage on it—
which is still all but impossible.

The slender hope these laws offer the Negro family is again
illustrated in the case of California, where there were two state
laws, the Hawkins Act which banned discrimination in publicly
assisted housing and the Unruh Act which prohibited discrimination in "all business establishments of any kind whatsoever"
and therefore applied to discriminatory practices by real-estate
brokers. One reason for the existence of these laws is that the
state by 1960 had 1.3 million nonwhites and another 1.4 million
of the Spanish-speaking minority, composing a formidable force
of voters.

The two laws were hardly strictures which a real-estate owner
should have viewed with trepidation. But California has had a

long history of anti-racial activities dating from the anti-Chinese campaign of the 1870's and the anti-Japanese outbursts in the decade that followed. Moreover, California's real-estate boards, which compose one of the most formidable lobbies in the state, have continuously favored race segregation. When, for example, the Supreme Court ruled against the racial covenant, the Los Angeles Board was the first to broadcast eight ways of evading the decision. It simultaneously sought a state constitutional amendment to validate the covenant but did not succeed.

The situation changed in 1963 when a local ordinance was introduced in the city of Berkeley—a community generally considered liberal—which proposed to ban racial discrimination by property owners. Largely because the bill carried a possible prison penalty, it was defeated. The defeat lent courage to California's real-estate interests and, shortly after the Berkeley fiasco, the California Real Estate Association, representing 173 local boards, announced its plan to initiate a constitutional amendment barring any anti-bias laws in housing. The proposed amendment, cleverly framed, provided that

Neither the State nor any subdivision or agency thereof shall deny, limit or abridge, directly or indirectly, the right of any person, who is willing or desires to sell, lease or rent any part or all of his real property, to decline to sell, lease or rent such property to such person or persons as he, in his absolute discretion, chooses.

The California Real Estate Association was soon backed by the powerful National Association of Real Estate Boards which not only gave its nationwide support to its affiliate but also joined the campaign and helped finance it. An advertising agency was hired to guide the campaign, and a fund reported to run well over one million dollars was raised to assure victory.

California now became the battleground for a nationwide campaign to end, once and for all, the long struggle for equal access to shelter. Anti-Negro propaganda circulated freely, and fear of Negro invasion of white neighborhoods was whipped up throughout the state. As a prominent industrialist put it: "In the real estate industry there were a number who were motivated by racial bigotry, others by their concern for property values and some who won't buck the stream. But at the bottom of it all is racial bigotry."

Proposition 14 rolled up a surprising 4.5 million votes in its favor to less than 2.4 million against it. The votes for the proposition exceeded those polled by President Johnson by more than 350,000. President Johnson received almost 1.8 million more votes than those cast against the proposition, indicating that many voters saw no conflict in voting against Goldwater while protecting their own neighborhoods against the Negro scourge. "People just voted their prejudice" was Governor Brown's private comment.

Proposition 14 was also a great victory for the National Association of Real Estate Boards. Its official code of "ethics" up to 1950 had barred its member realtors from "introducing into a neighborhood members of any race or nationality, or any individual whose presence will clearly be detrimental to property values in the neighborhood."[3] The association had grudgingly modified its code of ethics in 1950 on the advice of counsel who may have feared that the Board could be charged with conspiring against the Civil Rights Laws. But despite the modification, there was little evidence that the official view had altered, and, nine days after Proposition 14 was approved, the NAREB Annual Convention in Los Angeles openly resolved that "government should not deny, limit or abridge, directly or indirectly, the fundamental right of every person to sell, lease or rent any part or all of his real property." The Convention called the California victory to the attention of other states "where the freedom of real estate practices may be imperilled."

The battle lines were thus drawn for a nationwide campaign. Detroit and Akron have followed California's example, while

---

[3] Violation of the rule exposed a member board to expulsion. Supplementing its official code, the association issued a brochure in 1943 entitled "Fundamentals of Real Estate Practice." This classed the Negro seeking an education with strange company:

"The prospective buyer might be a bootlegger who would cause considerable annoyance to his neighbors, a madame who had a number of Call Girls on her string, a gangster, who wants a screen for his activities by living in a better neighborhood, a colored man of means who was giving his children a college education and thought they were entitled to live among whites. . . . No matter what the motive or character of the would-be purchaser, if the deal would instigate a form of blight, then certainly the well-meaning broker must work against its consummation."

in 1965 Ohio, Rhode Island, and Indiana adopted the other course of banning race bias in private home selling and renting, with Maine barring discrimination in apartments only. This mixed record of victories and defeats suggests that, while the average voter will acquiesce when moral leadership is given to an anti-bias law by his legislators or Governor, he will vote his property rights against his moral scruples when put to the test in person. As long as ethical leadership is lacking, the supporters of property rights are in a position to win the tests, particularly if put to the people themselves, as in California.

Access of the Negro to decent housing is becoming the vortex around which his other rights revolve. Without housing in areas of his choice, the right of his child to an unsegregated school is meaningless; his right to a job will be impaired; his right to move and to secure shelter in a decent neighborhood will be an empty shell. The vote on Proposition 14 indicates that racial prejudice is still a potent political commodity in the nation, and it is not at all unlikely that the device may become the legal instrument for pitting the issue of property rights against civil rights in the years to come.

The extent to which the heated contest over Proposition 14 contributed to the anti-white emotions that burst forth into the Watts riot will be hard to assess. But this is certain: housing has and will continue to play a part, if not in Negro outbreaks against the whites, then in white outbreaks against the Negro. American history reveals a long string of such riots, dynamitings, and other forms of violence from the time Negroes began moving North in greater numbers. The toll in deaths and injuries is in the thousands, and property damage is in the hundreds of millions—the Watts riot alone destroyed $50 million in property. So far, violence has been confined mostly to the white sections of cities and to a few communities on the fringe of big cities. But since the urbanization of the Negro will not be complete until he has achieved suburbanization as well, a larger toll of violence can be expected as the Negro improves his income and begins to challenge suburban exclusion.

Although the expansion of the President's Executive Order may bring only a moral victory in the struggle against housing prejudice, moral victories are presently important. As long as the order remains incomplete, there will always be the implication that federal policy is indifferent to housing bias; real-estate groups will continue their efforts to win the right to exclude, school segregation will become the established pattern in the North, and racial frictions will accelerate.

Yet the Negro's housing problem can never be solved by laws and orders alone, for neither laws nor orders can reach the subtler and more effective forms of discrimination. Moreover, since Congress in the Housing Act of 1949 has guaranteed a "decent home in a suitable living environment for every American family" and has become the main force for creating and manipulating environment in the nation, the failure of the federal government to pass laws which relieve the Negro's housing problem is itself a form of discrimination, namely discrimination by omission.

The Negro is only 11.6 per cent of the nation's population, and about half of the American Negroes still live in the South. Although the presence of Negroes appears formidable because of exclusion and their concentration in the major cities, they would hardly be noticed in Northern and Western cities if the suburbs were opened to them, for there simply are not enough Negro families in the country to threaten white areas, even if the Negroes and other low-income families were subsidized to make their move possible.

To deal with the Negro's housing problem—as well as with school segregation—a meaningful housing program is needed for low-income families at costs they can afford. Despite official claims to the contrary, present programs cannot accomplish this. The public housing program hardly scratches the surface, and the local housing authorities that build the projects are generally located in the cities and lack the power to build beyond their legal boundaries. The states which could build without regard to local boundaries will not do so because of suburban opposition. FHA mortgage insurance is designed mostly for builders in suburban areas; besides, the housing it produces is too costly for most Negro families.

The two hundred million dollar authorization in rent supplements made available to families under the 1965 Housing Act represents one of the landmarks in the fight for better housing. Unfortunately, initiation of the housing operations will still depend on the will of private entrepreneurs or nonprofit corporations to venture into suburbia, and it will be a miracle if the program produces more than a token number of suburban dwelling units for Negro families. The best of intentions can always be forestalled by devious zoning ordinances or obstreperous building codes. Much will still depend on how much pressure can be brought to bear on the federal housing agencies so that they will be forced to challenge suburban bias.

The real answer is for the federal government to build directly wherever there is racial exclusion and housing needs for minorities are demonstrated. The federal government should not only insist that equal access to housing be provided in all federally assisted private subdivisions, but it should also combine direct building with rent supplements in order to bring the dwellings in suburbs as well as in cities within the means of lower-income families. Federal home building has a precedent in the housing constructed during World War I by the United States Housing Corporation and in the building of public housing and new towns during the New Deal. After their completion, the houses and new towns were sold as they should be under the formula proposed. Until Congress is ready to move in that direction, Negro slum life and neighborhood and school segregation will persist.

Simultaneously, the federal government must also meet the predicament facing the central cities. The migration into their centers of millions of low-income Negroes, combined with the presence of poor elderly families, is confronting these cities with social and economic problems with which they can no longer cope. Unlike the federal government, these cities cannot go beyond their boundaries in search of new levies to meet their rising costs. Since 1946 their debts per capita have trebled while federal costs per capita have actually gone down. The money which the federal government has given them for public housing and urban renewal is of small help when measured against the new burdens they have had to assume. Nor can they expect much help from the states whose debts have also rocketed and who are similarly limited in their taxing ability.

The much publicized poverty program is less a war on poverty than a series of well-intentioned skirmishes. Unlike the Peace Corps, it is not designed to assist, expand, and improve existing programs, but to innovate demonstration and pilot efforts. What the cities need are federal funds to support and improve their existing school systems as well as more federal help in meeting their housing, policing, relief, and other commitments.

Urbanization has confronted these cities with new tasks that are national in scope and origin. The Negro housing problem is only one of these concerns, and it involves much more than housing. It is also undeniably linked with making neighborhoods livable, safe, and socially solvent; creating schools, playgrounds, and social facilities which are better and more ample; providing homes that are within a reasonable distance of areas of employment and are within the means of low-income families. In short, the poverty of people and the poverty of cities are parts of the same problem. The plight of the city's people can be dealt with only if the cities are enabled to deal with them.

If the Los Angeles rioting reveals the underlying weaknesses of the current federal approach to segregation, poverty, and housing, and if it stimulates some fresh thinking on these problems, it may compensate at least in part for the terrible havoc it wreaked.

The Poorhouse State, by Richard M. Elman

Fascism "at its very best," wrote George Orwell, "is socialism with the virtues taken out." Precisely the same relationship exists between the Poorhouse State and the Welfare State to which an increasing number of Americans now belong and from which we can now "claim" a variety of benefits.

The Welfare State subsidizes the farmer; the Poorhouse State distributes his surplus product.

The Welfare State insures against old age; the Poorhouse State discourages dependency.

The Welfare State provides loans for small businessmen; the Poorhouse State provides retraining for the poor.

The Welfare State subsidizes the slumlord; the Poorhouse State subsidizes the tenant.

Source: Richard M. Elman, *The Poorhouse State*, pp. 3–28. © Copyright 1966 by Richard M. Elman. Reprinted by permission of Pantheon Books, a Division of Random House, Inc.

Not only are benefits under any given Welfare State program apt to be more generous and uniform than under a similar program of the Poorhouse State, but they do not customarily demand humiliation of the recipient. It is not the aim of the Welfare State to make its beneficiaries forfeit liberty and justice. By applying for assistance from the Poorhouse State, however, you must expect to forgo such privileges, for you will be treated as a social problem.

In the watery environs of New York City there are many small islands, nearly all of which serve this Poorhouse State. Hart's, Riker's, North Brother, and Welfare Island, among others, minister to individualized deprivations which have manifested themselves through misdemeanors and felonies, insane and addictive behavior, chronic illnesses, but for our largest category of deprivation—poverty itself—the City has created islands within its own precincts, racial and class ghettos in which one out of every fifteen New Yorkers lives on public assistance. In a period of unsurpassed national prosperity, their numbers are still increasing by an average of 5,200 persons a month. Even as the unemployment percentages drop, the relief rolls increase. In October, 1965, the Department of Welfare estimated that there were 512,497 such dependents in New York City. Out of narrow accommodation to—or perhaps self-protection from— the majority's problematical diagnosis of their indigence, they are often forced to lead lives as distinctively covert and habitual as those of drug addicts or any other members of the underworld.

The presence of so many public assistance clients has never been allowed to go unnoticed. They have been studied and lamented, analyzed and counseled. Occasionally, it has seemed as if their problems were distinctively urban or occupational in character, determined by their race, or their sex, or their uncertain family circumstances; but, like nearly all the eight million Americans presently living on public assistance these half a million New Yorkers could also be characterized as frustrated consumers. As such, their situation is unique. Their desires to consume have been overly stimulated, but their economic capabilities are underdeveloped. Moreover, they have to abide by a set of rules that tries to enforce their prudence. Enjoined to consume by some, they are subsidized to a bare necessity by others. When a corporation reaches such an impasse, it floats stock or obtains a defense contract; for people, there is only welfare. And whether they live in the Borough of Manhattan or in an agricultural village in Kansas, they may have to face suspicion, enforcement, and victimization; in return for the minimum subsidies they can expect to receive for food, rent, clothing, and personal care, these eight million dependents are regularly policed, punished, and rehabilitated, often with a complete disregard for their constitutionally guaranteed rights, which, in some cases, they are expected to forfeit in advance as conditions of assistance. Threats of ultimate institutionalization are made, and they are forced to live under constant suspicion of fraud. Applying for assistance, they are often greeted by an armed policeman. They also become acquainted with more subtle symbols of coercion throughout their dependencies. They are a target population in the War on Poverty, which as often as not seems to view them as the enemy.

Most of us can rationalize our behavior as consumers through a variety of harmless gambits. Either we say it is our pleasure, or our responsibility, or our compulsion, and we usually feel little guilt about the waste we are helping to perpetuate. But this presumption of competence is never extended to the consuming clients who are too young, too old, too sick, too unskilled, or too burdened down with dependents to earn the wages that would allow them to be full-fledged consumers; and there are few among the approximately 190 million Americans not presently in need of public assistance who would argue that it should be. What we do for these people we say we are doing in their own best interests, reasonably certain that their consumption must be limited because we are sure that we shall never be in their situation. Stigmatized historically as paupers, indigents, and vagabonds but more recently as AFDC, TADC, OAA, MAI, or HR,[1] their bureaucratically alphabetized miseries are deemed suitable for the pre-added budget and the as-needed grant (in administering which, the social service worker must

---

[1] Aid for Dependent Children, Temporary Aid for Dependent Children, Old Age Assistance, Medical Aid to the Indigent, and Home Relief are among the chief public assistance programs. County Welfare departments also offer aid to the blind and the disabled and assistance to veterans.

function as a detective) because it is assumed that their dependencies must be short-lived. And because the original programs of public assistance were created during the great depression for a caseload of skilled laborers (European immigrants and their descendants) who had been thrown temporarily out of work, the new clients—many of them dark-skinned, disadvantaged, perhaps unemployable under present circumstances—often find themselves at odds with this increasingly middle-class American polity because of their tendency to consume and still be dependent, which is considered alarming and which must, therefore, be controlled, suppressed, rehabilitated, even quarantined.

Dark-skinned people are only a minority in America. The dark-skinned welfare poor are a minority within that minority, lacking even the solidarity of its numbers, for the same majority that continues to make and administer the rules governing economic dependency commonly regards them as socially or morally, as well as economically, dubious; and the clients have been urged to agree with this diagnosis. It is, in fact, so prevalent that the Office of Economic Opportunity's insistence that it will not operate a "handout" program, when combined with its demands for the "maximum feasible participation" of the poor in all antipoverty programs, may prove out to be a cruel self-deception based on contradictory assertions. In what are these harassed unmarried mothers, children without fathers, old and disabled people, or men without futures expected to participate? They might, of course, begin to participate in a higher standard of living, commensurate with the general national affluence, if it were not so generally upheld by nearly the entire population that such people should not be coddled or everybody might aspire to the same deprivations.

There is no other group in America whose rights have been so often impugned and trampled upon as the citizenry of our Poorhouse State. In those states where racism has been official, Negro indigents have had to contend with racially, as well as morally, punitive statutes and policies that even now bar large numbers from minimum grants of public assistance. In general, the defenders of the working-class poor have not been shy, but the defenders of this *workless, shirking class* have been, respond-

ing only to the most blatant outrages. When Louisiana struck
some 22,000 illegitimate Negro children from the welfare roles
in 1960 to spite their parents, liberals and professionals had a
difficult time arousing any meaningful indignation from the
federal establishment against such policies. Even now, in New
York City, where as many as one thousand cases of Home
Relief are closed every month for unspecified reasons, such behavior on the part of public welfare officials is regarded as
routine.

These officials point out with some truth that they are under
constant pressure at the state and local levels to keep costs
down, but the indignities they must then administer become
routine as well as pervasive. Women with illegitimate children
can be examined in humiliating detail about the paternity of
their offspring before being granted aid. Although "separate but
equal" schemes of public education have been termed inherently
unfair by the Supreme Court, all the state laws governing the
economically dependent would appear to be, in this manner,
discriminatory. The costs of such a dependency can be charged
off against the applicant's legally responsible relatives (i.e., parents, grandparents, children, wives, and husbands), who must
also pay income taxes for the support of these same applicants.
To obtain assistance, the applicant must be prepared to sue his
relatives in court. If he balks at doing so, assistance will be withheld. If, moreover, the legally responsible relative is declared a
"putative" father and he defaults at acknowledging his paternity, he can be cited for contempt, tracked down, convicted, and
sentenced, perhaps, to a penal institution such as Hart's Island.

Historians of American welfare legislation are fond of tracing
its peculiarly punitive thrust to puritanical borrowings from the
Elizabethan poor laws, but such a purposeful vindictiveness
seems equally in keeping with our propensity for measuring success or failure in terms of economic mobility, of lauding the
success, despising the failure, and rating the course of every
human life in a kind of fever chart where a man is shown as
either one or the other. Many of our poor have never been allowed to be either. They have been required to consume without ever being given the means to participate in the presumptive
competence of those who consume in order to create the incen-

tives for more consumption. Elsewhere consumption is maximized, but they remain marginal men. Being so far behind, it is sometimes difficult for them to envisage how they can begin to participate in the consumer paradise, to which they so aspire, through mere labor.

But the majority of us do labor. We work hard. Despite machines, far too many of us are forced to gain our comforts through drudgery. It may not be physical labor. Increasingly it may be only the wretchedness of office work that consumes our lives so that we often feel deprived when we do not work. Faced, therefore, with a new leisure class that has never, apparently, earned the right to that leisure that we detest, we tend to become abusive of those who are not even sharing in the daily ordeal of work. Somehow, we think, they must be taught the value of work and the need to rise as a consequence of their own efforts, perhaps so we may begin to share in their leisure with a clearer conscience. It is not that we do not wish these "poor" to share our aspirations; we say we are only too willing to help them if they prove to us that that is their intention. But we want them to go the hard route, to be our taxi drivers, restaurant employees, secretaries, and factory hands so that they can support their families and thus improve their lives. We want them to believe in our values—and they do! But when they still seem dependent we become angry and abusive, and not always in the old, obvious ways. We know, in fact, that the leisure of the poor can be a misery, so we no longer try to chastise them for it but to uplift them from it. We tell those who deal with our poor not to pamper their weaknesses but to encourage their strengths. Yet our jargon seems curiously prone to images of violence; we describe this process as an effort to "break the circle of dependency."

If you regard taking money from others as a bad habit and you wish to "break" somebody of that habit, you usually do not encourage him to ask for more of the same. Thus Nathan Glazer[2] recommends that birth control can break the circle of dependency of New York's Puerto Ricans on the theory that "the job at $50 a week, which manages to support such a small

[2] Nathan Glazer and Daniel Moynihan, *Beyond the Melting Pot* (MIT-Harvard, 1963), page 120.

family in the Bronx and which, compared with the $12 a week income that was left behind on the island, represents real advancement, is completely inadequate to support five children or more . . ." And Edgar May, Inspector General of the Office of Economic Opportunity, would like social workers to become "the turnstile guardians of relief."[3] Lamenting over the period he spent as a case investigator in Buffalo, May writes: "I was now part of the system . . . a system where help was measured by what it bought at the grocery and gave to the landlord. I had become a dispenser of checks and very little else."

As the administration of our Poorhouse laws has become more professionalized, the invidious character of much of our earlier vocabulary toward the poor has undergone some modifications; but we tend to want to be just as harsh in our judgments and just as niggardly in our allowances. Federal assistance programs provide only meager incentives for those to whom the word "job" has long been empty of meaning. Many training programs still "cream off" the worthy and allow the unworthy to go untrained. If no American now starves, many do go hungry supporting those who are still not eligible for assistance on their own niggardly assistance budgets, which have been devised by Pecksniffs with professional degrees on the theory that the poor man must be given the incentive to eat better by earning more. We ask the poor to consume along with us, but then we turn and ask only them to justify their consumption. If social service workers no longer divide their caseloads into the wise and the wasteful, they now tend to lay the blame for waste on "emotional disturbance," the "multiproblem family," the "female-centered family," or the poor man's propensity toward schizophrenia, which reduces our common human squalor to an exotic psychological squalor defined by class.[4] In his own best interests the person on public assistance is no longer threatened with the workhouse or the prison hulks, but he can be forced to accept "counseling" as a condition of eligibility, or he may be

[3] Edgar May, *The Wasted Americans, Cost of Our Welfare Dilemma* (Harper & Row, 1964).

[4] One New York City Department of Welfare survey in 1962 diagnosed more than sixty per cent of the caseload for one health area as "emotionally disturbed."

asked to place his children in a home as another condition, or he may himself be committed to a mental institution. Throughout his dependency, his alleged character deficiencies will be used to explain why he is unable to obtain better service from the bureaucracy; and his defects of personality will come to justify his continuing squalor. He will be urged, cajoled, coerced, and exhorted to seek help, or to restore himself to productive citizenship, or to break the circle of dependency—a condition that may be problematical to everyone but himself—and when he asks for more help (i.e., more cash) he may be accused of being "manipulative," and he will be punished, perhaps by the withholding of that same help.

Too often, what is most problematical to the recipient is his demonstrated lack of resources. Through the scrupulously administered "means test" his lack of work or other resources has been certified so that he has been given a professional status—that of Welfare recipient—and, as the constant reinvestigation of his need continues, he is still willing to cling to this profession as tenaciously and with as much energy and commitment as if he were some aspiring employee in the mail room of a large firm. But although he must operate within the Welfare system with as much aggressiveness as the clerk seeking to rise above his fellows, the Welfare system will invariably punish him whenever he shows too much aggressiveness as a consumer. If he seeks to move out of his slum into a decent neighborhood, his apartment security may be withheld. If he asks for more money, his need may be reinvestigated. If he shows a taste for beefsteak, he will be reminded that he should use surplus foods. Dinned into his ears are the new federal slogans stressing "Rehabilitation instead of Relief." The pervasiveness of our highly advertised consumer culture is such that even he, in his aggrieved state and with his limited prospects, understands that no one would be so obsessed with his joblessness or lack of skills or with the fact that he was a school dropout, or came from a broken family, or was mildly schizophrenic if he could boast a Diners' Club card, an M.A. degree in English Literature, or 5,000 shares of American Telephone and Telegraph. But it is usually impossible for him to convince the functionaries that the priority of his needs calls for money before any other form of assistance. Too often the functionary has been given a mandate to define the person as defective simply by his application for assistance and to justify his invasions of privacy in the same way. Just as often it has been made organizationally feasible for the functionary to combine a great deal of advice with a minimal amount of assistance. In New York City, for example, the more senior caseworkers are always placed on "intake" because it is assumed that they will be more discerning in rejecting Welfare applicants. Such rejections are, of course, thought to be rehabilitative, since they return the applicant to the job market.

For the rejected applicant, rejection creates the necessity for poorly paid work, which, in turn, creates poverty; but for the successful applicant the situation is apt to grow just as nightmarish as he becomes more deeply involved in the Poorhouse State apparatus. Confronted continually by hierarchies of functionaries who have been endowed with extraordinary discretionary powers, the recipient will learn to accept the "social plan" by which he is to live out his dependency, take himself off Welfare, or be punished for failing to comply with a set of regulations that are sometimes at variance with state and federal policies. If he chooses compliance, he must get used to a continual interrogation about his resources, his friends, his family relationships. Rarely will he be given any record of these transactions. Although all the information he gives is to be regarded by regulation as confidential, so as to insure his privacy, this is usually used as a device to insure the privacy of the functionary and to conceal his activities. He can still judge and punish his client whenever he fails to act in accordance with a given policy. Thus, the woman who tells her investigator that she has parents in South Carolina, for example, may find that she must remove herself to South Carolina if she is to receive assistance.

If only we could guarantee stable and rewarding jobs for everyone who needs to work, the daily perjuries that take place at any Welfare office might be illegitimate, and such extensive scrutiny might make sense; but the increase in jobs has not kept up with the influx of people into the job market. Moreover, government economists seem to get the inflation jitters whenever the employment rate dips below four per cent. If we can no longer hope to guarantee employment for all, the problem will be especially crucial among Negroes, which—along with a gradual lessening in discrimination against them when they apply for Welfare—accounts for their increasing access to Welfare. The Negro comes to Welfare cynical and bitter, a defeated man. Often he does not come at all but sends his family. Through what is believed to be the temporary application of Public Assistance payments, the assumption is that such "families" will be able to restore in six months or a year what has been taken from them over generations. Our impatience grows when we see that they fail to perform as we had hoped on subsistence incomes and substandard living conditions. But, if we are now sufficiently appalled with their performance to disguise some of our most angry impatience in a psychiatric or social scientific *newspeak*, this has little save a punishing effect, finally, on the lives of our newest class of dependents. Even when finally "rehabilitated," many may not be more than a few pennies better off. Lacking money or real political and social organization to uphold their rights as the recipients of public assistance, they are still held in the residual thralls of that older Poorhouse system, which rewarded virtue and punished vice and which regarded the continuing prospect of a person's economic dependency as the *prima facie* evidence of his improvidence, incompetency, and illegitimacy.

Thus, although all Americans are free to cross state boundaries and choose their residences to their liking, special residency laws are always being enacted—in one form or another—by nearly all the states denying this guarantee to the person who applies for public assistance after coming from another state.

(In California a one-year residency is required of women with children; three years is demanded of single persons. In New York State a modified residency law, or Welfare Abuses Act, was passed in 1962, allowing the functionary to decide whether a person has come to New York for the purpose of collecting Welfare and to reject him if he can be shown to have done so.)

Although Americans need not fear illegal searches and seizures or the arbitrary violation of their privacy, the person on Public Assistance (or living in a low-income public housing project) can protect himself against such actions only at the risk of disqualification (or eviction).

*For more than a hundred years all Americans have been pro-
tected against "involuntary servitude," but the functionaries
who are engaged in city and state offices of "employment rehabilitation" do not interpret this to mean that their clients
have the freedom to accept or reject work.*

Violations of constitutional guarantees are endemic to many
aspects of our Public Welfare programs. Some localities maintain work relief programs that verge on "peonage." In the 1960s
many states passed "suitable home" laws, which denied assistance—in violation of the equal protection clause of the Fourteenth Amendment—to women with illegitimate children. Still
other states adopted "substitute father" provisions, which give
the states the right to cut off assistance to unmarried mothers—
in violation of both due process and equal protection—if they
have a relationship with any male who could be considered a
substitute father. In 1961 the Department of Health, Education
and Welfare ruled that states would have to abandon their
"suitable home" laws unless other means were provided to support the children. At present the NAACP is also attempting to
bring an action against the states of Arkansas and Georgia so
that HEW will rule similarly in the case of "substitute father"
provisions.[5]

*When the beneficiary of a Poorhouse State program appeals
some violation of his rights, some new affront to his dignity, he
is not guaranteed an impartial trial by a jury of his peers but is
made to come before an administrative tribunal that can function with only the most perfunctory regard for due process of
law.*

Within recent years the rapid growth of the Welfare State
has been the cause of some alarm, particularly among political
conservatives, whose ultimate fear seems to be that they will be
treated as subjects of the Poorhouse State; but these fears have
little basis in reality. Only for women who mother illegitimate
children while on Welfare have our legislators ever proposed
involuntary sterilization. Only for such families has Congress
ever contemplated making child desertion a federal offense.

[5] For a good discussion of these two issues in particular, see Winifred
Bell's *Aid to Dependent Children* (Columbia University Press, 1965).

These are also the only Americans for whom it has been recently suggested that corporal punishment be reintroduced as a possible deterrent to welfare recidivism.

At present, therefore, citizenship in the Poorhouse State—unlike enrollment under a program such as social security—still manages to be rigidly restrictive and subject to the power fantasies of other humans. Whenever efforts are made to eliminate the distinction between claiming benefits and applying for assistance, even responsible organs of public opinion are likely to express great outrage. Vermont Senator Winston Prouty's recent bill to extend social security benefits to recipients of old-age assistance (who are among the 1.8 million persons over seventy presently ineligible) was greeted editorially by the *New York Times* as a "hare-brained idea" and a "share-the-wealth scheme."[6] "Mr. Prouty's prodigal measure is not limited to proffering relief to those who need it . . . the proposal offers blank coverage to everyone reaching three score and ten."

The paradox of such reasoning is that only eight million Americans of any age have thus far been certified for assistance, although some believe that two to three times as many may be eligible. Not only do the various federal statutes by which people qualify for public assistance echo with contaminations of the "deserving poor" categories (and even some of the humiliations) of the pre-New Deal local poor laws, but they have also been made operative under state welfare codes, which tend to be even more restrictive in attempting to define and determine need; and then they have been placed—along with the usual emphasis on rehabilitation—under the administration of state and local functionaries who are jealous of their prerogatives, anxious to use discretion, and subject to greater political pressures from their local communities than from the generally benign federal establishment.[7] A veteran Welfare worker gave me as a rule of thumb of Welfare administration that "the Feds propose, the

6 *New York Times* editorial, March 10, 1966, "Perverting Social Security." At this writing, the Prouty bill narrowly has gotten through the Senate, but stiffer opposition is expected from the usually more conservative House.

7 Legislators, professionals, and administrators of an earlier generation rewrote the Public Assistance sections of the New Deal Social Security Act of 1936 so there were no nationwide income policies established. It was felt in the South that a uniform federal income subsidy would destroy

states oppose, and the localities dispose" of new programs. In the matter of eligibility, however, the applicant usually finds himself at the combined mercies of these three interest groups, each of whom is equally interested in conserving funds. No two counties are likely to have the same eligibility requirements, but residence laws will penalize the person who "shops" for benefits. Since all three levels of government participate in welfare funding on a matching basis, all are subjected to the same widening circle of indifference or active hostility, which means that disagreement at any level may immobilize a given program. The matching formula was initially devised to preserve local autonomy and federalism, but its chief appeal has been to further exaggerate our selfish individualism by assuring prosperous farmers that they are not bearing the costs of urban improvidence and vice versa.

Administratively the Welfare system is cumbersome and grants a great deal of local discretion where it can be easily abused; but it also places obstacles before the well-intentioned functionary. Recently, for example, a liberal New York City Welfare Commissioner announced that his department was considering eliminating the means test in favor of "relief by affadavit." He also announced at the same time that he was hoping to increase the amount of money a man could earn and still collect assistance. "Just Sign Up, Collect Relief While on Job," a *Herald Tribune* headline blared; but the Commissioner had tried to anticipate such criticism by stating that his new policy would not cost the City any more money, "at least at first." If, as he pointed out, applicants would no longer be subjected to the lengthy means test interview, workers would be free to focus on their clients' rehabilitation, he asserted, and no longer would there be the need for checking and cross-checking every request of the clients. Assistance would be granted on the client's testimony, and the caseload would then be subjected only oc-

---

already depressed low-wage-paying industries such as agriculture. The result has been a crazy quilt of benefits whereby New York was recently paying out $41.38 per dependent child per month and Mississippi paying out $8.91. As Schneider and Deutsch pointed out at the conclusion of *The History of Public Welfare in New York State* (University of Chicago, 1941, p. 355): "The Social Security Act of 1936 was essentially a compromise measure embodying several contradictory principles as a result of amendments forced by conflicting interests."

casionally to "spot checks" to attest to their veracity. The Commissioner stressed that what he was considering initially was a "pilot program" at only one Welfare center. He also made it clear that he would have to seek federal and state approval for funding such a program. But whereas the federal bureaucracy has vaguely put itself on record as endorsing simplified eligibility requirements but has not yet provided any incentives, the state has been far less generous. Even as the Commissioner was announcing his proposals, the State Department of Social Welfare was recalling retired welfare workers to serve as "quality control" experts within local welfare departments. These people were to read and study the case records of all those declared eligible and report back any ineligibles directly to the state, which could then hold up its matching fund reimbursements on the basis of such reports.

In general, the federal-state-locality nexus maximizes administrative discretion at the expense of clients' rights. In some states only so much money is appropriated by the Welfare system through this arrangement, only so many clients can be granted benefits. Federal law stipulates that aid can be given to the dependent child and mother, the aged person, the disabled, the veteran, or the blind person,[8] if a state so chooses, but uniformly, and according to a plan devised by each state. But, though rights are vaguely articulated for the recipient in nearly all these state programs, they continue to be vested most clearly in the state and county (or city) size bodies choosing those programs they will consent to administer. Even after a program is adopted, with need as the chief criterion for eligibility, the people who administer our Poorhouse laws are often not able to adjudicate need to their satisfaction through the present means test; they protect themselves against criticism from the press and other generally conservative groups by superimposing further bureaucratic criteria, which are even more selective, so that they can arrive at a satisfactory restrictive definition of who is needy and who is not.

[8] There are also deserving poor among the deserving poor, to judge from annual reports of New York City's Department of Welfare. In 1962 New York City spent more than $50 million on some 32,000 old persons while 212,000 mothers and their dependent children received approximately $121 million. Least deserving of all were the better than 37,000 on Home Relief, who were given only a little more than $17 million.

Suppose we say that the needy are those who present no extraneous behavioral problems to the functionary. It becomes, then, a very simple matter of moral arithmetic to subtract from the candidates' lists those who, for one reason or another, can be described as troublesome, or potentially troublesome, or troubled, and, therefore, undeserving, or to make their eligibility for a particular benefit contingent upon their good behavior. Thus applicants for public welfare in New York are regularly rejected for such reasons as "obnoxious behavior" or because they are deemed employable (by whom?); and applicants for any of the scarce units of low-cost public housing in the city may be denied admittance if they have ever been evicted from private housing, if they show irregular work histories, if there are out-of-wedlock children, if the husband and wife have been separated two or more times in the past five years, or if any members of the family are mentally retarded. They can also be admitted conditionally upon their acceptance of counseling, and once they become residents they can be evicted for poor housekeeping or if any members of their family are arrested. At the hearings to review these charges they can be asked about anything that reflects to their discredit. In a memo to its supervisors, the New York City Housing Authority recognizes that there just is not enough public housing for everybody, for it states that its major objective in making these seemingly arbitrary discriminations against those who have been defined as in need is to "create for its tenants an environment conducive to healthful living, family stability, sound family and community relations and proper upbringing of children." But a prime result of such policies is that while New York State voters continually defeat propositions to increase the number of units of low-income public housing, public housing authorities become increasingly defensive and discriminatory in the selection of tenants, so that many poor find it impossible to be admitted or, once admitted, difficult to maintain their residence. In New York City they must reside in the blocks of deteriorating tenements[9] which, in many instances, are owned by the city in re-

[9] In 1964 there were 43,000 tenements erected before 1900, which housed approximately 900,000 persons—nearly twice as many as those presently living in public low-income housing.

ceivership or are wholly subsidized by the Poorhouse State through its Department of Welfare.

Welfare is a way of life for some. It is all the mobility they have. In New York a Negro woman can collect more from Welfare than she could earn by doing housework in Alabama or Georgia; but living standards tend to make such comparisons meaningless. If, by nationwide standards, New York is considered such a liberal branch of the Poorhouse State that it tends to attract the indigent from other states, they do not fare any better once they get here. In Syracuse they can be issued food vouchers instead of cash. In Albany they are encouraged to use surplus foods by pegging cash benefits below the minimal living standards; in Buffalo they are not allowed to use their food vouchers to purchase beer or cigarettes; and within New York City, they have difficulties getting special grants, even for such things as carfare reimbursements (30¢). None of New York's social welfare policies toward the dependent consumer is deliberately biased, but they are all unfair because they do not acknowledge the poor as consumers and because they are subject to unchallenged interpretation by local administrators. "Liberal" New York State has two legislative committees on public welfare and many hundreds of interested community and voluntary groups. It will expend nearly $500 million in 1966 on public assistance alone, of which more than half will go to New York City. Augmented by its share of federal and local funds, the city's welfare budget will be larger[10] than the state's, which is not surprising if one realizes that there is a city of paupers the size of Buffalo within the crowded 319.1 square miles of the five boroughs. The largest group of dependents is children under eighteen. They are among the clients about whom the New York City Department of Welfare, in its official manuals, advises its employees that it is dangerous to manifest "an exaggerated solicitude and over-willingness—even anxiety—to 'do things.' " The state also has some rather niggardly attitudes toward these clients which it wishes to see enforced. It is because

[10] In January, 1966, the then Acting Welfare Commissioner asked for $663,607,986, approximately a third of it to come from each level—federal, state, and city.

of its insistence upon proper and frequent investigation of the caseload that New York City welfare employees were until recently told during their training sessions that the applicant for public assistance must forfeit his right to privacy and choice.[11]

A fifteen-minute subway ride from Times Square will take you to Manhattan's Lower East Side, a welfare ghetto. Officially more than ten thousand paupers and their dependents now occupy this congested area, but there are probably even more.

Once almost exclusively a system of overlapping ethnic ghettos from which the Jewish, Irish, Italian, Hungarian, Polish, Greek, and other immigrant groups struggled for economic mobility and assimilation, achieved through their own sweated labor, the Lower East Side (with its socialist past and high-camp bohemian present) has in large part become a dependency ghetto, a kind of seedy familial extension of the nearby Bowery. The new influx consists of highly visible recent immigrants from Puerto Rico and Negro migrants from the rural South; most arrived with many of the same ambitions as earlier generations to find themselves increasingly superfluous or redundant in an economy that no longer needs their unskilled labor. If many of these people have remained resourceful, others have revealed all the weaknesses resulting from generations of poverty. There is a good deal of what we choose to define as antisocial behavior (i.e., high rates of drug addiction, illegitimacy, alcoholism, felonious assault) and a pervasive system of credit bilking, consumer frauds, and other forms of mercantile corruption. For more than four years an ambitious federally funded social work program called Mobilization for Youth has been in the area, attempting to give the newcomers "a stake in conformity" by helping them to organize themselves and by providing their children with skills and opportunities. Of all "colonialist" operations among the poor this has probably been one of the most benign, the most willing to yield some of its sovereignty to its constituents; the extent of its success has varied from program to program. If it has enhanced the reading skills of some youngsters or the job prospects of others, it has not been given the

[11] Federal law stipulates one investigation a year. In New York four are considered mandatory for all categories of public assistance but Old Age and Veterans Assistance. The department visits those they deem untrustworthy even more regularly and without notice.

resources to create any of the vitally needed public services (housing, health, and child care), and it has not yet been able to change any of the prevailing power relationships of the area. When it attempted to do so there were denunciations in the press and attacks on its personnel.

Still largely powerless, the new residents of the Lower East Side have become increasingly dependent on public largess which claims to view their dependency as a social pathology but which, through its procedures of scrutiny, confidentiality and rehabilitation, treats it more often than not as if it were a psychological aberration. As one woman on public assistance told me: "When I am in arrears (to the landlord), you should see how angry they get at the Welfare. When I want a pair of eyeglasses for my daughter, hell can freeze over."

In comparatively liberal New York the Poorhouse State functions differently than it does in thrifty New Hampshire or racist Mississippi; its procedures differ from the city of Newburgh to the Borough of Manhattan and, in some of its behavior, from welfare center to welfare center.

In New York some 5,000 social investigators, augmented by a special grand investigations bureau, serve the requests of such clients. Many of the investigators are so new to the department that they have not had time to learn the multiplicity of regulations under which they are said to be operating. Among residents of the Lower East Side, they are known simply as the Welfare, DW, or the man from *Bienestar* (Welfare); and they help to account for the many thousands of Welfare disqualifications within the city every month.[12] In addition, an average of two out of five applicants for public assistance are rejected when they appear at the intake desk to apply; and every day, in nearly every center, injustices are recorded for which there is apparently no redress. In fact, in the entire city of New York there are only

[12] The ratio of Welfare workers to Welfare clients is greater than the ratio of police to the citizenry of New York at large. In 1962 the Department spent nearly four times as much for salaries (approximately $48 million) as it gave out in grants to persons on Home Relief. Welfare job classifications are under civil service except for the unclassified and more highly paid fraud investigators. In general, Welfare salaries are considered low. Starting pay for a social investigator (case worker I) is $5,750 per annum, approximately three times as much as he can give out in a year to a family of four on public assistance; but I was told that a major problem of the Department is petty theft among employees.

about fifteen formal appeals (or Fair Hearings) made from
Welfare decisions every year. These injustices are, in the main,
so petty and routinized that the caseworker may not even regard
his conduct as problematical; and the recipient, ever mindful of
his precarious status, will not be likely to jeopardize it by taking
the caseworker to task. To the citizen of the Poorhouse State,
the need to consume is so unsatisfied and the possibility of punishment always so imminent that he is not likely to complain
about the daily degradations, the violations of his privacy, the
errors that are buried and made unremediable, the arbitrary
handling of his problems. He may not even complain when he
has a toothache because he will not wish to travel all the way
to Queens for his dental care; and he may be afraid to ask his
caseworker to make other arrangements. Despite well-meaning
programs of legal advocacy on behalf of such people, the in-
timidation of the poor remains pervasive, in part because the
Poorhouse State apparatus still reserves the right to see its clients
unencumbered by the presence of lawyers, translators, or social
workers, in a sanctity that is policed only by the discretion and
good intentions of the caseworker and in part because services
are so scarce that those on welfare must always beg for whatever they get. Thus the responsibility rests with the caseworker
to discern worthy and unworthy petitioners. If many workers
use this discretion judiciously and well while others are so preoccupied with petty paper work that they use it only sporadically
(if at all), it is in the nature of his dependency for the client
to regard his worker as an enemy who can deny him what he
needs. But most cannot afford to act upon this recognition.
When at any moment after such a meeting, a determination can
be made affecting your destiny—during the process of which
you will normally be consulted only to incriminate yourself—
prudence dictates that you "sit back and just take it." More
often than not, the bad news will later arrive by mail.

FOR FURTHER READING

The literature on housing is enormous. For the problems discussed
here, Charles Abrams, *Forbidden Neighbors* (New York: Harper
Bros., 1955) is particularly relevant. Also useful, but in the broader

context of world problems, is his *Man's Struggle for Shelter in an Urbanizing World* (Cambridge: Massachusetts Institute of Technology Press, 1964). A lively, dramatic treatment of housing based on first-hand experience is Jane Jacobs' *The Death and Life of Great American Cities* (New York: Random House, 1961). An overall view of conditions in the slums is provided by David R. Hunter, *The Slums: Challenge and Response* (New York: Free Press, 1964). A critical discussion of programs to rebuild the city is in Staughton Lynd, "Urban Renewal—For Whom?" *Commentary* (January, 1961). Several chapters in Alvin L. Schorr, *Slums and Social Insecurity* (London: Nelson, 1964), are related to housing for the poor.

A competent and useful survey of welfare systems in America may be found in Sar A. Levitan's *Programs in Aid of the Poor* (Kalamazoo: W. E. Upjohn Institute for Employment Research, 1964). Harry M. Caudill offers perceptive observations on the application of welfare standards to the poor in Appalachia in his *Night Comes to the Cumberlands* (Boston: Little, Brown, 1963); the chapter on "The Rise of the Welfare State" is especially pertinent. The student may also want to consult Charles E. Silberman, *Crisis in Black and White* (New York: Random House, 1964), particularly the chapter "The Revolt Against 'Welfare Colonialism.'"

RACE, POVERTY, AND THE LAW

Loren Miller

Scott Briar

Whether he is renting an apartment, buying on the installment plan, or seeking welfare aid or unemployment insurance, the poor person seldom escapes the legal pitfalls involved in such activities. The day-to-day business of living is apt to bring him into direct contact with the police, the courts, and the arbitrary decision-making power of public welfare agencies. The poor person senses that he is trapped by a legal structure he cannot comprehend. He may well agree with Anatole France that "equality before the law" really means that neither rich men nor poor are permitted to sleep under bridges on rainy nights. The poor who are also Negro view the law as white man's law, justice as white man's justice. For them, white man's legality is encompassed in the term "The Man."

Yet a few advances have been made. In several major cities Legal Aid Societies assist poor clients; the Vera Foundation seeks to provide bail for defendants without funds; and Mobilization for Youth in New York has established a legal aid unit. Unfortunately, certain sectors of the legal profession have protested that these efforts violate the lawyer's Canon of Ethics (despite the fact that such projects have received the support of major bar associations). These people complain that legal advice is being offered to plaintiffs, an unheard of service to the poor. But to protect their rights, the poor badly need just such services—whether to force a landlord to make repairs in a decrepit building, or to void an essentially fraudulent sales contract.

This section is a combination of the two articles from "The Law of the Poor," a special issue of the *California Law Review*. Loren Miller is a judge of the Municipal Court of Los Angeles. Scott Briar is Associate Professor, School of Social Welfare, and Research Associate in the Center for the Study of Law and Society at the University of California, Berkeley. His study was supported by the U.S. Department of Health, Education, and Welfare and the California State Department of Social Welfare.

᠅ᢒᢒᢒᢒ᠅

Race, Poverty, and the Law, by Loren Miller

The proudest boast of American lawyers is that all men stand equal before the law. The boast is a noble and useful one even if it isn't quite borne out by the facts. Too much of that equality is of the kind described by Anatole France when he said that the laws of his country were fair: They forbade both rich men and poor men from sleeping under bridges on rainy nights. Recent events in the South have brought the realization that all men aren't equal before the law in some southern courtrooms and have occasioned soul searching to find out whether persons of differing economic circumstances are always equal before the law.

Senator Robert F. Kennedy, former Attorney General, insists that the "poor man looks upon the law as an enemy . . . . For him the law is always taking something away." Nicholas deB. Katzenbach, . . . [who succeeded Kennedy as] Attorney General, puts it that, "To us, laws and regulations are protections and guides, established for our benefit, and for us to use. But to the poor, they are a hostile maze, established as harassment, at all costs to be avoided."

Source: *California Law Review*, LIV, 2 (May, 1966), 62–82. Copyright © 1966, California Law Review, Inc. Reprinted by permission.

Racial identity, particularly for Negroes, has always been as troublesome a factor as poverty in the quest for equality before the law. Most Negroes, the overwhelming majority, are poor. The poor Negro has trouble on his hands when he seeks to surmount the twin obstacles of race and poverty and attain that equality guaranteed alike by federal and state constitutions and ingrained in American hopes.

One of the biggest obstacles to a frank national confrontation of this problem is the general American reluctance to admit that the original Constitution condoned and permitted discrimination against Negroes and that there was a great leeway for racial discrimination under late nineteenth- and early twentieth-century construction of the Civil War amendments. Racial inequality before the law affects all Negroes, no matter what their economic status or station in life. Jim Crow laws catch the affluent as well as the impoverished Negro in their nets. To complicate the matter, few persons believe that the Negro is entitled to full equality. Working class suburban cities and towns voted against a 1964 Fair Housing law in Los Angeles County, California, in about the same proportion as middle-class and upper middle-class suburbs. An analysis of a vote in Berkeley, California, showed a majority of white citizens with college degrees or better education opposed that city's fair housing ordinance.[1] Large law firms have always drawn the same color lines against ambitious young Negro lawyers as have other employers.[2]

HISTORICAL PERSPECTIVES

Most persons would deny vigorously that they entertain racial prejudices in any degree. Their denials are not contrived fictions; they are believed by those who utter them. Americans simply have a double standard of judgment as to rights of white per-

[1] An unpublished survey taken in 1962 by California Research Associates showed that of a sampling of 368 Berkeley voters, 201 opposed a fair housing ordinance and 167 favored it. About 58% of white college graduates opposed the measure.

[2] A casual check will show no Negro lawyers in any of California's top law firms. These firms deny discrimination, of course. All nonemployers of Negroes also deny discrimination. All give the same reason for the non-employment of Negroes: Merit alone is the only test used!

sons as contrasted to those of Negroes. To them, white persons are born vested with that vast array of rights and privileges vaguely thought of as natural rights. Negroes, on the other hand, are regarded as entitled to such rights as the white majority grants them. It is commonly said that Negroes must "earn" the rights they would enjoy. That attitude is deeply rooted in our history.

Heeding the admonition of James Madison that it would be "wrong to admit, in the constitution, that there could be property in man," the Constitution makers fashioned a document that makes no mention of slaves, slavery, or race. Yet that great instrument protected slavery in the states where the institution existed, provided for the return of escaped slaves to their masters, devised a formula for counting slaves in the apportionment of members of Congress, prohibited Congress from taxing slavery out of existence, and preserved the African slave trade for twenty years. The slave trade and taxing clauses could not even be amended before 1808. The Founding Fathers heeded Madison's advice so well that the layman cannot identify the articles dealing with slavery without the aid of an historian. In fact, few lawyers can turn the trick.

Every Fourth of July and every Bill of Rights Week, orators shout themselves hoarse and teachers exhaust themselves telling Americans, adults and children, that the original Constitution and the Bill of Rights protected the rights and liberties of *all* Americans. This bit of pleasant folklore is arrived at by taking all the language of the Constitution at face value. In truth, the equalitarian guarantees explicit and implicit in the Constitution and amplified in the Bill of Rights offered absolutely no protection to the approximately 700,000 persons held in slavery at the birth of the nation and, as the Supreme Court was to hold later, little more protection for the some 60,000 free Negroes of the North and South. The Constitution, Chief Justice Roger B. Taney said in the *Dred Scott* case, decided in 1857, was made by and for white men. Negroes, he elaborated, "were not intended to be included, under the word 'citizens' in the Constitution, and can therefore claim none of the rights and privileges which that instrument provides for and secures to citizens of the United States." He went further to say that free Negroes were "not even in the minds of the framers of the Constitution when they were conferring special rights and privileges upon the citizens of a State in every other part of the Union." Citizenship extended to Negroes by some states, he said, did not and could not confer national citizenship on them. Distinguishing state citizenship from national citizenship, the Court held that the states were in entire control of civil rights and that the citizen of a state must look to the state for protection of those rights.

Of course, the Chief Justice's construction of the Constitution ran directly counter to that contended for by anti-slavery lawyers and theoreticians, but his was the practical construction put upon the document prior to and at the time of the decision. A portion of the hue and cry raised against the majority opinion in the *Dred Scott* case was the normal reaction of men who wince and cry out in pain, real or simulated, when their deeds are described in apposite language. The interpretation of the Constitution advocated by Chief Justice Taney as regards the rights of Negroes, free and slave, prior to the Civil War has had enormous consequences for the nation.

The most important principles that suffused the Constitution and undergirded stability for the political institutions created by it were the dignity of the individual and the inviolability of the rights and privileges recognized in that instrument and protected against governmental infringement. Those principles demanded that every man be treated as, and function as, an individual, as a *person*, in constitutional language. By such reckoning no person had group identity in the eyes of the law; he was neither Jew nor Gentile, Catholic nor Protestant, rich nor poor. He was a person, and as such he could claim the rights, privileges, and protections of the Constitution and the Bill of Rights.

The Constitution vindicated those principles for white Americans, but recognition and protection of slavery inflicted a mortal wound as far as the Negro was concerned. For the word slave was for all practical intents and purposes synonymous with the appellation Negro. The Constitution as construed and as applied imposed legal disabilities on the slave; he was stripped of his individual dignity simply because of his race and stood not as a *person* but as a slave before the law of the land. The slave existed beyond the pale of the protections of the original Constitution and the Bill of Rights. He was a stranger in a strange land; his status as a Negro was itself an invidious classification.

Nor did the freeborn or emancipated Negro escape the disabilities laid on his slave kinsman. The existence of Negro slavery was an ever present reminder that every free Negro was a *freedman,* not a *free man,* to whom rights or privileges might be extended or denied at will. Again, such an attitude ran counter to the beliefs and theories of anti-slavery lawyers and theorists; again, it was the practical construction upon which northern and southern states acted as they enacted laws barring free Negroes from schools, places of public accommodation, the ballot box, and other facilities open to white Americans.

In spite of theory, and from the earliest days, there were classifications of white men based on economic distinctions which impaired equality before the law assumed to be the birthright of free men. The right to vote or hold office often depended upon property qualifications; the debtor could be imprisoned; the appellant in a criminal trial might be denied a transcript of his hearing unless he could pay for it; a poor defendant could be forced to trial without a lawyer; a litigant desirous of a jury trial in a civil matter might be required to deposit costs. The vagabond, the roamer, the idle, the beggar might be denominated a vagrant and penalized because of his status—indeed, he still faces that possibility in many states.[3]

It is only in these latter days—very latter days—that some Americans have come to see that economic classification of a citizen may be disabling even where it is not specifically condemned by the Constitution. Most Americans are still blinded to a full realization of the importance of that fact by the belief that has so long sustained the nation that ours is an equalitarian society in which only the lack of ambition, thrift, and desire keep some in poverty. Deep in their hearts, a majority of Americans believe that any man can find a job if he has a mind to do

[3] See Hicks v. Dist. of Columbia, 383 U.S. 252 (1966) (dissenting opinion). Vagrancy laws in some Southern States are fashioned to penalize what are believed to be shortcomings of Negroes, and were formerly used to further peonage. See Stephenson, *Race Distinctions in American Law* 58, 275 (1910).

so, that with a job he can save money, buy a home, and ultimately become a middle-class member of the affluent society.
Within that context they nurse the belief that an economic
classification is temporary and hence permissible—they hope
that the penalties poverty exacts may even spur ambition. By
that same token, they are uncomfortable over the fact that the
individual cannot shed his race or vanquish his color as he can
his poverty, and they are happy to say, and hear the judges say,
that racial classification is suspect.

In a constitutional sense, racial classification as a device to
impose disabilities is worse than suspect: It is forbidden by the
Civil War amendments, or at least it was forbidden until the
Supreme Court revised the meanings of those amendments. The
precise purpose of the amendments was to abolish all invidious
racial distinctions tolerated by the original Constitution, as
interpreted by the Supreme Court, and to provide a new constitutional basis for congressional action to establish equality
whenever states or individuals were laggard or insisted on imposing racial disabilities.

After the ratification of the thirteenth amendment in 1865,
Congress enacted the first Civil Rights Act of 1866 in response
to the threats of the Black Codes[4] to reduce Negroes to semi-
slavery. Congress codified the sweeping legislative command for
equality as contained in the 1866 Civil Rights Act in the constitutional shorthand of the fourteenth amendment, ratified in
1868. In 1870 it proposed and secured ratification of the fifteenth amendment. Each of the amendments provides that
Congress shall have power to enforce the provisions by appropriate legislation. Congress exercised its newly established power
in the sweeping and searching Reconstruction legislation that
culminated in the Civil Rights Act of 1875.[5] "[H]ereafter," said
Charles Sumner, "there shall be no such word as 'black' or
'white,' but that we shall speak only of citizens and men."

Then the Supreme Court took over. In *The Slaughter-house
Cases*, it restored the *Dred Scott* doctrine that there are two

[4] McPherson, *Political History of the United States During the Period of
Reconstruction* 29–44 (1871).
[5] The Civil Rights Act of 1875 was the final civil rights law of the Reconstruction era. There was no similar legislation until 1957.

categories of citizenship, national and state, and gutted the privileges and immunities clause of the fourteenth amendment of all meaning. In *United States v. Cruikshank*, it restored control of civil rights to the states. In *United States v. Reese*, it severely restricted the scope and reach of the fifteenth amendment. In the *Civil Rights Cases*, it further cabined the meaning of the fourteenth amendment with its ruling that Congress could not proscribe an individual's discriminatory conduct. In *Virginia v. Rives*, it validated the indictments and verdicts of all-white juries in the absence of specific objections and proof by a Negro defendant of systematic and purposeful racial exclusion, and thus it set up a rule which allowed extensive discrimination in jury selection. In *Williams v. Mississippi*, and later in *Giles v. Harris* and *Giles v. Teasley*, it gave its blessing to state constitutional and statutory provisions deliberately and professedly designed to circumscribe the franchise. In *Plessy v. Ferguson*, it approved a state's racial classification, undertaken to establish the separate-but-equal rule in the use of state facilities or public utilities. In *Berea College v. Kentucky*, it approved state statutes proscribing interracial association for innocent purposes. In *Gong Lum v. Rice*, it approved separate schools. In *Corrigan v. Buckley*, it validated racial restrictive covenants and by indirection approved judicial enforcement of such agreements. In *Grovey v. Townsend*, it decided that state political parties could exclude Negroes from primary elections.

It is important to realize that prior to the Civil War amendments, the degradation of the Negro as tolerated by the Court after the addition of those amendments was consistent with constitutional theory and practice. The long list of disabilities just recited would have excited no opposition from pre-Civil War lawyers except from anti-slavery theoreticians. Chief Justice Taney's statement in the *Dred Scott* case that a Negro had no "rights which the white man was bound to respect" was a trifle too sweeping, but it is literally true that a Negro had no civil rights except those conferred on him by white men. The obvious and often expressed aim of the framers of the Civil War amendments was to confer those rights on Negroes through the Constitution and to obviate the power of white Americans to dole out such rights as they chose. Their view of the way to achieve that end was to vest the same rights in Negroes as were vested in white persons.

Those rights were conceived of as the natural rights of man as a member of the body politic. The Negro was made a citizen and hence vested with the same rights as a free born white man. His rights were a part of his birthright. None could take them from him because he was now a free man. None could detract from them. Among free born men vested with natural rights, race and skin color were to be an irrelevance. If any state trenched on these rights, there was a remedy, but, as Senator Oliver P. Morton of Indiana pointed out, that "remedy . . . was expressly not left to the courts. The remedy was legislative because in each case the amendment itself provided that it shall be enforced by legislation on the part of Congress."

The Supreme Court, however, had its own notions as to its power. It ignored the congressional fiat and interpreted the amended Constitution in the light of precedents that were based on the implicit concept of its original interpretation of the Constitution that the Negro, free or slave, lacked the full attributes of citizenship.

The net result of the Court's post Civil War decisions was to return Negroes to a modified second class citizenship of the kind that obtained prior to the Civil War and to resurrect the dictum of the *Dred Scott* case that "the unhappy black race were separated from the white by indelible marks. . . ." This separatism was said to be based upon racial instinct as the Court noted in the *Plessy* case: It intoned that "legislation is powerless to eradicate racial instincts or to abolish distinctions based upon physical differences . . . ." Social Darwinism had been assimilated to the amended Constitution; the William Graham Sumner dogma that law-ways cannot change folkways had become constitutional doctrine. Fortunately, the Court has repudiated most of the holdings that have just been cited, but they were the law of the land during the critical and formative years from the early 1870's to the middle 1930's, and during that sixty-year period were among the prime factors in institutionalizing racial segregation and discrimination.

As the first Justice John Marshall Harlan observed in his dissent in the *Civil Rights Cases*, the majority opinion in that case postulated a basis for establishing a color caste system with one "class of human beings in practical subjection to another class with power in the latter to dole out to the former just such privileges as they may choose to grant." That, of course, is precisely what happened, with white Americans doling out to Negroes "just such privileges as they [chose] . . . to grant." Or as he put it in the *Plessy* case, "we have yet, in some of the States, a dominant race—a superior class of citizens, which assumes to regulate the enjoyment of civil rights . . . upon the basis of race."

The belief that whites retain the "power . . . to dole out" to Negroes "just such privileges as they may choose to grant" flourishes in contemporary society; it finds expression in the vulgar judgment that "Negroes are moving too fast" or "asking too much" in their demand for civil rights; in a Supreme Court decision postponing the enjoyment of an admittedly vested and, therefore, *personal and present* constitutional right until recalcitrant school boards bestow it on its possessors with "all deliberate speed"; and in the enactment of a California constitutional provision protecting the right of white persons to discriminate in the sale or rental of real property. Because few white Americans subscribe to the proposition that Negroes are born with the same rights which they believe inhere in white Americans, most of them, even persons of goodwill, accept the popular judgment that it is quite proper for the majority to "regulate the enjoyment of civil rights . . . upon the basis of race" until that mythical day when the "hearts and minds of men," even the most backward, have changed and all racial prejudices have disappeared.

These historical facts with their intrusions into current thinking must be borne in mind and assessed if a discussion of race, poverty, and the law is to be invested with substance and realism. It must also be borne in mind that racial classification has rarely been benign in purpose or intent in American law. Rather, it has been a means of enforcing restrictions or restraints.

Despite the restrictive interpretations put upon them, the Civil War amendments have always been construed to prohibit discriminatory racial legislation by the states or their political subdivisions and to interdict imposition or support of racial disabilities by the executive and judicial branches of state govern-

ment. Even separate but equal legislation or administrative
practices made elaborate bows in the direction of equality by
proscribing white use of "Negro" facilities as well as Negro use
of "white" facilities, with the courts finally arriving at the curious conclusion that where interracial association was proscribed,
the equal protection clause of the fourteenth amendment was
served by imposing the same penalty on both the white and
Negro offender. Troublesome questions often arose as to the
equality of separate facilities, but the courts assuaged the constitutional conscience of the nation with the doctrine of substantial equality in which, for example, a one-room ungraded
school for Negroes was said to be "substantially equal" to a ten-
room graded school for whites, or a wooden railway car with no
running water or air conditioning was said to be "substantially
equal" to Pullman accommodations. The command for equality, the courts said, did not require the furnishing of identical
facilities.

Where the separate but equal concept could not be applied
but the desire to restrict Negro participation was present, every
effort was made to posit desired restrictions on permissible classifications which would encompass as many Negroes as possible
while netting a small number of white persons.[6] Because poverty
has always been one of the hallmarks of Negro life in the United
States, economic classification has proved very useful.[7] Thus
Negro voting was circumscribed by requiring a poll tax payment
as a prerequisite for voting. Property qualifications were imposed
as a condition of jury service in some Southern States.[8] When
Mississippi led the southern revolt that disfranchised Negroes in
the late nineteenth century, it "swept the circle of expedients"
by classifying as ineligible persons convicted of such crimes as
vagrancy, assault, and like offenses of the poor. Finally, the
Southern States hit upon classification of illiterates and those
lacking ability to read, understand, and explain state and federal

[6] Guinn v. United States, 238 U.S. 347 (1915) (all persons eligible to
vote prior to January 1, 1866, and their descendants, entitled to vote; all
others must pass literacy test); Williams v. Mississippi, 170 U.S. 213
(1898) (literacy tests for voting and jury duty).

[7] It is no secret that welfare payments in most Southern States are kept
low out of a desire not to "coddle" or "spoil" Negroes.

[8] Property qualifications as to the right to vote were almost universal at
the time of the adoption of the Constitution.

constitutions as persons unfit to exercise the suffrage—the illiterate and the lacking in understanding were, of course, the poor. These fair-on-their-face laws were enforced in such a discriminatory manner as to disfranchise almost the entire southern Negro population—a practice that gained nationwide acquiescence and drew approval from the Great Commoner, William Jennings Bryan.[9]

POVERTY AND RACE

Any economic classification that affects the poor as a group will include a disproportionate number of Negroes simply because a disproportionate number of Negroes live below the poverty line in American life. If disabilities attend economic classification, Negroes will be disadvantaged, no matter how nondiscriminatory the legislation may appear to be. Fair-on-their-face statutes, such as a levy of a poll tax as a condition of voting, will not vary that result. Uniform bail schedules lay a heavier burden on the poor than on the well-to-do and inevitably leave a disproportionate number of Negroes in custody. The same hardship results from use of a uniform fine schedule for traffic violations and other misdemeanors. Laws which penalize owners who are unable to secure and maintain public liability and property damage insurance on their automobiles hit the poor hard and fall with a heavy hand on proportionately more Negroes than whites. There are many situations in which classification does not seem to rest on poverty but in which economics intrudes. Thus it has been said that the application of juvenile delinquency statutes is "heavily weighted against the poor family." There, again, the disproportionate amount of poverty in the Negro ghettos operates to disadvantage the Negro youngster. Of course, the same observation may be made of the application of criminal statutes to the adult.

The preponderant number of Negroes caught in these legal nets is almost invariably pointed to by the unknowing or by the hostile to "prove" Negro criminality, or irresponsibility, or in-

[9] "The white man in the South has disfranchised the Negro in self-protection, and there is not a white man in the North who would not have done the same under the same circumstances." Speech by William Jennings Bryan, Cooper Union, N.Y., 1908.

feriority. In their proper turn, such attitudes serve to persuade law enforcement administrators that rights and privileges ought to be doled out rather sparingly to Negroes to prevent them from "going too fast" or "demanding too much" in the way of privileges they are believed to be ill-equipped to exercise. The result is a difference in the quality of law enforcement as between white persons and Negroes, particularly as far as the poor are concerned, a difference that is reflected in the almost universal hostility of the poor Negro to law enforcement officials. The poor Negro sees that his friends and neighbors, indeed, members of his own family are more often caught in the toils of the law than the white person, that the burdens of the law's penalties are more onerous for them, and that law enforcement officials can misuse him at their whim. In his own shorthand, he describes all of these inequities as "police brutality." And just as the unobservant white person lays the Negro's shortcomings to race without weighing economic and other factors, so the Negro poor tend to lay all of their ills to what they regard as racial prejudice. It is in this atmosphere that welfare laws operate and are administered.

A. *The Negro Poor Under Welfare*

Welfare legislation and its administration are critical in Negro life because so many Negroes are affected—again, because a disproportionate number of them fall into those categories of the poor for whom assistance is designed and necessary. Provision for welfare is an almost exclusively legislative function with legislators having almost free rein. There is comparatively little case law on the subject, but there is a welter of administrative rules and regulations, most of them designed by the administrators to win legislative favor and approbation. The legislature which pays the piper calls the tune.

Welfare legislation in American states traces back to Elizabethan poor laws with overlays of humanitarianism, enlightened flashes of public conscience, weak and wavering realization that a nation as rich as the United States can well afford an adequate standard of living for all of its citizens, and that failure to nurture the young and care for the ill and the aged is costly public policy. Nevertheless, the ill, the handicapped, the aged, the jobless (after unemployment benefits are exhausted), the deserted mother, the fatherless child are often treated as beggars and mendicants at best or as rogues, vagabonds and vagrants at worst. The welfare administrator who keeps as many applicants as possible out of benefits is in a fair way to win the approbation of his community and of its establishment. All too often, rules are administered to exclude apparently qualified applicants, and every effort to utilize existing regulations in such a manner as to obtain benefits is branded as "fraud." A Los Angeles superior court judge who could find no legal fault in utilization of some of the rules in order to maximize benefits fell back on the charge of "moral fraud" on the part of some beneficiaries. Current mores condone, even honor, the rich taxpayer whose lawyers and accountants find loopholes in the law that enable him to avoid income tax payments, but the welfare recipient who finds a loophole that enables her to increase aid to her children is an object of public wrath. The taxpayer is entitled to whatever savings he can effect; the welfare recipient is not "entitled" to aid provided for him.

Undergirding popular attitudes toward the needy poor is the premise that the poor are the authors of their own woes and ills, and are sponging on the rest of society. The hope is that if sponging can be made as disagreeable as possible they will do as others have done, and are doing, and earn their keep in the sweat of their own brows. The public insists on maintaining a close watch over them and continually demands more stringent local control so that doles can be kept a shade below local standards.[10]

Community hostility toward welfare recipients is heightened by administrative sub-classification of these poor on ethnic lines. When such racial classifications are made, it is at once discovered that the Negro ratio is high, considerably higher than the population ratio. The discovery looses a great clamor even though it is well known that Negro unemployment hovers around two to three times that of white workmen and that what

---

[10] This attitude rests on the belief that by reducing the lot of the welfare recipient to disagreeable poverty, we will force him to find one of the jobs assumed to be available to those who want to work.

is described as employment for Negroes is all too often marginal work that requires supplemental aid or assistance. Given the almost pathological American preoccupation with race and the demand for racial explanations for every social ill involving Negroes, it is not surprising that it is somewhat widely believed that a high percentage of Negroes prefer relief to steady jobs. By way of proof, examples are constantly dredged up of the Negro who prefers drawing seventy-five dollars per week on relief to accepting a dead-end job that would pay him $58.45 weekly.

The current horrific example of supposed racial exploitation of public assistance is the Aid to Families with Dependent Children (AFDC) program. In the classic case, aid was furnished for the children where the father was absent, although now help may be given where the father is unemployed. The father may be absent because of death, desertion, or incarceration, or because there has been no formal marriage. Lack of formal marriage makes the child illegitimate according to old and built-in notions of morality, and illegitimacy is one of the oldest and most disabling of legal classifications, tainting both mother and child.[11] To the everlasting surprise of everybody—and nobody—the slightest inquiry uncovers the fact that illegitimacy is higher among Negroes as such than among the general population, in a nation which has been trying to destroy the Negro family for the past three hundred years.

Under slavery there were neither valid marriages nor Negro families; the Negro woman was simply a brood mare used to produce as many valuable slave children as possible. The succeeding plantation and sharecropping systems placed a high value on a large number of children who could help in cropping; the law made no effort to fix responsibility for support on the father or fathers of the woman's children. White men (ordinarily the privileged members of society) who fathered a great many of the illegitimate children of Negro women had no legal responsibility whatever. In an increasingly urban society, the Negro woman could, and can, find a job where the Negro male

---

[11] The bastard child is held in low esteem; the mother of the bastard is held up to ridicule and shame. The bastard rarely inherits from the father and is subject to all manner of legal disabilities.

could not, and cannot, and she has thus been assured of family primacy. Until quite recently when aid to the Negro family became a burden on the white taxpayer, urban law enforcement authorities, north or south, made very little effort to compel the putative father to support his children. White fathers are still not compelled to support their illegitimate Negro children in southern or border states.

Public knowledge of the imbalance of Negroes on welfare rolls depends on the keeping and dissemination of racial statistics by welfare administrators. There is, however, no more legal warrant for the keeping and dissemination of these statistics, as such, than there is for compilation and distribution of religious data on recipients of old age assistance or aid to dependent children, and the fact that the figures are kept and so widely distributed is testimony to deeply rooted beliefs that race is a telling factor in human conduct. What has happened is that the social work establishment has created a racial classification within the economic classification required by law to determine eligibility. This is not to say that racial statistics should never be kept by state agencies; there are times when such figures can be justified as an aid to identification. My own view is that the Constitution is color-blind when discrimination is practiced against persons because of their race, but color-conscious when persons have special needs as a result of prior racial discrimination. There is, however, no evidence that the color-consciousness exhibited by social work agencies has been utilized to correct the disabilities of Negro recipients that arise as a result of racial discrimination.

Racial statistics are so badly kept that they are useless and meaningless. Illegitimate children of a Negro mother and a white father are classified as Negroes, and illegitimate children of a white mother and a Negro father are likewise denominated as Negroes, in conformity with the blood theories of Nazis and white supremacists. Statistical comparisons are invidious since all Negroes are lumped in together and matched against all white persons—the illegitimacy rate in the Negro slum is, in effect, compared with the illegitimacy rate in the upper-class white suburb. Nobody has tried to make a comparison between such rates among the Negro middle class and its white prototype. Nobody compares the Negro slum with the white slum. Current comparisons are as true and as meaningless as the similarly true and meaningless statement that American Negroes suffer less from beri-beri and leprosy than their remote African cousins.

One of the presumably unintended results of administrative racial classification of welfare recipients has been to arouse legislative hopes that a permissible social classification can be found to reach the constitutionally impermissible end of racial discrimination. Thus the Louisiana legislature enacted a statute lopping off or curtailing assistance to dependent children when the mother had an additional illegitimate child. Legislators were frank in saying that the laws were aimed at Negro families. Of course some whites would have been caught in the net, but the success of Southern States in administering fair-on-their-face statutes in voting and other areas leads to the suspicion that errant white mothers had little to fear. Federal intervention was necessary to scotch some of these schemes. No such bald attempts at discrimination are apt to occur in Northern States where Negroes have access to the ballot box, but undoubtedly the constant harping on racial imbalance in welfare rolls persuades legislators to keep benefits at a minimum. Nor can there be any doubt that the figures incite white public opinion and help to preserve and create racial stereotypes.

In 1960 at the height of a campaign to disfranchise Negroes, Louisiana denied the vote to persons who had "lived with another in 'common law' marriage," persons who had "given birth to an illegitimate child," and persons who had acknowledged themselves to be the "father of an illegitimate child" within five years preceding the passage of the law. The obvious intent was to deprive Negroes of the vote through penalizing them for social conduct believed to be more common among them than the general population. The belief was that public opinion was so inflamed against illegitimacy among Negroes that such a measure would enlist wide support and ultimately win judicial approbation. The state's long success in administering other apparently fair statutes in such a manner as to include Negroes and exclude white persons doubtless encouraged belief that few white offenders would be affected.

Welfare administrators are intimidated by the very figures they keep and cite. All too many of them adopt the attitude that it is their function to limit the number of recipients by technical interpretation of rules and regulations. Sometimes they achieve their end by making application for and acceptance of welfare benefits as difficult as possible. In Los Angeles prior to the recent riot, Watts residents had to make their applications and apply for welfare adjustments in adjoining lily-white suburbs which were difficult and expensive to reach. In other situations, the very concept of fairness may be made to serve discriminatory ends: Discretionary budget figures may be set in areas of Negro occupancy at exactly the same [level] as those in other areas although transportation, food costs, and rents are higher in the protected sellers market sheltered by the ghetto. Every administrator knows about the hue and cry against excessive numbers of Negroes on welfare rolls, and it is not at all remarkable that not a few foresee advancement if they can reduce that disparity.

The McCone Commission investigating the Los Angeles riots suggested that some California relief recipients may have migrated to the state because relief payments are higher than in other states. The between-the-lines inference was that southern Negroes may leave that section for California to take advantage of the state's relatively liberal payments to dependent children. Politicians took the cue and converted the suggestion to an accusation with the connotation that there was something reprehensible in such migration. Of course, Europe's poverty stricken streamed to the United States by the millions in the late nineteenth and early twentieth centuries with the almost certain knowledge that if they failed to find employment they would certainly secure a far higher measure of charity than in their homelands. The prime motivation for the migration of a Mississippi sharecropper to Los Angeles or San Francisco is to find employment which is disappearing in his home state before onrushing mechanical farm implements. The knowledge, if he has it, that California will give him more assistance for his children if he can establish residence and is unable to find a job is certainly no deterrent factor in his decision to migrate. Just why it should be is never made plain. The curious idea that he should remain in Mississippi where he is jobless and where his dependent children must subsist at a starvation level presupposes that he ought to prefer a state which denies him almost every conceivable citizenship right over one where his rights are held in higher esteem. Very few people who urge him to make that judgment would make it themselves—even if it meant some relief for a California taxpayer. Citizenship is national and a citizen has an absolute right to move from one state to another. That right cannot be denied or curtailed because he is an indigent person.

B. *The Law and The Poor*

Undoubtedly the poor have failed to secure the fullest measure of their legal rights because they have not been able to afford the services of lawyers. The very paucity of judicial precedents and the lack of decisions construing the rights of welfare recipients testify to the fact that their cause has seldom been presented to the courts. Welfare administrators have been left free to interpret the legislative command almost at will. Such appeals as have been taken have generally been decided by lay persons within the concerned agency. It is only in recent years that there has been any attempt to invoke constitutional safeguards against intrusions on the rights of the welfare recipient —indeed, there has been little realization that he has any "rights." He has been regarded as a beggar and, as everybody knows, beggars can't be choosers.

It took almost two decades of Supreme Court litigation to establish the very simple fact that a poor man accused of serious crime is entitled to a lawyer as a matter of right. The nation is still pretty well satisfied with a bail system under which a presumptively innocent person may lose his job, his home, and his family while he remains in jail in default of what is thought of as "reasonable bail," even when there is reason to believe that he would appear for trial if released on his own recognizance. At best, uniform bail schedules are uniform for the affluent and the poverty stricken defendant under the pretext that uniformity in application means equal protection of the law. At worst —and circumstances are ordinarily at their worst in misdemeanor courts where the poor appear most often—bail may be set at the caprice of the magistrate who often becomes panic stricken in the face of public sentiment in a crisis.

When arrests mounted in the Los Angeles riot, all bail was increased over the uniform schedule, and for a panic stricken moment there was a serious suggestion that rioters be held without bail even where there was no proof or charge of homicide. The effect of the increase was to burden the poor defendant with an additional bondsman's fee of from one hundred to three hundred dollars or to make sure of incarceration during which he ran the risk of losing his job. Many defendants later released or held on only minor charges did lose their jobs.

Bail may also be used to work direct racial discrimination. Southern courts often hold Negro misdemeanants to high bail in civil rights disturbances and release white offenders on very low bail.

There is a much larger body of precedential law in the area of civil rights of racial minorities than in those areas where poverty lies at the root of conflict with the law. Most civil rights law has been accumulated in the past forty years since the NAACP entered the field in a planned and orderly way. However, only a small portion of present civil rights law pertains to the problems that grow out of the Negro's economic status, as such; emphasis has been on use of public accommodations, attendance at schools, segregation in transportation, and like questions. Indeed, as the Urban League's Whitney Young has suggested, there is some danger that the Negro may wind up with a mouthful of civil rights living in a hovel on an empty belly.

There is a need for an orderly and well conceived program to meet the legal needs of the poor and, of equal importance, to put them on a legal parity with the affluent members of our society. At the same time, care must be exercised to see that today's poor can become tomorrow's affluent and that legal safeguards designed to protect their current status do not hinder or hamper such progress.

Some equalitarian notions are going to have to be re-examined. For example, there has to be a facing up to the fact that the one hundred dollar bail and the one hundred dollar fine of the uniform bail and fine schedules do not fall with equal impact on the ten thousand dollar a year junior executive and the four hundred dollar a month father of a family of five, even if both have violated the same statute in exactly the same manner. The public defender system is an excellent device in the quest for justice for the underprivileged—if the public defender is given staff and funds that will enable him to match skill and wits with the public prosecutor. Welfare recipients need counsel, perhaps as a class, as laws, rules, and regulations become ever more complicated. The social worker can no longer serve as counsel as she did in the days of direct handouts. The slum tenant and the preyed-upon installment buyer need lawyers.

The poor person who bears the burden of unpopular ethnic identification in our society is doubly put upon in all too many situations. He is poor and black in a world attuned to the needs and interests of the affluent and the white. His is not entirely an economic problem; nor is it entirely a racial issue. It is both and it must be dealt with simultaneously at both levels. The Negro's classic civil rights problems may be safely left to the civil rights organizations. What needs attention, and badly, is that complex of problems, which becomes one problem, arising out of the Negro's economic status and classification as intertwined with and complicated by racial classification. Americans have lived in a fictional "separate but equal" world so long that they tend to talk and think in racial terms. Social workers and legislators talk about "Negro" illegitimacy, for example. Of course, there is no such thing. There are many factors that affect the rate of births out of wedlock. Poverty is one of those factors. It makes formal divorce too costly for the poor; it makes access to birth control information difficult; moreover, it actually keeps the mother and the unwanted child together and the necessity for securing public assistance makes illegitimacy highly visible and the subject of conversation. My own preliminary studies on the basis of census data indicate that the illegitimate birth rate varies little as between racial groups within the same income range. There is every probability that the same thing is true as respects juvenile delinquency and crime rates.

There are, however, other figures which show wide disparities between Negroes and whites in the same economic groupings. President Johnson cited statistics in June 1965, showing that thirty-five years ago the unemployment rate for white job seekers was about the same as that for Negroes but that the present rate for Negroes is roughly twice that of whites; that the relative income of Negro working men to white workers is on the decline; that the median income for the Negro family as compared to white families has declined some four per cent in the past half-dozen years; and that the number of white families living in poverty has declined about twenty-seven per cent since 1947 while the number of Negro families has dropped only about three per cent. There is what he called a widening gulf between the two racial groups. These figures reflect the increasing alienation of the Negro poor from American society and the striking failure of the welfare state to close the gap that has existed between whites and Negroes since the days of slavery.

Legislation which is effective in relieving the burdens of the poor will inevitably assist a disproportionately large number of Negroes for the reason already observed that a proportionately large number of Negroes fall within poverty classifications. That is all to the good in the effort to vanquish poverty on the widest possible scale. But such assistance could well leave untouched the gap that now exists between the two racial groups. There is a rising demand for compensatory measures to close that gap.

The critical question is whether the color-blind constitution which equalitarians have always demanded will tolerate such compensatory measures. Some assail the very suggestion as a proposal for discrimination in reverse or a new kind of Jim Crow directed against white persons. This is no place to consider the inquiry in exhaustive detail, but the short answer is that the command of the fourteenth amendment is a command for equality. "It is clear," says Jacobus tenBroek in a study of the fourteenth amendment, "that the demand for equal protection cannot be a demand that laws apply universally to all persons. The legislature . . . must impose special burdens upon, or grant special benefits to, special groups or classes of individuals. Classification determines the range of persons to be affected by the special burden or benefit of a law not applicable to all persons." It is plain that the command for equality voiced in the fourteenth amendment can be effective only after corrective measures have been taken to eradicate the inequality resulting from past discrimination. The framers of the fourteenth amendment, who were most insistent that the Constitution as amended was color-blind, had no constitutional qualms about enactment of remedial legislation such as the Freedmen's Bureau Acts, which were designed to assist Negroes and newly freed slaves. It seems then that compensatory legislation designed to benefit Negroes as a class is constitutionally permissible.

In a realistic sense, current poverty legislation is compensatory. The poor are classified as such, and beneficial laws—or what are thought of as beneficial laws—are enacted to enable them to overcome handicaps and facilitate their entrance into the affluent society. Such classification earns no strictures and arouses no constitutional doubts because it is viewed as benign and as compatible with the American thinking that everybody is entitled to an even chance in life—nobody is to be ill-fed, or ill-clothed, or ill-housed. Many persons who boggle at similarly benign racial classification designed to relieve Negroes *as Negroes* misread the real meaning of the equalitarian dictate of the amended Constitution: The fourteenth amendment was designed to cure the ills of omission as well as commission, and Congress has power to legislate in either sphere. Poverty legislation cannot effectively aid the Negro poor until disparities between the white poor and the Negro poor are erased.

As the President has put it: "You do not take a person who, for years, has been hobbled by chains and liberate him, bring him up to the starting line of a race and say, 'You are free to compete with all the others,' and still justly believe that you have been completely fair." He added that "it is not enough just to open the gates of opportunity. All of our citizens must have the ability to walk through those gates." That is true of all the poor who seek equality in the affluent society; it is doubly true for the poor Negro who must surmount two hurdles to find equality in that society.

In historical perspective it is apparent that the Negro's long attempt to attain what he calls first class citizenship has been, and is, an attempt to be dealt with as an individual, as a *person* in constitutional terms, when he seeks a job, or tries to buy a home, or votes in a local, state, or federal election, or eats in a restaurant, or reads a book in a public library, or joins the Air Force, or attends school, or even swims in the ocean. The problem of how to make constitutional guarantees meaningful and fruitful is the problem inherent in an inquiry into race, poverty, and the law. There are no sure guidelines; in fact, the issues are not yet clearly defined. What has been said here is only an introduction. The road to solution lies through unchartered constitutional territory.

Welfare From Below: Recipients' Views of the Public Welfare System,* by Scott Briar

I think the Welfare Department is too soft, too lenient. They don't make investigations to see how the welfare money is being spent. If the workers went to the house more often they would be able to tell if people are cheating. They could go to the home anytime they want to, day or night. If the person isn't guilty, then they shouldn't care when the worker comes.

These are not the words of an irate taxpayer or public official concerned about the rising costs of public welfare programs. On the contrary, this statement was made by a poorly educated welfare recipient living in the Negro ghetto of an industrial city. But the importance of this statement is that these views are not atypical of the opinions expressed by the more than ninety welfare recipients interviewed in the study reported in this article.

In the growing body of literature on what has been called "the law of the poor," little attention has been paid to the conceptions held by the poor themselves about their relationship to the law and to legal and quasi-legal institutions. This omission is partly due to the lack of systematic data on this subject, a lack which is only beginning to be remedied. Another explanation, one which partly accounts both for the inattention to the conceptions of law held by the poor and for the lack of research on the subject, is found in two assumptions which appear in some of the recent literature on the law of the poor: (1) that one of the basic *social* problems in this area is the lack of legal services;

* This article is based on research supported by Grant No. 230 E–5–141, Welfare Administration, U.S. Department of Health, Education, and Welfare and in part by a grant from the California State Department of Social Welfare to the Social Welfare Research Projects Office, School of Social Welfare, University of California. The author acknowledges the assistance of Miss Mildred Alexander in the development of the interview schedule used in this research and the contribution of Mrs. Naomi Streshinsky to all stages of the work reported here.

Source: *California Law Review*, LIV, 2 (May, 1966), 46–61. Copyright © 1966, California Law Review, Inc. Reprinted by permission.

and (2) that if legal services are provided, the poor will use them. The former assumption is well supported, but the validity of the second is in doubt.

While some programs designed to extend legal services to the poor have reported success, others have not, for reasons which appear to be due in part to the attitudes of potential users among the poor. An example is Sparer's description of the problems arising because of the sentiments and attitudes held by potential users of the Mobilization for Youth Legal Services Unit; for example, he notes that "they felt too unsure of themselves to argue with—or insist upon anything with [officials] . . . ."

Thus one reason for conducting studies in this area is that knowledge about the views of law held by the poor may be useful in designing effective programs for extending legal services to them. Second, such research may shed light on the effects of the legal order on the persons directly affected. The experiences of the poor may be particularly instructive in this regard since the poor are more likely than others to be directly affected by certain major legal institutions, particularly the police, the courts, and the correction agencies.

This article attempts to contribute to both of the above aims by describing the findings of a study concerned in part with welfare recipients' views of the welfare agency. It should be emphasized that welfare recipients constitute only a portion of the population living in poverty, and therefore the findings reported here cannot be generalized to the nonwelfare poor. The welfare poor tend to be more impoverished and to be afflicted by other problems to a greater extent than the nonwelfare poor.[1] Most

[1] There have been few systematic studies of the differences between welfare and nonwelfare poor. Robert Stone, of the Institute of Social Science Research, San Francisco State College, in a study still in process, attempted to find a matching, nonwelfare sample for comparison to a sample of AFDC-U, *Cal. Welfare & Inst'ns Code* §§ 11201, 11250, families. After much effort, he had to settle for a nonwelfare group which, although it was otherwise comparable, had a higher average income than the AFDC-U sample. Sydney Bernard found that the essential difference between welfare applicants and nonapplicants in a homogeneous low-income neighborhood was that the nonapplicants had more financial resources of various sorts available to them than the applicants. Bernard, The Economic and Social Adjustment of Low-Income Female-Headed Families, May, 1964 (unpublished, Florence Heller Graduate School for Advanced Studies in Social Welfare, Brandeis University).

important, the welfare poor live dependent on the operations of an institution, the public welfare agency, established to administer welfare legislation.

THE STUDY

The study reported here is part of a continuing project concerning the impact of public welfare policies and operations on family life. As part of the exploratory phase of this project, intensive interviews were conducted with more than one hundred recipients of AFDC-U (the program which provides aid to intact families with dependent children in which the father is unemployed). These interviews, which ranged in length from three to six hours extending over two to three sessions, probed systematically and in depth each recipient's experiences with the agency, his conceptions of the agency and its operations, his perceptions of his rights and obligations vis-à-vis the agency, his attitude towards certain welfare policies and issues, and the effects of recipient status on his family life.[2]

The findings presented in this article are based primarily on interviews conducted with a systematically selected sample of ninety-two AFDC-U recipients, consisting of forty-six married couples heading family units in recent receipt of AFDC-U funds. Since the husbands and wives were interviewed separately (using the same interview schedule), and since the husband and wife in the same family frequently differed in their responses to questions about the agency and their separate experiences with it, the data are reported for individuals rather than families.

The recipients were selected from the official rolls of the county welfare department in inverse order of date of application, beginning with the most recent applicant prior to July 1, 1965. A quota sampling procedure was used to yield an equal number of recipients in each of the three major ethnic groups in the county studied; thus the sample includes thirty Caucasian

---

[2] A structured schedule was used in these interviews to insure that comparable data were collected from the respondents. So far as possible, responses were pre-coded (on the basis of pre-test interviews). In addition, all interviews were tape recorded so that each recipient's free responses also would be available for analysis.

(fifteen families), thirty Negro (fifteen families), and thirty-two Mexican-American (sixteen families) AFDC-U recipients.[3] In many instances the *distribution* of responses obtained from these three groups are, in effect, identical; consequently, findings are reported for the total sample, except where significant or systematic differences among the three ethnic groups were found.

In a study of this sort the question of response validity always must be considered. Did the recipients report their "true" beliefs and opinions, or did they say what they thought the interviewers wanted to hear? Important as these questions are, they are difficult to answer categorically. Nevertheless, in this study there are a number of reasons for believing that the responses obtained reflect the recipients' own opinions. First, in approaching recipients, interviewers identified themselves as being with the University of California and took great pains to make clear that the study was not connected with the welfare department. Second, recipients frequently made comments about the welfare agency and their experiences with it that they would have been unlikely to make had they believed the agency would have access to their responses. Third, Negro recipients were interviewed by a Negro interviewer, and Spanish-speaking interviewers were used with the Mexican-American recipients. Fourth, the interviewers spent from three to seven hours (in more than one session) with each respondent. Fifth, the dominant responses reported herein were contrary to what the interviewers privately had hoped and wanted to hear; the responses revealed a state of affairs which was a source of frustration to the interviewers and which made it necessary to caution the interviewers to check their desires to educate and inform the recipients about their "rights." Finally, the most convincing test of validity is the extent to which the responses obtained are consistent with other known beliefs and behaviors of the group studied; this aspect is considered following presentation of the findings.

[3] The actual proportions of these three groups in the AFDC-U population in the county studied, as of July 1964, were: Caucasian, 50.3%; Mexican-American, 10.8%; and Negro, 38.9%. California State Dep't of Social Welfare, *Research and Statistics.* Comparison of the study sample with known characteristics (for example, family size, age, education, and usual occupation of the unemployed parent) of the AFDC-U population in the community studied revealed no great differences between the two groups.

The welfare department in the county in which this research was conducted has acquired a reputation both locally and nationally for its progressiveness. Thus the recipients interviewed in this study are somewhat atypical in that their welfare experiences have been with a department which is unusual in the degree of its commitment to a professional and client-oriented approach to welfare services. It is not known, however, to what extent or in what respect recipients' perceptions of the welfare system vary in relation to the character of the welfare department—these questions require further research.

It should be noted that the AFDC-U family is a recent phenomenon in public welfare programs—in California the program did not begin until February 1964. Prior to that time, intact family units with dependent children in need of public assistance had two options: (1) general assistance, or "relief," which is dependent on county funds, provides extremely low benefits, and for all practical purposes is unavailable in many localities and difficult to obtain in many others; and (2) separation of husband and wife so that the mother and the children could become eligible for benefits under the AFDC program. Thus the AFDC-U program provides assistance to a portion of the "able-bodied poor," one of the groups for which society traditionally has been most reluctant to provide stable financial assistance—partly out of fear that to do so would undermine their incentive to seek gainful employment.[4]

THE VIEW FROM BELOW

A. On the Edge of Disaster: Becoming a Welfare Recipient

The typical AFDC-U recipient-father,[5] when he appears with his wife at the welfare agency to apply for aid, has only about

[4] Part of the political support for the AFDC-U program in California came from groups that hoped this program would: (1) curb "immorality" among AFDC recipients, and (2) remove an incentive for the unemployed father to desert his family.

[5] It should be emphasized that the composite picture of the recipient presented in this paper is limited to the sample interviewed in this study. No wider generality can be claimed at this stage in the research. Consequently, whenever a finding is reported about "recipients" the qualifying phrase "in this sample" is implied.

ten dollars left in his pocket, has been out of work for three
weeks or more, and has three or four children (five or six if he
is Mexican-American) to feed and care for. He is comparatively
young (thirty to thirty-five), and when he last worked was
earning less than four hundred dollars per month in a job requiring few skills. His wife is not employed, and for a while
they got by on unemployment compensation or with the help
of small loans and gifts from friends and relatives, but these
resources are exhausted. Moreover, given his usual income,
he is deeply in debt (thirty-nine per cent have debts in excess
of one thousand dollars) and is worried about how he will
meet his monthly payments as well as feed, clothe, and house
his family.

He is not a stranger to this city. Chances are that he has lived
in this community for ten years or more—though he moved to
his present address less than two years ago—and he has lived
in the state over fifteen years. He has not applied for welfare aid
before (sixty per cent in this sample had not), and he was reluctant to do so. But his friends and relatives, and finally his
wife, have urged him to go to the welfare department, and
eventually he agreed.

When applicants arrive at the welfare department—or Social
Service Department as it is called in this country—they first
meet the receptionist. She asks them some factual questions
(for example, "What is your name?" "Where do you live?"
"Have you ever applied for aid here before?") and then directs
them to the waiting room. In this room—light, windowless, but
reasonably pleasant—an applicant may begin to experience the
sense of estrangement evident in the responses of most recipients
interviewed. As one father described it, "I looked around [the
waiting room] and saw a bunch of old people and Negroes—I
felt I should be someplace else."

But few recipients were this sensitive and perceptive about
their personal reactions to the experience of becoming and being
a welfare recipient. For most, this sense of estrangement is expressed in a less subtle way: Our respondents almost never (and
most respondents never) referred to welfare recipients as "we"
but as "they." This characteristic estrangement—also manifest
in a tendency to view oneself as an atypical recipient, a self-
conception which seemed to be held by nearly all the recipients

interviewed[6]—reflects the desire of these recipients to dissociate themselves from the image they have of other recipients. Our respondents expressed opinions about other public welfare recipients which usually have been associated primarily with conservative, anti-welfare groups. For example, fifty-eight per cent of the recipients interviewed believe that more than twenty-five per cent of all welfare recipients remain on welfare longer than necessary, and nearly one-half believe that over twenty-five per cent of all recipients "cheat" the welfare department.[7]

In addition, the recipients seemed to use their own situations as a standard for evaluating the claims of other recipients. For example, each recipient regarded as justifiable his own reason for seeking welfare assistance, but often judged other reasons depending on their similarity to his own situation. Thus in response to specific questions asking whether a person would be justified in requesting assistance under various specified conditions, Mexican-American recipients (a number of whom were farm laborers) were more likely to say that a farm laborer is justified in requesting aid during the off-season than were Negro and Caucasian recipients. Negro and Caucasian recipients were more likely to say that recipients should not be expected to take farm labor jobs than were Mexican-American recipients. And the Mexican-American and Negro recipients were much more apt than were Caucasians to say that a man is justified in requesting welfare assistance if he cannot find work because of discrimination.

B. Welfare Assistance: A Right or Charity?

Returning to the typical (or, more accurately, composite) recipient couple that we followed into the waiting room of the

[6] Few clear exceptions to this generalization were found. One was a woman in a small group of persons (not included in the data reported in this paper) whose applications for aid were denied. This woman had previously been a welfare recipient and had re-applied for aid. Subsequent to denial of her re-application, she became a community organizer in an OEO project. When interviewed, she spoke of welfare recipients as "we."

[7] A report of a fifteen-month survey of welfare fraud conducted by the California State Department of Social Welfare and released in December 1965 found that established fraud amounted to a "fraction of 1/30th of 1 per cent of the total Aid to Families of Dependent Children caseload." California State Dep't of Social Welfare, News Release, Dec. 10, 1965.

welfare office, after a wait of from one-half to two hours[8] a lady (the intake social worker) appears, takes them into an office in the inner recesses of the building, and begins the application interview. What are the recipients' expectations of this situation? What are their conceptions of the request they are making?

Welfare assistance under federally assisted programs such as AFDC-U is a right in that entitlement is defined by statute and not by the arbitrary (however well-motivated) decision of a charitable organization. If a family meets the statutory requirements the agency is obligated to grant their claim for assistance.

While this conception of the federal assistance programs is held by the social workers in the department studied, our findings suggest that few recipients regard welfare assistance as a right. One indicator, though a rather marginal one, is that none of the recipients interviewed could define "AFDC-U." Thirteen per cent gave a partially correct definition (for example, "Aid to Families of Dependent Children—Universal"), but seventy-eight per cent said they had no idea what the term meant.[9] A better, more direct indicator is the manner in which the recipients refer to the aid and whose property it is. The statement of one recipient defending the social worker's close scrutiny of recipients' lives characterizes the attitudes of most recipients: "You are going to them for money . . . *they* are supporting you." A more convincing piece of evidence, because it is quantifiable and less anecdotal, is the recipients' perceptions of who has control over the assistance grant once it is given. Asked whether the social worker has a right to know how the aid money is spent, sixty-six per cent said yes. (Responses of two recipients

[8] It must be emphasized that throughout this section, we are attempting to present experiences as they were perceived by the recipients. Actually, in the agency studied, applicants rarely have to wait more than thirty to forty-five minutes to see the intake social worker.

[9] Another indicator of this sort is the difficulty we encountered, in the pre-test stage of this study, in wording questions asking whether a person in certain specified situations is entitled by law to receive aid. This concept of entitlement proved to be exceedingly elusive for recipients. After trying various wordings, we finally settled for "Is he [the person in the specified situation] legally entitled to aid?" It still was necessary, however, to explain the meaning of this question to many recipients, and it was not always clear that recipients were able to distinguish between what the person was legally entitled to receive and what the agency would in fact "give" him.

typify this view: "The social worker's job is to find out that the money is being spent right," and, "They [the social workers] are supposed to know all about a person on welfare.") Asked what the agency would do if the social worker found that aid funds were not being spent properly, seventy per cent of the recipients said that aid would be terminated. And asked whether in their opinion aid *should* be cut off under these circumstances, seventy-six per cent of the recipients said yes. In the eyes of these recipients, "the new property"—Reich's term for the property to which people are entitled by virtue of government benefits—belongs to the welfare agency.

Thus the stance these recipients adopt toward the welfare agency is not that of a rights-bearing citizen claiming benefits to which he is entitled by law but that of a suppliant seeking, in the words of a number of recipients, "a little help to tide us over until we can get back on our feet again." Moreover, the "little help" they sought was modest indeed. Of those recipients who were able to specify the amount of aid they expected when they applied for assistance, sixty-four per cent said they expected to receive less than one hundred dollars. Since over fifty per cent of the recipients actually were given aid in excess of one hundred dollars, it is not surprising that most recipients were satisfied with the amount they received and that only seventeen per cent reported that the amount of aid granted was less than they had expected.

C. Agency Decision-Making

For most recipients, decision-making in the welfare department is a mysterious process, one which they do not understand and one which—as they conceive of it—is not visible to them. According to their descriptions of the application interview, the worker asked a great many questions, many designed to find out if they were telling the truth: "They have to check on what you say, so they have to ask all these questions. They can't just give money to anybody who walks in and says they need it, or they would be in trouble. If she'd given it on my word, she'd been a fool."

In the application interview, the social worker also begins the complicated task of calculating the "budget," a crucial step in the determination of need and of the amount of aid, if any, to which the applicant is entitled. This process is difficult for the staff to master and harder still to interpret to applicants.[10] In the words of one recipient: The intake worker "sat there and figured and figured a whole bunch of things. All the time she was figuring, I wasn't paying any attention." "Why weren't you paying attention?" "Because I felt uncomfortable being there."

The next stage in the application process is deciding whether the recipient is eligible for aid. Actually, this stage—within the agency—involves a number of steps and may follow one of several different pathways, but these complexities need not concern us here. As the recipients perceived it, *a* decision was made—yes or no. The recipients were asked who made the decision; their responses are presented in Table 1.

TABLE 1

The Locus of Aid Decisions as Perceived by Recipients

	NUMBER	PER CENT
Social worker and someone else	48	52
Social worker, on his own	27	29
Other	7	8
Don't know	10	11
Totals	92	100

Table 1 indicates that recipients divide into two major groups in their responses. The larger group believes that someone other than the worker is involved in the decision to grant aid: "The social worker just helps you fill out the papers—how much family you have, and so on. Then she gives the forms to her boss who says yes or no whether you can get aid." The second

[10] As part of this research, we observed a number of application interviews. Although the research observers were trained, experienced social workers, even they found the budgeting process difficult to follow at points. To fully understand the steps involved, the recipient had to be able first to understand interpretations by the worker which might include technical terms such as "participation maximum" and second to comprehend anomalies such as the discrepancy between the amount the worker has calculated and has told the applicant is his *minimum need* and the lesser amount the agency will grant him.

group attributes to the social worker the authority to make this decision: "The worker has the right to decide if there is need for aid."

Regardless of the recipient's belief about who makes the decision, it may be of little significance insofar as his view of the legal status of his request for aid is concerned. Compare, for example, the following two statements, representing the two groups of recipients:

Worker, on his own:
The worker decided herself. She is very experienced and knows from experience how much a family needs. She is smart and all out to help the needy.

Worker and someone else:
There is someone she [the social worker] has to confer with, a committee or something that agrees. Well, they're the ones—I guess they vote on it or something like that and they say who gets it and who don't.

In either event, the decision is one over which the recipients appear to feel they have—or apparently even expect to have— little control.

In view of these and other findings presented earlier, it is hardly surprising that forty-six per cent of the recipients report that they were not told about their rights on welfare and that sixty per cent said they were not informed about the right to appeal. The point is not whether they were told about these rights—our observations indicate that many, if not most, of these recipients probably were given this information by the social worker—but rather that this information probably is not particularly meaningful and useful to a person who sees himself as a suppliant, and therefore it may be ignored or soon forgotten. An example of their lack of a clear conception of the appeal procedure is seen in the recipients' responses to a question asking to whom a recipient should appeal if he disagrees with a decision made about his case by the welfare department.[11] These re-

---

[11] Actually, initiation of the appeal procedure is relatively simple for the recipient. He simply writes or calls a field office of the State Department of Social Welfare. And as noted in the text, most, if not all, recipients are told that such a procedure is available and also are given a brochure which includes information about the opportunity to appeal.

sponses are presented in Table 2. As the data in this table indicate, nearly one-third of the recipients did not know where to
appeal, the remainder lacked a consistent conception about

TABLE 2

*Recipients' Perceptions of the Person to Whom an Appeal
Should Be Made*

	NUMBER	PER CENT
Don't know	28	30
"Person in Sacramento"	15	16
"Head of the Welfare Department"	13	14
Social worker's supervisor	8	10
"Person in —" (city in which the central administrative offices for the county welfare department are located)	7	7
Social worker	6	7
District attorney	4	4
Other	11	12
Totals	92	100

where to initiate an appeal, and very few considered appealing
to a resource outside the welfare system. The "other" category,
which includes a variety of responses (for example, "State Personnel Board"), does not include a few recipients who said they
would see an attorney; but as one of these respondents said, "I'd
go to a lawyer, though I don't know what he could do."

D. *The Welfare Department—A Benevolent Autocracy*

The recipients' vague, diffuse, and limited conceptions of their
own rights and of the welfare department's obligations to them
contrast sharply with the well-crystallized views most of them
have of the welfare agency's rights and of their own obligations
to the agency. Some evidence to this point is presented earlier,
namely the findings showing that most respondents believe that
social workers have a right to know how recipients spend the aid
money and, further, that aid would and should be terminated if
not spent properly.

The agency, however, also is seen as having legitimate authority over recipients extending considerably beyond the surveillance of aid expenditures. This can be illustrated first by further examination of the agency's authority over the management of money. We asked a series of questions on this subject, including a set addressed to the following situation: "Suppose the social worker suggests that a couple on welfare come in once a week for budget counseling." The questions and the responses obtained are given in Table 3.

As Table 3 indicates, not only did most recipients believe that the agency could make budget counseling a compulsory condition for receiving aid, they were virtually unanimous in their belief that couples *should* be expected to come in if the worker suggests such counseling.

Similar sets of questions were asked about areas of agency authority less directly related to management of the aid grant. For example, if the social worker suggests that a recipient see a psychiatrist, seventy-six per cent of the respondents said that the recipient should be expected to go and sixty-six per cent said he must go in order to continue receiving aid. But the recipients perceived some limits to the range of the welfare agency's authority. While sixty-seven per cent of the recipients said that a recipient should go if the social worker suggests marital counseling, only twenty per cent believed that a recipient's aid would be cut off if he refused to follow this suggestion.

However, the findings which most dramatically indicate the extent of authority these recipients confer on the agency and which best illuminate their reasons for granting the agency extensive authority over their lives are those obtained in response to a series of questions about the use of night visits as a means of checking on recipients. These questions and the recipients' responses to them are shown in Table 4.

As the data presented in Table 4 indicate, over two-thirds of the recipients favor night searches by the welfare department. The reasons the recipients gave for favoring this practice are anticipated by findings reported earlier: (1) The agency has a right to know how aid funds are spent; and (2) many recipients cheat or continue to accept aid after they no longer need it.

However, the data of greater interest in this table concern the

TABLE 3

Recipients' Opinions about Budget Counseling

SUPPOSE THE SOCIAL WORKER SUGGESTS THAT A COUPLE ON WELFARE COME IN ONCE A WEEK FOR BUDGET COUNSELING:	YES NO. %	NO NO. %	DON'T KNOW NO. %	OTHER NO. %	TOTALS NO. %
1. Would they have to come in?	57 (61)	24 (27)	11 (12)	– —	92 (100)
2. Would their aid be cut off if they refused to come in?	55 (60)	22 (24)	14 (15)	1 (1)	92 (100)
3. Should the couple be expected to come in?	88 (95)	4 (5)	– —	– —	92 (100)

TABLE 4

Recipients' Opinions about Night Searches by the Welfare Department

	YES NO. %	NO NO. %	DON'T KNOW NO. %	OTHER NO. %	TOTALS NO. %
1. Should the welfare department make night visits?	63 (69)	24 (26)	3 (3)	2 (2)	92 (100)
2. Does the recipient have a right to refuse to let the worker come into his home at night?	46 (50)	40 (43)	5 (5)	1 (1)	92 (100)
3. Are there any other times when the recipient has a right to refuse to let the worker enter his home?	34 (37)	49 (53)	6 (7)	3 (3)	92 (100)
4. Is there a law that says you can refuse entry to your home to anyone who does not have a search warrant?	53 (87)	5 (8)	3 (5)	– —	61[a] (100)
5. (If yes to #4) Does this law apply to welfare recipients?	35 (66)	9 (17)	9 (17)	– —	53[a] (100)

[a] These two questions were added to the schedule after the first 31 interviews had been completed.

233

recipients' views about a recipient's right to refuse entry to the social worker at night. Nearly ninety per cent of the respondents say
that there are laws which give a person the right to refuse entry
to anyone who does not have a search warrant, and over two-
thirds believe that these laws apply to welfare recipients. Yet
only one-half the respondents say that a welfare recipient has a
right to refuse entry to the social worker on a night visit. How
can the seeming inconsistency in these findings be explained?
Why (as further analysis of these data not reported here reveal)
do a substantial proportion of the recipients who say that there
is a law that permits the recipient to refuse entry to the worker
at night also say that the recipient has no right to invoke this
law? Analysis of the recipients' responses to these questions
reveals a common theme: The recipient has an *obligation* to let
the worker come into his home at any time because the welfare
agency is supporting him: "You are going to them for money.
They got the right to go and look in your house without no
questions—they're supporting you." And this theme appears in
the statements of those recipients who said that the recipient
does have a right to refuse entry at night: "According to the
criminal law, they [the recipients] do have the right, yes—I don't
think it's right, but they do have that right." "All people have
the right not to let someone enter their home if they don't want
them to. But in the case of the social worker, one ought to let
her in." In other words, most recipients favored the practice of
night visits—they tend to differ only over the necessity for the
agency to obtain a search warrant.

Conclusion

Before considering the meaning and significance of these findings, the limitations of the research should be noted. The welfare recipients interviewed in this study were drawn from one aid
program as administered in one locality. It is not known to what
extent these findings hold for recipients of other public assistance programs or for recipients in other communities in which,
among other things, the character of the public welfare agency
may be quite different. Nevertheless there is reason to believe
that some of the findings may have wide generality.

For one thing, the conservative (in the sense that assistance is perceived as a privilege rather than a right) views expressed by these recipients on certain welfare issues are not surprising. The prevalence of political and social conservatism and of submissive attitudes toward authority among persons in low-income groups has been documented in a number of studies. Moreover, while social workers and others concerned with promoting the expansion of welfare programs have long advocated that public assistance should be provided on a basis of entitlement rather than privilege, public welfare recipients have had few opportunities to be exposed to this view.

For these are people with limited education and limited access to the publications and forums in which this view is expressed. Nor are more than a few recipients exposed to organizations which attempt to inform them of their rights and of the welfare agency's obligations to them—in fact, few such organizations exist. In view of these conditions, only if these recipients had expressed a welfare ideology markedly different from the views reported here would there have been reason to suspect that this group of recipients is atypical.[12]

Secondly, although public welfare departments differ greatly in many ways (including the service orientations of the social work staff and the liberality of assistance grants), certain characteristics are common to many of them: the elaborate complexity of determining eligibility and especially of budgeting (including both the determination of need and of the amount of assistance to which the recipient is entitled); the low visibility, for the recipient, of agency decision-making processes and of appeal opportunities and procedures; the comparative powerlessness, from the recipient's viewpoint, of the line social worker—the person with whom he must deal—in the decisions made about his assistance grant; the linkage of financial assistance to other services so that the aid recipient also automatically becomes a client who, at least partly at the discretion of the

[12] It should be emphasized that the recipients interviewed were not all of one mind on welfare issues. In this article, we present the dominant and modal responses obtained from the sample studied. The characteristics of those recipients who expressed divergent opinions—for example, the small group who did *not* favor night visits—will be examined in subsequent reports by the author.

agency, may become the object of other services (for example, counseling and psychiatric treatment); and review and surveillance of recipient's expenditure of aid funds beyond that necessary to establish eligibility and detect possible fraud.

Our findings suggest that the presence of these characteristics —common to many public welfare agencies—serves to reinforce and thereby perpetuate recipients' conceptions of themselves as suppliants rather than rights-bearing citizens. Moreover, the presence of these characteristics may obliterate the effects on recipients of the distinctive attributes of specific welfare departments. Thus the dimension which has received the most attention in comparative studies of welfare agencies, namely the extent to which staff are committed to a professional versus a bureaucratic service-orientation, may, in the presence of the other characteristics enumerated above, have little effect on recipients' conceptions of their rights. In a paradoxical way, commitment to a professional orientation by public welfare workers may, *when the above characteristics are also present in the agency*, reinforce the suppliant role. For the practices of the welfare agency together with the beliefs about public welfare which many recipients hold when they go to the agency appear to evoke a sense of obligation to the agency; this sense may be accentuated if the agency is benign and the social worker is kind, sympathetic, and understanding.

These considerations suggest that to the extent that one objective of public welfare programs is to help recipients become "responsible citizens"—an aim presumably shared by both proponents and critics of more liberal welfare programs—the public welfare agency must be organized and operated in such a way that it at least does not generate or reinforce attitudes of submissiveness and suppliance on the part of the recipients. More than that, however, these considerations imply that public welfare agencies—because of their strategic position vis-à-vis the poor—could become positive instruments for the inculcation in recipients of a conception of themselves as rights-bearing citizens, with all of the benefits this may have for increasing self-confidence and hope among these people. To accomplish this would appear to require, at the very least: radical simplification of the eligibility and budgeting processes so that they are comprehensible to recipients with limited education; high visibility of agency decision-making in individual cases to reduce its apparent arbitrariness (from the recipient's viewpoint) and to make accessible to the recipient the information necessary to understand and review agency decisions affecting his claim; high visibility and accessibility of appeal procedures; and a redefinition of the social worker's role away from that of an instrument of agency rules and regulations towards one of an advocate who, because he is informed and knowledgeable about the applicant's rights and the agency's obligations, can assist the applicant to secure the maximum benefits to which he is entitled. For as Edgar and Jean Cahn have stated, "Law is made not merely through statutes and legislative programs, but also through modes of official behavior." The mode of official behavior necessary to inculcate in recipients a conception of themselves as rights-bearing citizens is one which provides them with "the means and the effective power wherewith to criticize, to shape, and even to challenge the actions or proposed actions of officials." This perspective, if implemented in the public welfare agency, has the potential of becoming the agency's most effective means of enhancing the dignity and self-respect of the persons it seeks to serve.

FOR FURTHER READING

As might be expected, much of the discussion on poverty and the law takes place in the pages of various law journals. Excellent articles, too numerous to list here, have appeared in the *Yale Law Journal, Wisconsin Law Review, Pennsylvania Law Review*, and others. Perhaps the best single introduction to the way legal problems affect the poor is Zona Fairbanks Hostetler, "Poverty and The Law," in Ben B. Seligman, ed., *Poverty as a Public Issue* (New York: The Free Press, 1965). For a study of the poor as consumer and tenant, the student should consult David Caplovitz, *The Poor Pay More* (New York: The Free Press, 1963). Other useful works, though generally legalistic in their discussions, are Earl L. Koos, *The Family and The Law* (New York: National Legal Aid Association, 1952); Arnold S. Trebach, *The Rationing of Justice* (New Brunswick: Rutgers University Press, 1964); and Elliot E. Cheatham, *A Lawyer When Needed* (New York: Columbia University Press, 1964).

THE DESIGN OF

ANTIPOVERTY

STRATEGY*

Sar A. Levitan

Sar Levitan, research professor of economics at the George Washington University, is one of the most knowledgeable persons in Washington on issues relating to the War on Poverty. He is now preparing a detailed history of the antipoverty campaign under a grant from the Ford Foundation, and the article reprinted here is part of that study. It is an analysis of the origins of the Economic Opportunity Act, relating in detail the administrative and legislative anguish that went into its creation.

Washington legend attributes the beginning of the War on

* The author is indebted to Roger H. Davidson of Dartmouth College and three active participants in the design of the war on poverty—Paul Jacobs, Daniel P. Moynihan and James L. Sundquist—for valuable critical comments on the manuscript. Dr. Davidson has also collaborated in the research on this article. His version appears in John Bibby and Roger Davidson, *On Capitol Hill: Studies in the Legislative Process* (New York: Holt, Rinehart and Winston, 1967), pp. 219–251. The research assistance of Robert J. Hanson II is also gratefully acknowledged.

Source: Sar A. Levitan, *The Design of Federal Antipoverty Strategy*, pp. 1, 8–52, published by The Institute of Law and Industrial Relations, University of Michigan and Wayne State University, 1967.

Poverty to President Kennedy's reading of a remarkable article by Dwight MacDonald in *The New Yorker* magazine. But much more than persuasive journalism was needed. Legislative preparation, administrative bargaining, and an excited public response were all required before the Economic Opportunity Act was passed. Poverty became a major concern of public officials and academics across the land. Yet despite all the frenetic activity, the War on Poverty was not so revolutionary. It was bounded by traditional concepts of social welfare, shaped by the demands of the groups desiring action, and molded by the politicians who had to give their approval.

It is instructive to find out how the program got started. Dr. Levitan's report is undoubtedly the best source for this story. Some Washington cognoscenti will say he gives too much credit to the former chairman of the Council of Economic Advisers, Walter Heller, and not enough to CEA staff experts; but these are details for historians to quibble about. The main point is that the Office of Economic Opportunity became a specific commitment of the government to eradicate poverty in our time. In itself that was a step forward. Evaluating the extent of that commitment is another task.

✦

The Vision

On August 20, 1964, Lyndon B. Johnson signed the Economic Opportunity Act—the most dramatic and highly publicized of the Great Society's programs. Five months earlier, when the President presented his Antipoverty Message, he urged the American people as "citizens of the richest . . . nation in the history of the world" to declare war on poverty. "Having the power," he exhorted Congress and the nation, "we have the duty." In signing the bill, the President declared that the passage of the Economic Opportunity Act was a commitment of a "great nation . . . to eradicate poverty among its people."

The aspiration of eliminating poverty is not new. Though the Bible enjoins us that "Ye have the poor with you always," the hope of eliminating poverty in society has been often expressed. And this was not a dream cherished by social reformers alone. Two generations ago the influential British economist,

Alfred Marshall, expressed the belief that "poverty and ignorance may be gradually extinguished . . . during the present
century."[1] Herbert Hoover anticipated an early victory over
poverty when, in accepting the Presidential nomination in 1928,
he declared, "We shall soon, with the help of God, be in sight
of the day when poverty will be banished in the nation."[2] Even
the slogan "war on poverty" is not new: David Lloyd George
requested funds from the British Parliament to wage "warfare
against poverty" nearly six decades ago.[3]

. . . . .

THE ECONOMIC OPPORTUNITY PACKAGE

"War on poverty" is clearly an inflated description of [the]
recent effort to help the impoverished. Even a casual inspection
of the legislation reveals that the "war" cannot meet . . . expectations. By the time the Economic Opportunity Act was passed,
society was allocating about $15 billion annually to welfare pro-
grams with need criteria. The exact cost of the welfare system
cannot be determined, because many of the programs are closely
interwoven with general government activity. The Economic
Opportunity Act may therefore be viewed as a supplement, albeit a significant one, to [existing] welfare programs. The Act
added some $1.3 billion annually for welfare expenditures during
the first three years of the "war," even though the President's
Council of Economic Advisers had estimated that there were
some 34 million poor people in the country. It was presumed
therefore to fight poverty with an average annual expenditure
of less[4] than $40 per person. Obviously, this amount fell far
short of the President's commitment to an "unconditional war
on poverty."

[1] Alfred Marshall. *Principles of Economics,* 3rd Edition (London: Macmillan and Co., 1895), p. 2.
[2] Quoted in Herman P. Miller. *Poverty: American Style* (Belmont, California: Wadsworth, 1966), p. 5.
[3] Statement made in 1909. Quoted in *Encyclopaedia Britannica* (1950
ed.), Vol. 18, p. 220.
[4] George H. Dunne, S.J., ed. *Poverty in Plenty* (New York: J. Kennedy
& Sons, 1964), p. 122.

In rejecting income support to the poor, the President indicated a disdain for the "hand-out." This was in harmony with traditional American economic values. "The days of the dole in our country are numbered," the President declared upon signing the law. "Our American answer to poverty is not to make the poor more secure in their poverty but to reach down and help them lift themselves out of the ruts of poverty . . ." However, it may not be entirely irrelevant to suggest that "hand-outs" were rejected because they are costly: a meaningful program based on cash payments would run into billions of dollars. Indeed, it was soon commonly conceded that even the most successful implementation of the Economic Opportunity Act at its current levels of funding could not eliminate poverty, and that some income maintenance schemes would be needed to achieve this end.

Nevertheless, it was hardly surprising that despite its limited funds the new legislation was sold as a "total war on poverty." Such salesmanship follows the Washington habit of assuming a priori that any new piece of legislation will resolve the problem which it is designed to attack. Thus, legislation enacted in 1962 providing some work projects for persons on relief and limited expansion of social services to the poor was hailed by President Kennedy as a new approach to combating poverty. In this tradition the claims made for the Economic Opportunity Act were quite understandable.

The Economic Opportunity Act is a series of programs, some experimental and others conventional. Reflecting the complexity of the causes of poverty, the new legislation concentrated on the needs of some groups and passed over the needs of others. Meaningful help for the 5 million aged poor, for example, was precluded by budgetary constraints. Obviously, the aged could not be motivated, trained, or "rehabilitated." Income maintenance provisions and health care would have been the only effective ways to aid the poor, and these were left out of the program. Other legislation planned by the Administration did seek to meet the needs of the elderly, and a year later Medicare and Medicaid were enacted by Congress.

The Economic Opportunity Act thus concentrated on helping young people. The hope was to "break the chains of poverty"—an objective to be achieved, in the words of President Kennedy, through "rehabilitation instead of relief." Accordingly, the antipoverty programs focused on providing employment and services which would hopefully help motivate the poor to escape poverty. More specifically, the Act provided for the following series of major programs:

1. To help prepare the poor to obtain jobs in the competitive labor market, the Act provided for the creation of jobs paid by government funds. Separate programs provided jobs to youths from impoverished homes and work relief for adults, particularly indigent unemployed parents.

2. To provide a "last chance" for youths who failed to obtain a rudimentary education in school and who were not properly prepared for the world of work, the Act established residential centers where youths could acquire a basic education and learn marketable skills.

3. To mobilize and coordinate community resources to combat poverty as well as improve and to expand welfare services available to the poor, the Act called for the creation of Community Action Programs. On the assumption that self-help is the most effective means of aid, it specified that representatives of the poor be involved in the planning and administration of these programs.

4. Finally, to foster self-employment of poor people, the Act provided for separate loan programs for impoverished rural residents and for small businessmen.[5]

POVERTY BECOMES A FEDERAL ISSUE

It is not easy to explain why a war on poverty was launched in 1964 and why it gained such immediate and widespread support. Although unemployment remained at about 5 per cent, general prosperity prevailed; for the third consecutive year the economy showed rapid expansion, and incomes for the bulk of

[5] The 1964 Act also provided for employment of college youths from impoverished homes, in order to permit them to continue with their education. A year later this program was transferred from the Economic Opportunity Act to the Higher Education Act of 1965. This change and others which followed indicate the eclectic character of the programs included in the 1964 antipoverty package.

the population were the highest in history. This was hardly a propitious atmosphere for inaugurating a war on poverty. The social welfare legislation of the thirties, for example, had been stimulated by a deep depression and mass unemployment. If the overall economic conditions were not conducive to new social legislation, the explanation must be found elsewhere.

The problem of poverty was largely ignored during the post-World War II years. Widespread fears that the end of the war would bring mass unemployment led to passage of the Employment Act in 1946, which committed the government to maintaining high employment and purchasing power. This legislation remained largely an exhortation in the general prosperity that prevailed during the postwar years, and the Act was not implemented. Social welfare legislation held low priority during the years following World War II, and no important laws were enacted during the period—the exceptions being modification in minimum wages, extension of coverage under unemployment insurance, and Old Age, Survivors and Disability Insurance. The eight years of Eisenhower's "Great Crusade" put the stamp of respectability upon the New Deal programs, but produced very few innovations of its own.

In this climate it was not really respectable to talk about poverty. When Senator Hubert H. Humphrey announced his candidacy for the Democratic Presidential nomination in 1959, he declared that he would be the "poor man's candidate." The press simply regarded this as an unsubtle reminder that Humphrey's three major rivals for the nomination were multimillionaires. Even candidate Kennedy's call for a "war against poverty" during the 1960 campaign went largely unnoticed.[6] Such talk was taken as normal campaign rhetoric.

Rediscovery of Poverty

Herman P. Miller observes, "A myth has been created in the United States that incomes are gradually becoming more evenly distributed. This view is held by prominent economists of both

[6] U.S. Congress. Senate. Committee on Commerce. *The Speeches of Senator John F. Kennedy, Presidential Campaign of 1960*, 87th Cong., 1st Sess., S. Rept. 994, Part I (Washington: Government Printing Office, 1961), p. 18.

major political parties. It is also shared by the editors of the influential mass media."[7] This view was being nourished by influential economists, including Arthur F. Burns, Chairman of President Eisenhower's Council of Economic Advisers, and Paul Samuelson, one of President Kennedy's leading economic advisers. It was taken for granted that in a "laboristic" or welfare state this was a "natural" trend.

However, there were a few who dissented from this optimistic view. Most prominent in the 1950's was John K. Galbraith, who did call attention to the inequality of income distribution and deplored the failure to take measures which would lead to the reduction of poverty.[8] In 1950 and again in 1955, Senator John J. Sparkman of Alabama documented the persistence of rural poverty during extensive hearings of the Joint Economic Committee.[9] Beginning in 1955, Senator Paul H. Douglas of Illinois continued to point to the anomaly of depressed areas and pockets of deprivation in an economy of abundance.[10] An attempt by Governor Averell Harriman in 1957 to focus upon problems of poverty in the Empire State[11] did not advance beyond the research stage. When Harriman was defeated for reelection in the next year, the effort was dropped by his successor. In 1959, a Special Senate Committee on Unemployment, headed by Senator Eugene J. McCarthy of Minnesota, disclosed serious economic deprivation in many areas of the country.[12] Systematic statistical analyses of the incidence of

[7] Herman P. Miller. *Rich Man, Poor Man* (New York: Thomas Y. Crowell Co., 1964), p. 37.

[8] John K. Galbraith. *The Affluent Society* (Boston: Houghton Mifflin Co., 1958), p. 73.

[9] U.S. Congress. Joint Committee on the Economic Report. *Low-Income Families and Economic Stability*, 81st Cong., 2d Sess., S. Doc. 146 (Washington: Government Printing Office, 1950); U.S. Congress. Joint Committee on the Economic Report, Subcommittee on Low-Income Families. *Low-Income Families*, Hearings, November 18, 19, 21, 22, 23, 1955, 84th Cong., 1st Sess. (Washington: Government Printing Office, 1955).

[10] The Douglas campaign to aid economically depressed areas is summarized in Sar A. Levitan, *Federal Aid to Depressed Areas* (Baltimore: The Johns Hopkins Press, 1964).

[11] New York State. Governor's Message to the Legislature, January 30, 1957.

[12] U.S. Congress. Senate. Special Committee on Unemployment Problems. . . *Report on Unemployment Problems*, 86th Cong., 2d Sess., S. Rept. 1206 (Washington: Government Printing Office, 1960). This Committee

poverty were developed by Robert J. Lampman of the University of Wisconsin in a 1959 study made for the Joint Economic Committee of Congress,[13] and again by a group of University of Michigan economists and the Conference on Economic Progress three years later.[14]

The evidence of economic imbalance piled up, but few paid attention to the Congressional hearings or the scholarly monographs. And even the impassioned argument of Michael Harrington's *The Other America* for an "integrated and comprehensive program . . . [to] overthrow America's citadel of misery" was at first hardly noted.[15]

The first item that created a noticeable stir was an article by Dwight MacDonald which appeared early in 1963 in *The New Yorker*.[16] The article, "Our Invisible Poor," reviewed the major literature on poverty. It reached the White House and was read by Theodore Sorensen and presumably by the President himself. Harrington's book was also given to the President by Walter W. Heller, then Chairman of the Council of Economic Advisers, although it is not known whether the President read it. Thus the notion of the persistence of poverty continued to spread, and the phenomenon of mass poverty received in-

also printed nine volumes of hearings, a compendium on unemployment problems, *Readings in Unemployment* (Washington: Government Printing Office, 1960) and a volume of essays, *Studies in Unemployment* (Washington: Government Printing Office, 1960).

[13] U.S. Congress. Joint Economic Committee. *Low-Income Population and Economic Growth*, 86th Cong., 1st Sess., Study Paper 12, December 16, 1959 (Washington: Government Printing Office).

[14] James Morgan, Martin David, Wilbur J. Cohen and Harvey Brazer. *Income and Welfare in the United States*, A Study by the Survey Research Center, Institute for Social Research, University of Michigan (New York: McGraw-Hill Book Co., 1962); and Conference on Economic Progress. *Poverty and Deprivation in the United States* (Washington: The Conference, 1962).

[15] The story of this volume (New York: The Macmillan Co., 1962) offers an excellent barometer of the interest in poverty. The book was published in March 1962 and sold only a few thousand copies during the balance of the year. After review by Dwight MacDonald in *The New Yorker*, some 7,000 copies of the second printing were sold out. The paperback reprint of the volume, released in the fall of 1963, sold several hundred thousand copies.

[16] Dwight MacDonald. "Our Invisible Poor," *The New Yorker*, January 19, 1963, pp. 82–92.

creased attention. The next step was to place the problem on the agenda of the federal government's policymakers.

Poverty Reaches Kennedy's Attention

This was accomplished by Lampman, then a staff member of the Council of Economic Advisers (CEA). Every good story must have its hero, and it was Lampman who performed the role of catalyst in bringing poverty to the attention of the "highest governmental level." Lampman in turn found in CEA Chairman Walter W. Heller a sympathetic and encouraging ally. In a series of memoranda, Lampman called the attention of Heller and his colleagues to the fact that the "New Frontier" had failed to live up to its promise to aid the poor. Lampman stressed that the investment tax credit of 1962 and the then pending massive income tax cut were of little help to large groups of the poor. He predicted that even if the pending income tax could bring the economy back to full employment, additional programs would be needed before the aged poor, the disabled, and the fatherless families could rise above the threshold of poverty.

Similarly, the social welfare legislation enacted under the Kennedy Administration was of little help to these groups. The Area Redevelopment Act, which provided aid to depressed areas; the Accelerated Public Works Act, pumping development money into the same areas; and the Manpower Development and Training Act—these were of aid at best only to the poor who were in the work force. The limited data that were available at that time suggested that these programs were reaching very small numbers of the poor.

Another staff paper prepared by Lampman demonstrated that after 1956 a decline of poverty had been sharply arrested. During the decade 1947–1956 the proportion of families living in poverty—families with a total annual income of less than $3,000—declined by about 1 per cent a year, from 33 per cent to 23 per cent. But in the following five years the proportion of poor families declined by only 0.4 per cent annually, while the absolute number of people living in poverty actually increased. In transmitting this information to President Kennedy,

Heller commented that he found the data "distressing." This memorandum, dated May 1, 1963, started the discussion within the Administration of what later became the "war on poverty."

But the recognition of poverty was a long distance from the design and implementation of a program aimed at combating this social ill. The facts supplied by the intellectual community were necessary to help to identify and focus on the problem, but political forces were necessary to weld a program together. The most potent of these forces was the civil rights movement. In 1958 John Kenneth Galbraith asserted, with much justification, that there was no political payoff in fighting poverty. "Any politician who speaks for the poor is speaking for a small and inarticulate minority," he claimed.[17] However valid this observation may have been in 1958, it certainly did not hold true five years later. To be sure, the civil rights struggle was initially waged in terms of social and political rights—spurred by increasing numbers of Negro and white militants, aided by an activist Supreme Court, and supported after 1960 by a sympathetic administration. Yet the issue of civil rights inevitably led to the problem of poverty, for economic deprivation was an integral part of overall discrimination and injustice suffered by Negroes.

The increasing amount of statistics generated on the Negro question made transparently clear that a disproportionate number of Negroes were to be found in the ranks of the unskilled, the unemployed, and the poverty-stricken. Most significant were the data developed by Herman P. Miller, a Bureau of Census expert on income distribution. On the basis of an exhaustive analysis of the 1960 Census data, Miller concluded that, contrary to popular belief, the income gap between Negro and white had not narrowed during the post-World War II period. He estimated that lifetime earnings of nonwhites were about two-thirds those of whites in the same occupation with similar educational attainment.[18] The close relationship between economic and political discrimination was expressed succinctly by President Kennedy, who insisted (in a message to Congress on June 19, 1963) that equal employment opportunities must be

[17] *Supra*, footnote 3, p. 328.

[18] Herman P. Miller. "Is the Income Gap Closed? 'No!'" *The New York Times Magazine*, November 11, 1962.

included among the Negro's civil rights. "There is little value," the President stated, "in a Negro's obtaining the right to be admitted to the hotels and restaurants if he has no cash in his pocket and no job." Thus the civil rights movement, which became a potent power by 1963, could have supplied the political pressure for a program in aid of the poor. And the administration was responsive and sympathetic to this pressure.

The President's Economists Take the Initiative

In early summer of 1963, when Heller and Lampman initiated the Council discussion on poverty, there was little public interest in a comprehensive governmental antipoverty program. In June 1963, Heller tried out the idea before a presumably sympathetic audience at the annual convention of the Communications Workers of America. His address hammered at a double theme: the need for a tax cut, and for policies ". . . to open more exits from poverty."[19] The minutes of the convention indicate that Heller received the usual applause at the end of his address. But union president Joseph Beirne, in thanking Heller for his address, indicated support for the tax cut but made no reference to the antipoverty program. Heller's own reaction was that the union members were interested in the tax cut, but that he lost his audience when he spoke about poverty. Later that same summer, Heller tried to interest reporters in the topic. Except for one press association story, the reporters seemed uninterested. One reporter from a newspaper that publishes "All the news that's fit to print" took special pains to collect information and background data, but returned to inform Council staff members that the topic would have no appeal.

Administration advisers themselves were divided about the wisdom of mounting an antipoverty program. In the summer of 1963, Heller called together a group of White House aides and other executive officials to discuss the feasibility of including new measures in aid of the poor as part of the administration program for the coming year. The reaction was mixed,

[19] Communications Workers of America. *Proceedings of the 25th Annual Convention*, 1963, p. 141.

ranging from outright opposition to lukewarm support. Although none of the participants objected in principle to an antipoverty program, several questioned the wisdom of raising the issue close to the 1964 election campaign. The time to raise the issue, according to one Cabinet secretary, was in 1960 when the Democrats were out of office and not campaigning for reelection. A nationally known economist of unimpeachable liberal credentials, happening to be in the White House dining room where the meeting took place, joined the discussion and rejected the idea of a program as ill-timed and politically unsound. (Later he claimed credit for being an initiator of the antipoverty program.) But the idea also had supporters, including Presidential aide Theodore Sorensen, who thought the antipoverty program was both morally sound and a good political issue for 1964, Charles L. Schultze (Bureau of the Budget), and Wilbur J. Cohen (Department of Health, Education, and Welfare).

During the early fall of 1963, the notion of launching an antipoverty program received a temporary setback. There was widespread talk about white backlash as a reaction to the civil rights movement. Apparently some outside advisers reached President Kennedy, urging him to inaugurate a program focusing on problems of suburbia as a central campaign theme for 1964. For a while, Kennedy seemed to question the political wisdom of making an antipoverty program a theme of his prospective reelection campaign.

But the problem of poverty could not be ignored. On October 20, 1963, *The New York Times* published a penetrating survey of deprivation and want in eastern Kentucky.[20] The report described the region as "a vast ghetto of unemployables" where children went hungry and schools were "unfit for cattle." It is known that Kennedy read and was deeply moved by this article.

Heller and his staff persisted with the development of an antipoverty program. Although he encouraged these efforts, Kennedy refrained from committing himself to such a program until his last meeting with Heller—on November 19, 1963. At

[20] Homer Bigart. "Kentucky Miners: A Grim Winter," *The New York Times*, October 20, 1963.

that time he instructed his chief economic adviser to formulate legislative proposals for the following session of Congress.

Meanwhile, Heller began a series of consultations with key officials whose departments or agencies were responsible for the administration of welfare programs—at the same time keeping top White House aides advised of his activities. To augment his own small staff, Heller pulled in the Bureau of the Budget to help design a program of action for 1964.[21]

During the summer and early fall of 1963 the Council of Economic Advisers–Bureau of the Budget task force concentrated on informational and analytical needs for designing "an attack on poverty." No attempt was made to devise specific programs and, in the absence of an explicit commitment from the White House, the task force had no basis upon which to estimate the magnitude of the program that might be launched.

It is apparent, however, that the staff people were not disposed to "think big." While they raised the right questions, the general trend of their thinking was in the direction of pilot projects. In their defense, it must be remembered that there was no indication that the White House would favor a major new program.

Heller's goal was to submit a tentative program to the White House by Thanksgiving. With this target in mind, he circulated a memorandum on November 5, 1963, to heads of the major departments and agencies involved in administering welfare programs, requesting suggestions for a 1964 legislative program aimed at "Widening Participation in Prosperity"—the tentative title for the program to attack poverty.[22] Heller invited the administrators to suggest "imaginative new programs," redirection

[21] The key people during the summer and early fall were Theodore C. Sorensen and Meyer Feldman from the White House staff; William M. Capron, Robert J. Lampman, Burton A. Weisbrod, and Rashi Fein (who left the Council in September 1963) from Heller's own staff; and William B. Cannon, Michael S. March, and Charles L. Schultze from the Bureau of the Budget.

[22] The memorandum was addressed to the Secretary of Agriculture, Secretary of Commerce, Secretary of Labor, Secretary of Health, Education, and Welfare, the Director of the Bureau of the Budget, and the Administrator of the Housing and Home Finance Agency. The Secretary of the Interior, whose department includes the Bureau of Indian Affairs, was apparently omitted by oversight and included later.

of existing programs, and to indicate, where necessary, the budgetary implications of the proposals. Heller was looking primarily for new ideas; budgetary constraints would be considered later.

Within two weeks Capron and Weisbrod, the two CEA staff members assigned by Heller to coordinate the agency proposals, were inundated with proposals which were obviously too ambitious for the Bureau of the Budget. One staff aide commented that the combined departmental proposals were enough to keep Congress busy for a decade, although many hardly deserved consideration. Encouraged by Kennedy's commitment to include an antipoverty program in his 1964 legislative proposals, the CEA–BOB task force was in the process of examining and analyzing the departmental proposals on Friday, November 22, when they received the news of the President's assassination.

JOHNSON—"THAT'S MY KIND OF PROGRAM"

The tragic event did not stop development of the program. Within two days after he took office, President Johnson met with Heller, and the first item on their agenda was the pending antipoverty program. The idea immediately received Johnson's unequivocal endorsement. As related by Heller, the President's comment was: "That's my kind of program. It will help people. I want you to move full speed ahead on it."[23]

The first task was to reduce the program to manageable proportions. While there was still no agreed-upon price tag for the program, obviously an initial multibillion-dollar program was not in the cards. The Agriculture Department's laundry list of previously rejected measures aimed at raising the income level of the poor in rural areas was rejected as unrealistic. HEW's income-maintenance programs received similar short shrift because they would have been too costly. Likewise, the task force was unsympathetic to proposals from the Housing and Home Finance Agency (now Housing and Urban Development Department), except for additional funds for the long-established

[23] Walter W. Heller. "American Poverty: Its Causes and Cures," Address delivered at the Seventh Annual Public Affairs Forum, Indiana State College, Indiana, Pennsylvania, March 25, 1965, p. 4.

public housing program. A proposal for rent supplements and relocation allowances for families displaced by urban renewal was also rejected outright, at this stage, only to be adopted in principle by Congress less than two years later. The Labor Department's programs received the kindest treatment. The reason was probably that Labor's memorandum included a list of priorities. Practically all of the items at the top of Labor's list had won prior approval of the Bureau of the Budget, and some were already pending before Congress.

Without passing judgment on the merits of the departmental proposals, the CEA–BOB task force found that imaginative proposals do not come cheaply. One of the department heads indicated the difficulty of developing a low-cost, "realistic" package which would not constitute merely a collection of a few miscellaneous small programs. His solution was to emphasize long-run programs and at the same time convey a sense of urgency about starting a war on poverty. He failed to indicate how this sense of urgency would help the poor—a problem which has continued to plague the antipoverty warriors ever since.

A Coordinated Community Action Concept

The solution to the task force's dilemma came from an entirely unexpected source and evolved from the combined experience of the Ford Foundation and the President's Committee on Juvenile Delinquency and Youth Crime. The Public Affairs Department of the Ford Foundation embarked in the late 1950's on a search for ways to help rejuvenate slum areas in large cities. Under the resulting Ford "Gray Areas program," a euphemistic title for aid to slum areas, the Foundation helped sponsor community improvement projects initiated and implemented by local organizations. Underlying the Gray Area program was the notion that rehabilitation of slum areas requires institutional changes including governmental reorganization. The needed transformation of slum communities could not be accomplished by "gobs of giving," according to Ford's Director of Public Affairs Program, Paul Ylvisaker. "It is not dependency we want to encourage," he explained, "but independence and choice."[24]

The need to attack problems normally falling within the purview of government imposed restraints upon the Gray Area program. As a private organization, the Foundation lacked the democratic mandate to impose its will upon public institutions; yet, at the same time, it wanted to assure that its funds would achieve maximum results. In a pluralistic society, this dilemma was not insoluble. The Foundation acted as a catalyst by establishing local private organizations which shared its views on slum rehabilitation and which would have sufficient local support to continue after the Foundation withdrew its aid. Thus, the Foundation insisted that private local agencies applying for funds have the broad support of community leaders and that the agency raise or promise contributions to match the Foundation's grant. To assure compliance, the Foundation withheld part of each grant to be released as acceptable programs were submitted and the conditions of the grant were met. However, the design and initiation of specific programs were left to the communities. A major aspect of these programs was an attempt to attack the problem of juvenile delinquency.

Closely related in concept and function to the Ford Foundation's Gray Areas program was the work of the President's Committee on Juvenile Delinquency and Youth Crime. The Committee was established in 1961 and was chaired by [the] then Attorney General, Robert F. Kennedy. Its goal was to reduce juvenile delinquency by developing the employment capacities of slum youth and by organizing communities to improve themselves. Needless to say, effective programs to combat juvenile delinquency and to make underprivileged youths employable required the coordination of diverse public and private institutions—welfare agencies, school systems, police, employment agencies, and employers, among others. Because the Committee's appropriations were limited—ranging between $6 and $8 million annually—it confined itself to making grants for the planning of community programs. Financing of these programs

[24] Quoted in Peter Marris and Martin Rein. *Community Action and the Professional Reformer* (New York: Harper and Row, in press).

was left to local agencies or to state and federal sources. By the end of 1963 the Committee had funded programs in more than a dozen cities. Its experience indicated that, once communities succeeded in developing effective plans, they encountered difficulties in obtaining federal funds distributed on a fragmented basis, each under different criteria and not easily adaptable to the multipurpose approach of the juvenile delinquency program.

The Ford Foundation program and the President's Committee shared with the nascent antipoverty program the goal of attacking the complex causes of poverty. David L. Hackett, Executive Director of the Committee, felt that the techniques developed by his program might be adopted to fight poverty on a broader scale. He believed that an effective antipoverty effort would require a coordinated approach not feasible under existing single-purpose federal programs. William Cannon of the CEA–BOB task force was persuaded of the soundness of this approach and converted others. Soon it became the focal point in the antipoverty planning.

Key people on the task force favored the proposal for a number of reasons. Not only did the newly proposed approach appear to have substantive merit, but it also lent itself to budgetary flexibility. The program could be sold as a comprehensive attack upon poverty which allowed experimentation and adaptability to local situations. Any number of communities could play, depending upon the extent of budgetary allocations. (At this stage, the planners did not take into account the usual tendency of federal programs to spread themselves thin. This occurred later.) The approach also provided a new area of experimentation for the coordination of general purpose federal grants in line with the President's later stress on "creative federalism."[25] Charles L. Schultze hit upon the name for this aspect of the poverty program—"Community Action Program."

The design of the conceptual framework was an important advance, but the edifice was far from complete. Crucial problems remained to be resolved. For one thing, the emphasis on

[25] Roger H. Davidson. "Poverty and the New Federalism," in *Dimensions of Manpower Policy: Programs and Research*, Sar A. Levitan and Irving Siegel, editors (Baltimore: The Johns Hopkins Press, 1966), pp. 61–80.

coordinated community action did not preclude single-purpose programs. And the advocates of expanded funding for education, housing, welfare services, and training—to mention a few major groups—presented persuasive arguments for their favorite programs. Spokesmen for federal funding of education argued, for example, that the antipoverty program presented an excellent opportunity to bypass the church-state controversy and provide federal aid for elementary and secondary education. This analysis was proved correct with the passage of the Economic Opportunity Act, which in turn opened the door for the passage of the Elementary and Secondary Education Act of 1965.

Another question arose over the components of the Community Action Programs. Spokesmen for the Departments of Labor and Health, Education, and Welfare—the two agencies whose traditional activities would be targets of a coordinated approach—were concerned that the new proposal would absorb their existing programs or serve as substitutes for their pending legislation. HEW officials even argued that no new legislation was necessary for planning coordinated community action programs. This objective could be accomplished, they said, under a 1956 amendment to the Social Security Act which authorized HEW to make grants for coordinated community services programs.[26] However, annual appropriations for these demonstration and research projects averaged less than $1 million out of a $5 million annual authorization, a fact which led a member of the CEA–BOB task force to observe that HEW "would make a molehill out of what is really a mountainous problem." On the other hand, representatives of the Department of Labor opposed the inclusion of a youth work component in the community action programs lest it serve as a substitute for the pending Youth Employment Bill.

Overriding all these substantive and parochial controversies was the realization that the program was going to be too small to satisfy all the competing and complementary needs. And, regardless of the size of the program, agency representatives were not inclined to surrender part of their domains, even if

[26] Public Law 880, 84th Cong., "Social Security Amendments of 1956," Title XI, Sec. 331.

they were persuaded by the soundness of the community action approach. Moreover, while the task force was trying to hammer out the antipoverty program, the President continued to preach and practice economy. At least one agency chief perceived a contradiction between the promises of cutting the budget and the planning of new programs. Logically enough, he hesitated to propose any expansion of his department's activities.

Finally, there was the problem of the administrative structure of the new program. This turned out to be the most hard-fought battle, since it touched on the very preserves of the actors involved in the drama. Some wanted to run the entire show; others fought for only a piece of the action. But all wanted something. Because Cabinet-level departments were involved, only the President himself could ultimately resolve this controversy.

Dividing a Small Pie

The dialogue—some would say squabble—over these difficult issues continued within the executive branch until the very moment the President sent his bill to Capitol Hill, on March 16, 1964. But some aspects of the controversy could not be delayed that long. The President is required by law to submit to Congress each January his proposed budget for the ensuing fiscal year. If the fiscal 1965 budget were to contain any reference to the war on poverty, a specific line item had to be provided early in January. The amount could be changed later, but a tentative decision on the magnitude, if not the scope, of the effort could not be postponed.

During the month of December, Budget Bureau analysts were actively engaged in "costing out" the alternative proposals. These estimates, some of which were sent to Theodore Sorensen in the White House, called for new expenditures in fiscal 1965 ranging from $389 million to $629 million, with projections of three to four times this range for fiscal 1969. All the proposals carried a uniform amount of $100 million for the implementation of ten community action programs, with $25 million for development and administration. The other funds were to be allocated to work projects for youth, medical care for needy children, and raising the federal share of Aid to Families with Dependent Children. At least one departmental representative consulted by the task force urged that in order to make the program "really dramatic" it should equal or exceed $1 billion.

The decision to ask Congress for a $500 million appropriation was reached by January 6, 1964. The budget contained only a single line item for this amount. But, in a memorandum to the Secretaries of Agriculture, Commerce, HEW, Interior, and Labor, and the Administrator of the Housing and Home Finance Agency, Heller and Gordon elaborated that the $500 million for the financing of community action programs be allocated as follows: (1) development and administration of local CAP's—$50 million; (2) assistance to local communities in providing summer work projects for youth, vocational rehabilitation, diagnostic care and health services, and funds for experimental programs—$275 million; (3) supplementary funds for existing and new programs—$175 million.

The last-mentioned amount was judiciously distributed among the six agencies with a proviso that the funds be used only in conjunction with approved community action programs. Agriculture, HEW, and Labor were to receive $40 million each, Commerce and HHFA $20 million each, and Interior $15 million. HEW was to use its money for adult work training, vocational rehabilitation, community health programs, and child care. Labor funds were to be allocated mostly for expansion of training, employment services, and aid to migrant labor. Agriculture was to use its funds for the expansion of food distribution, loans to farmers, and grants for housing rehabilitation. HHFA was to direct its funds for experimenting with rent subsidies, coordination of services in public housing, and urban planning. Commerce was to expand the area redevelopment program, while Interior was to allocate its $15 million entirely to the Bureau of Indian Affairs.

In addition, Heller and Gordon proposed that the five departments and HHFA allocate $625 million from existing or proposed new programs already included in the 1965 agency budgets to help carry out approved community action programs. In brief, the Heller-Gordon memorandum of January 6, 1964, outlined the substance, though not necessarily the detail, of what later became the Economic Opportunity Act.

The inclusion of the $500 million line item in the budget settled, at least as far as the federal officials were concerned, the debate over the magnitude of the new program. In light of this figure, departments and agencies intensified their lobbying to obtain the responsibility for implementing the proposal, as well as a maximum feasible share of the program for their respective clienteles.

The Agriculture Department maintained that, because nearly half of all impoverished families are located in rural areas, half of the antipoverty money should be allocated to the rural poor. The Department urged particularly a grant program for subsistence farmers, on the ground that most of these farmers are middle-aged or older and lack adequate education or training to obtain and hold jobs in an urban environment. The Department did not show how these subsistence farmers could be helped to escape poverty by a few thousand dollars, or how they would be able to compete effectively in an agricultural economy which is increasingly mechanized and concentrated. For that matter, no information was supplied as to how the proposal would mesh with national policies in an era when agricultural production had outpaced demand. Lowering its sights somewhat, Agriculture subsequently appealed for parity with Commerce, arguing that, since Heller and Gordon proposed to allocate $20 million to the Area Redevelopment Administration for stimulation of investment in commerce and industry, at least an equal amount should also be allocated for investment in farmers.

Commerce, on the other hand, was happy with the proposed $20 million allocation and promised to expand ARA from the thousand counties already in the agency's domain to encompass the entire country. Apparently no thought was given to the fact that ARA had already spread itself thin, or to how the Commerce Department expected to distribute the funds, $10,000 per additional county, for the purpose of offering technical assistance, loans for commercial and industrial facilities, and loans and grants for public facilities. Of course, all these funds were to be used specifically to fight poverty, but the Department supplied no information concerning the availability of entrepreneurs among the poor.

Interior also assured Heller and Gordon that it would have no difficulty in spending the proposed $15 million to combat poverty among the Indians—although the Department conceded that it had no specific plans at the moment. Interior also indicated a willingness to play a larger role in the program by offering the use of its facilities to provide summer camps for youths.

The sharpest conflict appeared to exist between the Departments of Labor and Health, Education, and Welfare. The former made it quite clear that it resented the encroachment of the newly proposed program upon its established domain. Labor was concerned that the proposed summer work projects would overlap with the then pending Youth Employment Act (passed by the Senate in 1963), and that the proposed community work and training programs would compete with the Manpower Development and Training Act (MDTA). The Department ignored the fact that only a handful of relief recipients had qualified for training under MDTA courses. In addition, the Labor Department urged that the war on poverty emphasize the extension of minimum wage coverage to retail, service, and agriculture, the enactment of legislation to aid migrant labor, and the strengthening of unemployment insurance.

The Department of Health, Education, and Welfare made the broadest claims upon the proposed $500 million. In fact, it indicated a willingness to spend all the money—conceding $50 million for creating summer jobs for high school–age youths to the Department of Labor, which for its own good and sufficient reasons did not want this program. HEW would have spent the bulk of the funds for community action programs, with the balance supplementing existing programs of the Department.

All the departments nominally endorsed the community action concept. Daniel P. Moynihan has suggested that at this stage of the legislative planning all the concept meant to the federal officials involved was a coordinated effort of disbursing funds.[27] A close examination of their responses to the Heller-Gordon memorandum discloses significant reservations even

[27] Daniel P. Moynihan. "What Is 'Community Action'?" *The Public Interest*, No. 5, Fall 1966, pp. 3–8.

about this narrow interpretation of the approach. HEW, which had traditionally operated programs through grants allocated to the states, wanted state agencies to be included in the planning and execution of community projects. Involvement of states was considered necessary and desirable, not only because they might contribute funds to community action programs, but also because they could provide technical expertise which many communities lacked. HHFA thought that the principle of coordinated community action was good enough at the local level but not for the federal establishment, and recommended that each participating agency administer its own traditional programs. In this approach the coordinator of the local action program, the chief executive of the locality, would be required to apply separately to the several federal agencies for funds to implement the local antipoverty program. HHFA also believed that, while it would take some time to plan community action programs, there should be no delay in implementing these programs; it therefore recommended that planning and action be funded simultaneously. It would appear that this agency did not expect that action required prior coordinated planning. Agriculture and Commerce also came close to denying the community action approach by arguing that the leadership of some localities would be either weak or indifferent to the whole program. These departments therefore urged a more activist federal role in some areas. The fears expressed by Agriculture proved correct in light of later experience, for many rural areas failed to apply for OEO funds. Taken together, it would appear that much of the support for the community action approach among executive agencies was more lip service than a full understanding of what the concept meant.

Administrative Structure

The most heated discussion focused upon the organizational structure of the proposed program. In their January 6 memorandum, Heller and Gordon indicated that no decision had been made on this point and declined to suggest any preference. This may have been a tactical move to focus on substantive proposals rather than administrative problems. Possibly they had not made up their minds. They did indicate, however, that two alternative organizational arrangements were being considered. One alternative would turn the administration of the antipoverty program over to the Department of Health, Education, and Welfare. This would have required the appointment of a new assistant secretary in the Department who would be responsible for the day-to-day administration of the program. This approach was similar to the one taken three years earlier in connection with the Area Redevelopment Administration, whose functions also cut across traditional departmental lines. The second alternative would be to establish a new agency, headed by a council composed of Cabinet members under the chairmanship of a Presidential appointee who was not himself a Cabinet officer. The chairman of the council would be responsible for administering the program.

Not surprisingly, there was no agreement on either of the suggested approaches, and new alternatives were suggested by the departments. Although quite naturally pleased with the first alternative, HEW urged the creation of an interdepartmental committee chaired by the Secretary of HEW and consisting of heads of the agencies having program responsibilities. To establish close ties with the White House, HEW also proposed that a special assistant to the President be assigned to maintain White House participation and liaison. For all practical purposes, however, this plan would have given to HEW the responsibility for the antipoverty program.

Labor opposed handing over the responsibility for the program to a sub-Cabinet official and urged that a single Cabinet officer be placed in charge. Needless to say, Labor was quite willing to assume that responsibility. Reminiscent of the true mother in the biblical story, however, Labor opposed cutting up the unborn babe and indicated that its second choice was HEW. Labor also conceded the need for program coordination and suggested that this function be assigned to a staff assistant of the President who would be responsible for general direction of the program.

On the other hand, HHFA favored that each agency administer its own program. Under the Presidential assistant would be field representatives who would be directly respon-

sible to him for coordinating purposes but with no power to
direct local programs. Otherwise, HHFA argued, lines of responsibility among the participating departments and agencies
would become confused and would hamper the program. Because HHFA favored comprehensive community action programs, it suggested that the responsibility for funding such
programs be vested in the Presidential assistant but that the
funding of components in implementing the plans remain the
responsibility of the separate departments—each supplying the
money for the "piece of action" in its own domain. HHFA
reasoned that to coordinate the funding of comprehensive
programs at the federal level would delay implementation of
the programs.

Agriculture and Commerce favored vesting responsibility
for the program with a Cabinet-level council chaired by a
special Presidential appointee, the second of the alternatives
suggested by Heller and Gordon.

From the interdepartmental dialogue there emerged consensus on the substantive aspects of the proposed program. The
attack on poverty would be coordinated at the local level under
the umbrella of the comprehensive community action programs.
The $500 million in new appropriations requested by the Presi-
dent would be divided as follows: $50 million for planning and
administration of community action programs; $275 million
for implementation of these programs; and the balance, $175
million, to supplement existing antipoverty programs coordinated with community action programs. The supplementary
funds were allocated to the various departments as proposed by
Heller and Gordon, except that in the process Labor lost $5
million which was allocated to a National Service Corps (later
incorporated as VISTA in the Economic Opportunity Act). In
addition, it was expected that another $500 million or more
would be transferred from existing departmental programs to
the community action programs.

No such agreement was reached concerning the administration of the program. Instead of the two alternatives proposed
by Heller and Gordon, there emerged three distinct alternatives, each having potent support within the executive establishment. All agreed that the central functions of the proposed

program would be vested in the director of a new community action agency. Special appropriations would be made to him for grants to local communities or for allocation to participating agencies in accordance with local community action programs approved by him. A Human Resources Council, chaired by him and composed of the heads of participating agencies, would be established to advise on policies and programs. Beyond this basic agreement, three major alternatives were considered in the organization of the program:

1. An independent agency. Proponents of this alternative argued that it would dramatize the administration's commitment to the war on poverty. Opponents countered that this arrangement would place the program at a disadvantage because the administrator of a single program is in a weaker bargaining position with Congress than is a department head. It was also suggested that the establishment of an independent agency would delay launching the war on poverty because of the time required to recruit an adequate staff.

2. A new unit in the Executive Office. Proponents of this approach argued that, in addition to the advantages of an independent agency, the program would gain added prestige from its location in the Executive Office, a fact which would presumably help the director in his dealings with the heads of other agencies. Opposition to this plan was centered in the Bureau of the Budget, which has traditionally opposed placing operating responsibilities within the Executive Office.[28] The Bureau of the Budget was concerned that placing the operating functions of the antipoverty program in the Executive Office might create a precedent for other interest groups wishing to push their projects to the same lofty position. Also, it was feared that opponents of the pending bill to establish a Department of Housing and Urban Development would be led to urge the establishment of an Office of Urban Affairs in the President's Office as a substitute for a new department.

[28] The major recent precedent for locating an operating agency in the Executive Office was the Office of Civil and Defense Mobilization (OCDM), established during the Eisenhower administration. But President Kennedy had transferred the major operating functions of OCDM to the Defense Department and retained in the Executive Office only the Office of Emergency Planning.

3. The Department of Health, Education, and Welfare. The major advocates of this approach were of course from that department. Their argument was that, since HEW would have the major responsibility for carrying out the antipoverty programs, it would be more efficient to place them in that department. Opponents saw this fact as their strongest argument against placing the program in HEW, arguing that the department's "old line" bureaucracy would oppose the new approaches envisioned in the antipoverty program. Another argument against having the antipoverty program in HEW was that it would preclude effective coordination of community action programs at the federal level.

Only the President was in a position to resolve this conflict among his major lieutenants. Accordingly, the chief protagonists and the Attorney General were summoned to the White House on January 23, 1964, to present their arguments before the President was to make his decision. Eight days after the White House meeting, on February 1, 1964, the President announced to everyone's surprise that he was appointing R. Sargent Shriver to plan the war on poverty.

Several factors may have accounted for postponement of the decision. Any final determination would have displeased some, if not a majority, of the Cabinet officers, and the new President may have wanted to defer such a potentially divisive decision. Another explanation is that the President wanted to give the future administrator of the program a chance to shape the program which he would administer. There was also a chance that another review of the issues would produce some fresh ideas or approaches. This was in line with Heller's recommendation to the President.

Finally, tactics may have suggested the wisdom of postponing the presentation of a bill to Congress. As long as the Council of Economic Advisers and the Bureau of the Budget were planning the program, little was reported about it in the public news media—although some news leaks, inadvertent or perhaps contrived, did appear. But the President's call for a "war on poverty" in his State of the Union Message, and the Council of Economic Advisers' report, were generating considerable public interest in the poverty problem. The appointment of a

Presidential aide to take charge of the program—inevitably the public news media called him a poverty "czar"—created an opportunity for educating the public and Congress about the problem of poverty and generating support for the contemplated programs.

THE SHRIVER TASK FORCE

A brother-in-law of the late President and a former Chicago businessman with a record of public service—he had been chairman of the Chicago Board of Education—Shriver had acquired an enviable reputation in dealing with Congress as Director of the Peace Corps from its inception in 1961. He was reported to be the only foreign-aid administrator who was able to obtain "not just almost as much as he wants but almost as much as he asks for the Peace Corps."[29] His effectiveness was not accidental. According to the same reporter, Shriver would absorb in public Congressional attack ". . . and then at night he will call up some power figure from . . . [the Congressman's] district and the next morning . . . [the Congressman] is unexpectedly slapped on the back of the head."[30]

Upon assuming his new assignment—he retained the directorship of the Peace Corps—Shriver created the impression that he was looking for new innovative ideas. "I come into this with an open mind," he declared, "I have been learning, sifting, and consulting . . ."[31] A member of the task force, James L. Sundquist, then Deputy Under Secretary of Agriculture, remarked on Shriver's open-mindedness: "I've never known anyone as open to ideas as Shriver is. If a man came in with an idea, he would seem to accept it right away and, if you objected, Sarge would say 'What's wrong with it?' and the burden of proof would be on the one who objected instead of the one who suggested the idea."[32] But another observer of Shriver during the period of the task force remained unimpressed by his apparent search for

[29] Murray Kempton. "The Essential Sargent Shriver," *The New Republic*, March 28, 1964, p. 13.
[30] *Ibid.*
[31] "Poverty U.S.A.," *Newsweek*, February 17, 1964, p. 38.
[32] Murray Kempton, *op. cit.*, p. 13.

new ideas, holding that his seeming tolerance of new approaches was simply an inability to sift sound suggestions from crackpot ideas. This observer described Shriver as a "dilettante with a propensity for schoolgirl enthusiasm."

Whatever Shriver's intellectual capacity for understanding the problem of poverty, he succeeded in fostering the image of bold innovation. Old welfare ideas were definitely out, and planning operations carried an almost mystic aura. A notion was conveyed that even jaded bureaucrats expected new ideas to emerge from the task force. Within six weeks after his appointment, Shriver claimed to have consulted 137 different people about the formulation of the poverty program. The list included leaders in agriculture, business, labor, and civil rights groups; officials of federal, state and local governments; an assorted group of college professors and administrators; and representatives from foundations. Social workers, welfare officials and experts were conspicuously absent from the list. Apparently there was nothing to be learned from the "old ways" of doing things.[33] There is little evidence that the "consultations" produced any usable ideas, nor even that ideas were genuinely sought. It is quite apparent that some "advisers" were brought in primarily to be seen and not heard—to win their support and to indicate to the public that all sorts of "creative" personages were involved in designing the program.

Shriver was particularly interested in advertising the fact that the business community supported the poverty program. The section of the above mentioned list devoted to "business and agricultural" leaders contained the names of one farm group leader and thirty corporate executives. According to a participant who was commissioned to carry the message of the antipoverty program to the business community, most of the business proposals dealt with tax cuts and removal of government restraints upon business enterprise. This might be one way of fighting poverty, but Sargent Shriver was not appointed to his post to reduce taxes. On the contrary, his mission was to find useful ways of spending public money.

[33] The President recommended that Shriver speak to a leading national authority on social welfare, a person with whom the President had consulted in the past. Shriver obliged but terminated the conversation after a few minutes.

Old Ideas—New Slogans

The scope and direction of the poverty program were determined during the two weeks following Shriver's appointment. Most of the ideas, moreover, came from old government hands (subcabinet officials and their advisers); only a few outside kibitzers or advisers participated in the process.

Within three days after his appointment, Shriver asked the Council of Economic Advisers, the Bureau of the Budget, departmental representatives and a few personal associates to brief him on the state of the program and to explore other alternatives. Heller opened the meeting by describing in detail the proposed community action concept. Wirtz attacked this approach as being too limited in scope and appeal and advocated an aggressive job-creation and training program as the most effective way to fight poverty. Of course, the community action concept did not preclude emphasis on job creation; presumably each community could determine its own program based on local needs. But in their planning, the Council of Economic Advisers and the Bureau of the Budget had laid heavy emphasis upon education, health and social service components. It was also argued that the adoption of the CAP approach would be time-consuming and that two years would elapse before most communities would develop operating programs. Several others in the meeting sided with Wirtz, and a consensus emerged: community action programs would be only part of the war on poverty, and the design of the legislation should stress the breadth of the approach.

Advocates of the broader approach were able to show that this could be accomplished with a minimum of extra funding. Instead of limiting the war on poverty to community action, the bill would include all the programs already approved by the President which focused on aiding the poor. This course had been considered by Heller, Gordon, and their associates, but in deference to established departmental jurisdictions they had not included these programs as part of the package. By transferring a few items from other budgetary requests, however, the war on poverty could be increased by $350 million without raising the administrative budget by one penny. Included in the transferred programs were Labor's Youth Employment Bill (later transformed into the Job Corps and the Neighborhood Youth Corps), HEW's Community Work and Training (work for persons on relief), and "special education projects" (later part of the adult basic education and work experience programs). The need to include a special youth program in the poverty program was accentuated by a widely circulated report which demonstrated a high rejection rate of draftees by the armed forces as being due to causes associated with poverty, particularly among Negroes.[34]

Nor was this all. To create the image of a broad attack on poverty, something had to be provided for everybody—or nearly everybody—as long as the costs were kept low. Though the Community Action Programs were intended to aid rural as well as urban poor, an explicit program for impoverished rural residents and subsistence farmers seemed politically desirable.

Within two weeks after his first meeting, Shriver reported to the President on the progress of his undertaking. Shriver's newly acquired staff prepared a memorandum to be transmitted to the President at this meeting. Although the statement was not intended for public consumption, it contained many of the slogans and cliches which have become the poverty war stock in trade. The memorandum informed the President that the "war cannot be either limited or cheap," and that "in the coming war, we *can* [underscoring in original] make a reconnaissance in force." In addition to its ambitious prose, the memorandum indicated that Shriver planned to propose the following expenditures for the first year of the program: $400 million for youth programs, $300 million for Community Action Programs, $50 million for rural grants and loans, and $50 million for adult work and training programs. Apparently the remaining $50 million had not been allocated.

The actual amounts recommended to Congress a month later were either the same as or close to these projections. As it turned out, the antipoverty bill proposed by the President requested $962.5 million instead of the $850 million envisioned by Shriver early in February. The major alteration was expansion of the work experience program from $50 million to $150

[34] The President's Task Force on Manpower Conservation. *One-Third of A Nation* (Washington: Government Printing Office, 1964).

million. A small loan program was also added with the theme of enabling the poor to help themselves. But this title of the Act cost nothing, because the loans were to come from the Small Business Administration's regular appropriation. The general framework of the bill, therefore, had already taken shape during the first week of the task force. The distinguished citizens "from all walks of life" who trooped through Shriver's office to share their wisdom may have contributed to his education, but they added very little of substance to the legislation.

On one substantive point Shriver did alter his position. In his memorandum to the President, he suggested that the National Service Corps—popularly termed the "Domestic Peace Corps"—which the President had already proposed, be withdrawn "so that prospective volunteers might be staged into the other projects." However, the bill which went to Congress retained this program under a new title, Volunteers for America. Shriver did not have to go far to seek advice on this point. His own brother-in-law, the then Attorney General, Robert F. Kennedy, persuaded him to include this provision in the proposed bill.

All this is not to conclude that Shriver and his associates did not seek or welcome new ideas from outside. What the experience did indicate was the paucity of approaches, at least within the predetermined budgetary restraints. When good ideas were offered they were gladly received. For example, early versions of the bill required that Job Corps centers be administered only by federal, state, or local agencies. John H. Rubel, one of the corporation officials whose advice was sought, suggested that the restriction be removed so that private companies engaged in developing new techniques and approaches in adult education or job training might contribute to the success of the Job Corps centers. The advice was accepted and turned out to be an important element in the later administration of Job Corps centers.

Drafting the Bill

Agreement on general principles is only the first requisite for legislation. Significant policy decisions are made at every step in the drafting process. In the case of the antipoverty bill this process was especially crucial because the legislation dealt with uncharted areas involving new substantive provisions and the coordination of established departmental jurisdictions. The drafting process was entrusted to old hands in the federal bureaucracy, who, as usual, neither expected nor received adequate credit for their labors.

The task force was subject to much turnover in personnel during its six-week life and it is difficult to identify all those who played a role in hammering out the legislation. Few had clearly identifiable tasks, and even within the short span of time their roles changed. Others were pulled in to perform specific chores. There were also those called in because they were recommended to Shriver or one of his key aides. Many of these found upon their arrival that no one had a clear idea of the functions they were to perform; and they departed without making any discernible contribution to the course of history. In this amalgam some stayed on and played definite roles and others who came for only a brief time made significant contributions. But since no record was kept of who did what, memories fade and individual recollections differ over the roles played by different participants. Any listing of the *dramatis personae* is therefore subjective.

As Special Assistant to the President for the war on poverty, Shriver was able to secure cooperation from the various departments who assigned representatives to his staff. Adam Yarmolinsky, a civil rights expert and a special assistant to the Secretary of Defense, was installed as unofficial chief of staff. (No one on the task force held formal titles and, needless to say, there was no table of organization.[35]) It became quite clear that important decisions had to be cleared with Yarmolinsky if Shriver was unavailable. The role of the other departmental representatives was somewhat ambiguous; it was not clear whether they were there to present and defend parochial departmental interests, or to strike off on their own. Included in this group were Harold W. Horowitz, a lawyer from HEW; Daniel P. Moynihan, Assistant Secretary of Labor; and James L.

[35] A *post facto* table of organization was constructed by Roger H. Davidson in Bibby and Davidson, *On Capitol Hill: Studies in the Legislative Process,* 1967.

Sundquist, Deputy Undersecretary of Agriculture. Hyman Bookbinder was assigned to the task force by the Department of Commerce, but since he was at that time serving on a consulting basis in that Department, his position was definitely not as a departmental representative but rather as an assistant to Shriver. As a former staff member of the AFL–CIO, Bookbinder also performed liaison functions with the labor movement. Finally, Richard Boone of the White House staff played an important role in shaping the Community Action Program.

The actual drafting of the bill required not only a substantive understanding of the proposed antipoverty program but also a thorough knowledge of the executive establishment. To head the team of lawyers, Shriver secured Assistant Attorney General Norbert Schlei. He was assisted by Harold Horowitz of HEW, Ann Oppenheimer of the Bureau of the Budget, and others. Christopher Weeks, a former Peace Corps official who had moved on to the Budget Bureau, was put in charge of preparing the Congressional presentation.

In addition, an assorted group of nongovernmental technical advisers and kibitzers played the role of critics and performed various other chores as the hectic situation required. Included in this group were Paul Ylvisaker, initiator of the Ford Foundation "Gray Areas" program, Frank Mankiewicz, a Peace Corps official, and social reformers Michael Harrington and Paul Jacobs.

Substantive Issues

Of the many technical and substantive issues raised in the drafting of the legislation, the most stubborn related to the Community Action Program and the coordination and administration of the several new programs. One problem arose in specifying the types of assistance to be included in the catchall comprehensive community action approach. The first complete draft version of the bill (February 24, 1964) listed fourteen activities as falling within the scope of the Community Action Program. These included development of new employment opportunities, rehabilitation of physically and mentally handicapped, diverse educational and counseling programs, and health services. Though the bill stated that the list was only illustrative, several agencies urged that their pet programs be included. Agriculture alone urged the addition of nine specific programs. Obviously, only a limited number of activities could be mentioned in what became known as the "CAP laundry list." Moreover, it was feared that any list might be further extended on Capitol Hill and might also suggest to some Congressmen the idea of making some programs mandatory, thus limiting flexibility in administering programs and the initiative of local communities. Thus it was decided to omit reference to specifically eligible activities.

Early thinking about the community action concept assumed that these programs would be limited to about ten to twenty urban and rural areas. The federal money would not only stimulate a coordinated approach to the diverse welfare, health, education and other services offered to the poor, but would make a significant contribution to the total available resources of the community. Such a pilot approach did not fit in with the "total war on poverty" envisioned by the Shriver task force. The proposed bill therefore imposed no limit on the number of communities eligible to receive assistance. This expansion process has often occurred in public programs. For example, the depressed areas program at first contemplated aid for a few score communities, but restrictions on the number of communities were dropped in the legislative process, and within a year after the legislation was enacted 700 different areas made the "depressed area list." Subsequently, the same phenomenon has appeared in the CAP's.

No doubt the most frequently quoted provision of the Act relates to the role of the poor themselves. The relevant provision is Section 202(a)(3), a portion of the definition of a community action program. One of the three criteria states that the program must be "developed, conducted, and administered with the maximum feasible participation of residents of the areas and members of the groups served." In light of later experience and the controversy generated by this phrase, it may be surprising that this language appeared in the first draft of the bill and was neither questioned nor commented upon by any of the departments that submitted detailed criticisms of the various versions of the bill. Nor was it considered significant enough to be mentioned in the official summary of the bill which was released, as is customary, when the bill was submitted to Congress. The advocates and planners of the community action concept were concerned, and some were determined, that the program would not exclude minority groups. A version of the bill prepared by the Department of Health, Education, and Welfare just prior to Shriver's appointment required that community and neighborhood groups must be represented on Community Action Program governing bodies. It was expected that this would overcome the problem of discrimination and would produce integrated community action boards. But this was considered inadequate by some of Shriver's task force members. During the first meeting of the task force on February 4, 1964, Richard Boone—who had served on the Ford Gray Area program and the President's Juvenile Delinquency Committee staff —urged that the poor be assigned a more definite responsibility in implementing community action programs. The final language of Section 202(a)(3) was the result. Whether anyone fully appreciated the implications of the language or the stir it might create is not known. To most of the task force participants, "maximum feasible participation" represented a nice sentiment and a means of giving the administrator of the program power to prevent segregation in community action programs.

The federal government's share of the funding—not only in community action but in such other programs as the Neighborhood Youth Corps—was another major problem area. In the task force's original draft bill, the federal government was to contribute from 25 to 50 per cent of the total cost of Neighborhood Youth Corps (depending upon the income level in the community) and two-thirds of Community Action Programs (with the proviso that the administrator could increase the federal share when it was deemed necessary). Most departments felt that state or local contributions of such magnitude would constitute a serious obstacle to the program, and that those communities most in need of help would not be able to participate at all. The federal share was therefore raised to 90 per cent of total cost, with the local contributions to be made either in kind or in hard cash.

Agriculture's proposal calling for the establishment of a new loan and grant program to low-income rural families was included in the bill. Many participants on the task force had reservations about singling out low-income rural families for special treatment, but apparently Agriculture's lobbying was sufficiently persuasive to retain this provision, arguing that few rural areas would participate in Community Action Programs. The program was yet another triumph for the Department in achieving special treatment for rural areas, and it appeared to have political appeal.

As expected, the most heated arguments centered upon organization and the division of administrative responsibility. Because neither Shriver's persuasiveness nor the passage of time served to resolve this controversy, it finally had to be referred to the President.

The Shriver task force managed to obtain agreement over the need for a new agency. There was no consensus, however, on the role the new agency would play. Shriver, who was destined to supervise the new program, favored operating responsibility rather than merely a coordinating role. The question then became how much of the total program should be placed in the new agency and how much delegated to established departments and agencies. Health, Education, and Welfare relinquished its claim on the Community Action Program, and in the absence of other claimants it was assigned to the new agency. Locating training and job creation programs was not so easy. Secretary of Labor Wirtz took a firm position that everything relating to work and training was within his Department's domain. HEW held that training of persons on relief was within its jurisdiction; and Shriver was bent on gaining control over the Job Corps—anticipating that it would yield quick results and favorable publicity. Knowledgeable Labor Department officials, foreseeing the difficulties in administering the Job Corps, did not share Wirtz's desire to have it assigned to Labor. The President finally divided the work and training programs three ways: the Job Corps went to Shriver, work relief and training to HEW, and the Neighborhood Youth Corps to Labor.

The status of the new agency was a final problem. Shriver insisted that it be placed in the Executive Office, on the assumption that this would give the leverage needed to coordinate the program. Objections came from the top echelon of the Bureau of the Budget, though some of the Bureau's subordinate officials thought that there was merit to Shriver's position. Again, the President sided with Shriver.

The major problems having been resolved, the legal aides lost little time in completing the draft bill. The total cost of the legislative package as approved by the President was $962.5 million. On March 16, 1964, the President sent the bill to Congress, reminding the solons that "Congress is charged by the Constitution to 'provide . . . for the general welfare of the United States' . . . Now Congress is being asked to extend that welfare to all our people."

CONGRESS REACTS AND DISPOSES

The President did not leave the fate of the antipoverty program to the whims of Congress. After sending the bill to Congress, he launched a successful campaign to persuade the public and Congress about the urgent need for the proposed legislation. The enlistment of outside support through the Shriver task force, the emphasis on traditional American values, and favorable publicity through the mass media all helped generate public awareness of and support for the proposed program.

More generally, Johnson cultivated the image of fiscal responsibility. Early in his Administration he asked Defense Secretary McNamara to cut defense costs and called for an overall reduction in federal jobs. Carrying on this theme, he assured the country that the proposed expenditures for the antipoverty program would be absorbed from "savings" in other governmental activities. Ironically, in light of later developments, the savings were to be achieved largely by trimming defense expenditures.

The President also used direct personal methods to sell the

bill. In a series of visits to depressed areas he emphasized the persistence of poverty and its debilitating effects upon individuals and communities. On a more pragmatic basis, he alluded to the prospect of forthcoming federal funds to communities and states that would result from the enactment of Great Society legislation. A number of communities—particularly several large cities which had participated in the Gray Area and Juvenile Delinquency programs and which were geared to expand their activities—began to press for quick passage of the legislation under the assumption that poverty funds would be distributed on a first-come-first-served basis. Congressional constituencies thus become aware of their stake in the poverty program. The efforts were so effective that only five months after the bill's submission to Congress it was the law of the land, an exceptionally short time for a piece of novel major welfare legislation.

Congressional Structure and Processing

The path of the Economic Opportunity Act through Congress presented special problems. Normally, when a bill is drawn by the Executive Branch, senior members of committees and/or their staffs are consulted about the general provisions and may also help in the drafting process. However, the poverty bill was generated and drawn up by the Executive Branch without Congressional participation. It was not even clear which committee in each house would consider the bill. Because the measure cut across jurisdictional lines—at least four committees in each house had jurisdiction over some part of the bill—the designers of the legislation did not know whom in Congress to consult.

During the drafting stage, it was assumed that each of these committees might claim jurisdiction to at least part of the bill. But the expected jurisdictional difficulties did not materialize. Before the bill went to Congress, the leadership agreed to assign it to the House Committee on Education and Labor and the Senate Committee on Labor and Public Welfare. The chairmen of the other committees raised no objections to this assignment of the bill. Inevitably, the two relevant committees were unable to assess thoroughly all parts of the bill. Like the Executive Branch, Congress was structurally ill-prepared to process the bill efficiently.

Some parts of the bill, of course, had been proposed in earlier legislation, but other provisions, notably the community action section, represented unfamiliar approaches or were in the domain of other committees. Often Congressmen and Senators acquire background during their tenure on committees which helps them appraise legislation embodying new ideas. In this case, few members on the Senate and House committees possessed the needed expertise to deal with the bill. Indeed, the fact of poverty had been buried for a long time before it suddenly burst into the limelight. It is not surprising, therefore, that few if any legislators had reflected on appropriate strategies to fight poverty. Congress, therefore, had to "play it by ear" in dealing with the Act.

The Administration's draft bill was introduced in Congress on March 16, 1964, and the next day hearings were begun by an Ad Hoc House Education and Labor Subcommittee on Poverty. Though the Subcommittee was chaired by Adam Clayton Powell, Chairman of the parent Committee, Phil Landrum of Georgia was asked to sponsor the legislation (H. R. 10440) in order to give the bill an aura of conservative support. In addition to the 1,741 pages of testimony, Chairman Powell commissioned a volume of facts relating to poverty to be prepared by technicians in the appropriate Executive departments.[36]

Administration strategy was to portray the bill as a thoughtfully conceived, comprehensive and integrated approach to combating poverty, even though it was really a series of compromises among various Executive departments. Appearing as the lead-off witness, Shriver outlined the program and defended it as responsible, comprehensive, and representative of a consensus of many individuals and groups. He stressed that the bill's sections were "designed to complement one another" and

[36] U.S. Congress. House. Committee on Education and Labor. *Poverty in the United States*, 88th Cong., 2d Sess. (Washington: Government Printing Office, 1964).

warned that defeat of any part could "jeopardize" the entire program.[37] For the next two weeks, a parade of the Administration's top brass appeared to nail down the case for the bill. The Secretaries of Defense, Labor, Interior, Commerce, Agriculture, and Health, Education, and Welfare, as well as the Attorney General, all testified in the same vein as Shriver.

Charges that the proposed authorization was too small to wage an effective war on poverty were cavalierly countered with the assertion that more funds could not be intelligently spent, at least during the first year. "We think this is a substantial first step," Shriver observed.[38]

Republican committee members found the hearings a frustrating experience. The great majority of witnesses favored the bill and were hesitant to criticize it. Of the sixty-nine primary witnesses who testified, only nine opposed the bill. Also, Chairman Powell's demeanor caused Republicans to complain that they were not being fairly treated. On one occasion, when government specialists testified on the extent of poverty in the United States, the Republicans on the committee tried to show that additional information was needed before effective legislation could be drafted. Powell cut short the hearings, responding to complaints by Republicans: "I am the chairman. I will run this committee as I desire."[39] Republicans consequently charged that the hearings were structured in the Administration's favor and that the opposition was gagged.

There appears little substance to the claim that the bill was rushed through Congress without giving the opposition adequate chance to present its views. The fact that Congress approved the Administration proposal with relatively few major changes appears rather to be due to the paucity of alternative ideas and approaches. Even the three academic witnesses who testified in opposition to the Administration bill failed to offer constructive alternatives. One deplored the CEA's definition of poverty, another asked that research design be built into the program, and a third criticized the bill for what he con-

[37] U.S. Congress. *Hearings on Poverty*, 88th Cong., 2d Sess. (Washington: Government Printing Office, 1964), Part I, p. 22.

[38] *Ibid.*, p. 58.

[39] *Ibid.*, Part III, p. 1150.

sidered its welfare state aspects. As a result of this dearth of constructive alternatives, the criticism tended to degenerate into negativism. One need not argue in favor of the Administration proposal to acknowledge that outright opposition was difficult. No witness wanted to argue against helping the poor.

As the debate progressed, Republicans indicated that they were ready to meet the Administration part way. Given any encouragement by Powell and the Administration, the antipoverty program might have gained bipartisan support and the legislation might have been improved. As it turned out, the Republican alternative (H. R. 11050, introduced by Peter H. Frelinghuysen) was an ineffectual substitute, authorizing the expenditure of $1.5 billion over a three-year period. The bill embraced the community action concept, but placed emphasis upon education and training programs by requiring that 50 per cent of the state funds during the first year, and a third during the subsequent years, would be spent on education and training programs. The money would have been distributed in grants to states by the Secretary of Health, Education, and Welfare, with each state submitting its own plans subject to authorization by the Secretary. H. R. 11050 would have required states to contribute one-third of total funds during the first year and one-half during the following two years, a provision which most likely would have deterred many states from taking advantage of the proposed legislation. The Republican bill was rejected by a 295 to 117 vote. Not a single Democrat voted for it, and 49 Republicans opposed their party's bill.[40]

Once the hearings were completed, Powell caucused with his Democratic colleagues on the Committee. The purpose was to reach a majority consensus and to present the Republicans with a final bill on a take it or leave it basis. By suppressing Republican criticism in the hearings and by excluding Republicans from the caucus, which considered a number of amendments, the Democrats prevented the Republicans from sharing credit for the bill. More tender treatment of the feelings of the minority members and a willingness to permit them to share credit for its enactment might have given the bill bipartisan support.

---

[40] *Congressional Record* (daily edition), August 8, 1964, p. 18042.

Two years earlier, for example, when the same Committee
considered the Manpower Development and Training Act, the
majority actively sought Republican support, giving the minority full credit for their contributions in drafting and passing
the legislation. The Manpower Development and Training Act
has been amended three times since then by Congress with
remarkable bipartisan support. Spokesmen for both parties
consider the legislation "their" creation. Powell's deliberate exclusion of the Republicans from participation in shaping the
poverty legislation may have provoked Republican hostility
towards the Economic Opportunity Act which still persists. The
winning of broader bipartisan support of the antipoverty bill
would have also required some substantive changes in the legislation. It is useless to speculate about the nature of these
changes. But in light of later experience, it would appear that
proponents of the bill might have welcomed some revisions.

Administrative Changes

The opposition directed much of its fire at the formal structure of the proposed war on poverty. Such criticism is sometimes valuable, but in this case alternative ideas were lacking.
The consequence was an undistinguished debate marked by a
great deal of carping.

One target of criticism was the unique administrative arrangement. Shriver's assertion that his proposed bill was a first
step in the war on poverty was vehemently denied, with considerable justification. Pointing to existing welfare legislation
with an annual price tag of billions of dollars, opponents reasoned that it was not necessary to establish a new superagency
to combat poverty. They raised the spectre that Shriver would
be a "poverty czar" who would have the power to ride rough-
shod over established agencies. Aware that several heads of
Executive agencies were concerned that the antipoverty bill
might encroach on their domains, opponents tried unsuccess-
fully to elicit criticisms from Administration witnesses. The
heads of departments replied that jurisdictional prerogatives
were inconsequential compared to the larger issue of fighting

poverty, and they assured that interdepartmental cooperation was both necessary and would be forthcoming.

A second line of attack dealt with states' rights. Fearful that some state governors would sabotage the program, the Administration bill drafters had bypassed the states and fashioned direct relationships between the federal government and the localities. Opponents argued that the governors should have a veto power over at least some of the poverty projects launched in their states. A Republican–Southern Democratic coalition succeeded in inserting an amendment authorizing governors to veto community action programs, Job Corps centers, and Neighborhood Youth Corps projects in their states. But though this coalition succeeded on the veto issue, it was unstable as far as the rest of the bill was concerned. In deference to Southern supporters of the antipoverty program, their Northern allies found it advantageous to ignore the civil rights issue. But when opponents of the bill tried to raise the issue, it was met head on—civil rights had lost its potency as an obstacle to legislation. For example, when Howard W. Smith argued in the Rules Committee for the rejection of the Job Corps because it would be racially integrated, Congressman Phil Landrum of Georgia acknowledged the charge but stated that this was "a matter of law over which neither you nor I can prevail."[41]

Another administrative amendment trimmed the powers of the program administrator in distributing community action funds. The Administration bill imposed no restrictions upon the director in allocating funds among the states. The amendment adopted by Congress established criteria for the distribution of funds.

Substantive Changes

Although much of the Congressional discussion concerned the formal structure of the war on poverty, the bill's substantive provisions were not entirely ignored. The Job Corps received closest attention, particularly in the Senate which had

[41] *Congressional Quarterly, 1964 Almanac* (Washington: Congressional Quarterly Service, 1965), p. 226.

approved similar measures in 1959 and in 1963. Because the members of the Senate Committee on Labor and Public Welfare were familiar with the issues involved, the arguments voiced during the Senate floor debate closely followed those of the earlier years.

The Job Corps proposed by the Administration in 1964 differed, however, from that proposed in the 1963 bill. The former called for the establishment of residential centers for youths where enrollees would receive educational and vocational training; the earlier bill in contrast emphasized conservation work. Aware of the "nature boy" lobbies represented by the federal Departments of the Interior and Agriculture and private conservation organizations, the drafters of the 1964 bill did not preclude the establishment of conservation centers. But they were intentionally vague on the subject, in order to permit maximum flexibility in the administration of the program. It became clear during the course of the hearings, however, that the pressures of the conservation lobbies could not be ignored, and the House Committee on Education and Labor specified two kinds of camps in the bill it reported (H. R. 11377, a revised version of H. R. 10440). Urban centers would stress vocational training while conservation centers would concentrate on basic education and conservation work.

The opponents' attack on the Job Corps program focused on conservation centers. It was argued that work in a rustic environment would not give corpsmen from slum areas meaningful preparation for their world of work. The potentially high cost of maintaining centers was also emphasized. Senator Winston L. Prouty of Vermont estimated, on the basis of a 1961 Department of Agriculture figure, that the annual cost of operating a hundred-man rural camp would amount to $8,263 per boy. These costs were said to be exorbitant, especially in view of the anticipated ineffectiveness of the rural camps.[42]

Defenders of the proposal replied that it was better to have these young people doing conservation work than hanging around the streets. Senator Hubert H. Humphrey, who originally proposed the Job Corps idea and sponsored the earlier

[42] *Congressional Record* (daily edition), July 31, 1964, pp. 16209–11.

Senate bills, said, "The main idea is to put these boys to work."[43] In addition there would be some tangible benefits accruing to corpsmen—such as better health, education, and frame of mind. Senator Humphrey estimated that the cost of the juvenile delinquency program was $25,000 per boy, considerably more than the anticipated cost per Job Corpsman. These arguments prevailed, and an amendment introduced by Senator Prouty to delete the conservation camps from the bill was defeated 61 to 33.[44]

It is noteworthy that there was little criticism of urban centers. Senator Prouty even argued for the elimination of conservation centers and for the allocation of all the Job Corps funds to urban centers. A less rigid position by the Democrats might have attracted Republican support for the Job Corps and still retain conservation centers. But the Democratic floor leaders refused to yield on the provisions relating to conservation centers. It has been suggested that the Republican attack on conservation centers was part of a maneuver to defeat the whole Job Corps program. It would seem, however, that with the support of Prouty and other Republicans the Democratic sponsors could have mustered sufficient support for the measure, even if some supporters of conservation centers had refused to compromise and had voted against the Job Corps.

The conservation lobbies were even more successful in the House where an amendment was approved requiring that 40 per cent of male Job Corps enrollees be assigned to conservation centers. This amendment was included in the final bill. Another amendment made girls eligible for enrollment in the Job Corps. Finally, Congress was also persuaded to add a loyalty oath requirement.

The novel community action concept was poorly understood by Congress, and as a result it stimulated little meaningful debate. Interestingly, the issue of participation by the poor in community action programs was completely ignored. The decision by the drafters of the legislation to omit a listing of the programs and activities that would qualify for assistance under community action proved to be wise. No doubt some members

[43] *Ibid.*, p. 16212.
[44] *Ibid.*, p. 16213.

of Congress would have opposed the inclusion of some programs and deletion of others. Congress thus left the adminis-
·trators of CAP maximum flexibility of operation—with one
exception, adult basic education.

The Administration bill did not contain a provision for adult
basic education. The failure of the Shriver task force to include
special provision for adult basic education is understandable. It
was anticipated that funds for this activity could be provided
from CAP grants. However, since an adult basic education bill
was pending in Congress for several years, the House Education
and Labor Committee added a section (Title IIB) authorizing
the director to make grants to states to operate adult remedial
reading classes and to develop new techniques for improving
the quality of instruction.

Another substantive issue dealt with CAP aid to parochial
schools, a hotly contested issue which until 1964 proved to be
a stumbling block to direct federal aid for primary and secondary schools. The Administration bill specifically prohibited
federal poverty aid to private schools. The intent, as Senator
Robert F. Kennedy (then Attorney General) and others had
pointed out in the hearings, was to exclude parochial schools
from the program. This met with strong behind-the-scenes resistance from Representative Hugh L. Carey of New York and
others. The bill as finally adopted prohibited general aid to
elementary and secondary education in any school (Section
205(b)), but the House Committee report specified that "other
programs could be carried on by nonpublic as well as public
institutions," permitting aid for remedial education but not
for "regular" education.[45] This compromise opened the door for
passage of the Elementary and Secondary Education Act of
1965.

The most sophisticated economic discussion dealt with loans
and grants to low-income rural families and the establishment
of corporations authorized to purchase and develop land for
resale to poor farmers (Title III). Opponents questioned the

[45] U.S. Congress. House. Committee on Education and Labor. *Economic
Opportunity Act of 1964*, 88th Cong., 1st Sess., H. Rept. 1458 (Washington: Government Printing Office), p. 19.

wisdom of making special allowances for rural folk and thus discouraging their mobility.[46]

Two important changes were made in Title III of the Administration bill. First, Senator Humphrey proposed on the Senate floor to delete a provision allowing direct grants to be made to impoverished farmers. However, he wanted to give the director discretionary authority to release debtors from loan obligations. His amendment was accepted by the Senate, but the House refused to allow loans to be forgiven, though it accepted the rest. Several factors accounted for the deletion of grants from the bill. Some legislators felt that the idea of direct grants contradicted the underlying theme of self-help. Also, the logic by which grants would be given to farmers compelled the giving of grants to poor people in cities. Since there was no apparent basis for discrimination against city dwellers, there was no reason to retain rural grants. Finally, some legislators, particularly those from low-income rural districts, feared that farmers qualifying for grants might be enabled to "leap frog" over other marginal farmers not qualifying for grants.

Second, Senator Frank J. Lausche of Ohio offered an amendment deleting the provision authorizing the establishment of corporations to buy land for resale to poor farmers. This provision was a revival of a New Deal program. Opponents argued that the measure smacked of collectivism and that the idea of cooperatives ran counter to the government's established policy of taking acreage out of production. Both arguments were fallacious. The intent of the legislation was to turn over commercially-operated land to subsistence farmers and would, therefore, not have expanded productive acreage. Nevertheless, the amendment was accepted.[47]

Congress also added a special section to the rural programs authorizing housing, sanitation, education, and day-care assistance for migrants and other seasonal agricultural employees.

Finally, Congress added a provision exempting the first $85 and half of additional monthly income earned by the poor

[46] U.S. Congress. *Hearings on Poverty*, 88th Cong., 2d Sess. (Washington: Government Printing Office, 1964), Part I, p. 530.
[47] *Congressional Record* (daily edition), July 23, 1964, p. 16203.

under the provisions of the Act (except work experience) from
income for purposes of determining basic needs under public
assistance programs. This provision was considered desirable
because in most states earnings by members of families receiving public assistance are deducted from the allowance a family
is entitled to receive. In the absence of this provision the incentive for the poor to participate in the antipoverty programs
would have been reduced.

One way to appraise the impact of Congressional amendments is to compare the funds requested by the Administration
with the actual authorization. The Administration called for a
total authorization of $962.5 million for the first year of the
legislation. Congress authorized $15 million less, reflecting the
deletion of the farm land redistribution scheme. The final authorization, as compared with the Administration request, was
distributed as follows:

		CONGRESSIONAL AUTHORIZATION	ADMINISTRATION REQUEST
		(Millions)	
Title I	Youth Programs	$412.5	$412.5
Title II	Community Action Programs	340.0	315.0
Title III	Rural Assistance	35.0	50.0
Title IV	Small Loans	— (a)	25.0
Title V	Work Experience	150.0	150.0
Title VI	VISTA and Administration	10.0	10.0

(a) No special funds authorized; loans were to be made from Small Business Administration funds.

The fact that the antipoverty bill passed through Congress
relatively unscathed was not due to a general consensus in
favor of the program. When the final vote was taken, Congress
was still divided. Were it not for the sustained pressure by
President Johnson, generating wide public support for the legislation, particularly among civil rights groups, the bill might
have failed. At the very least, it would not have been enacted
into law within five months and four days after President Johnson sent the antipoverty message to Congress. In the House,

the final vote on the bill (August 8, 1964) was 226 to 185. Republicans remained largely opposed to the program, with only 22 of the 167 Republicans voting in favor of the bill. In the Senate, sentiment for the bill was stronger. The final vote (July 23, 1964) was 61 in favor and 34 opposed. Ten Republicans joined 51 Democrats in favor, while 22 Republicans, 11 Southern Democrats and Senator Frank J. Lausche voted against the bill. In both houses Southern Democrats were equally divided on the bill.

President Johnson signed the Economic Opportunity Act (Public Law 88–452) on August 20, 1964. In signing the bill, the President declared:

The measure . . . offers the answer that its title implies—the answer of opportunity. For the purpose of the Economic [Opportunity] Act of 1964 is to offer opportunity, not an opiate.

FOR FURTHER READING

For other versions of the legislative process behind the Economic Opportunity Act, the student should consult Elinor Graham's "The Politics of Poverty" and "Poverty and the Legislative Process" in Ben B. Seligman, ed., *Poverty as a Public Issue* (New York: Free Press, 1965), and Roger H. Davidson's *On Capitol Hill: Studies in the Legislative Process* (New York: Holt, Rinehart and Winston, 1967). Some of the implications are discussed by David T. Bazelon in *Power in America* (New York: New American Library, 1967), and several of the essays in Sar A. Levitan and Irving H. Siegel's *Dimensions of Manpower Policy* (Baltimore: Johns Hopkins Press, 1966) are relevant. Congressional materials are available in the following reports and hearings (all published by the Government Printing Office): the Joint Economic Committee's *Low-Income Families and Economic Stability* (1950), *Hearings on Low-Income Families* (1955), and *Low-Income Population and Economic Growth* (1959); from the Senate Special Committee on Unemployment Problems, *Report on Unemployment Problems* (1960), *Readings in Unemployment* (1960), *Studies in Unemployment* (1960); and from the House Committee on Education and Labor, *Poverty in the United States* (1964) and *Hearings on Poverty* (1964).

POVERTY
AND POWER

Ben B. Seligman

As the War on Poverty proceeded, it became evident that major salients had bogged down in the mires of national and legal politics. While the Economic Opportunity Act specified that there was to be "maximum feasible participation of the poor" in community action programs, it was clear that most mayors preferred to attach the programs to their own political machines. As a result, some critics have described the War on Poverty as a war on the poor. The same power structure that had dominated existing social service agencies gained control of the community action boards; it looked as if the new antipoverty efforts were becoming mere appendages of old-line agencies.

There was resistance and turmoil, and much energy and effort were expended uselessly. Was all of this tumult—much of it still continuing—just "growing pains," or will the War on Poverty always be hampered by the exigencies of Washington and local

---

Source: Reprinted by permission of Quadrangle Books from Ben B. Seligman, *Permanent Poverty: An American Syndrome*, pp. 161–198. Copyright © 1968 by the author.

Professor Seligman is Director of the Labor Relations and Research Center at the University of Massachusetts. Among his other books are *Main Currents in Modern Economics: Economic Thought Since 1870* (1962), *Poverty as a Public Issue* (1965), and *Most Notorious Victory: Man in an Age of Automation* (1966).

politics? It may be too early to determine the direction in which our society will move. I have tried to present the background of this conflict in the following selections from my book *Permanent Poverty: An American Syndrome.*

๙ई॰

It would seem evident to most persons that poverty is of long standing, a phenomenon endemic to an affluent Western culture. Yet many economists and sociologists believed that the postwar era had brought an end to poverty: they hailed the fact that there were fewer poor people about than had been evident in the 1930's. It was difficult to become indignant over poverty in an affluent society.

Other writers responded with disgust to poverty amidst affluence. How else could they react when a society had pushed its gross national product to over $700 billion while tolerating low levels of income for thirty million of its inhabitants? Except for such writers—some social scientists and publicists—most Americans deluded themselves that there were no more poor around, or if there were, those few represented isolated instances that could be treated by the "case method." The prosperous years with their sprawling suburbias pushed the poor further back into the hills or left them isolated in the ghettos of the inner city.

Those who argued that the figures on income distribution did not tell the entire tale of poverty were ignored. Such critics were concerned with the quality of life, especially in contrast to the standards and expectations generated in modern society. Such a concern was expressed by Michael Harrington in his *The Other America*, a small book that helped arouse a furor over poverty.[1] His great service was to reveal a hitherto obscured subculture, one whose values are not adequately described by statistics. Unfortunately, Harrington's report did not upset many persons when it was first published. National attention was first called to it in a remarkable review by Dwight

[1] M. Harrington, *The Other America*, New York, 1962.

MacDonald in the *New Yorker* magazine (January 19, 1963).
Washington legend has it that Theodore Sorensen, special assistant to John F. Kennedy, showed the piece to the President,
urging that it underscored a potential political issue of some
consequence. Kennedy evidently required little to convince him
of the potency of the problem, for he had been to West Virginia during the primary campaigns that preceded his election
in 1960. Thus was born the War on Poverty, or at least its
beginnings.

On February 14, 1963, President Kennedy proposed a national youth service akin to the Peace Corps that had been
rather successful overseas. Public discussion and congressional
talk in the following months revolved about the idea of a domestic Peace Corps. Such a limited approach was characteristic
of Kennedy's caution in dealing with a recalcitrant Congress.
When Lyndon Johnson became President, it seemed doubtful
that much would be done to mount a program against poverty.
But in March 1964, hearings on a War on Poverty began in the
House of Representatives. Suddenly, poverty became "fash-
ionable"; Adam Clayton Powell, astute chairman of the House
Committee on Labor and Education, opened the hearings personally, one of the few occasions when he had been present in
Washington. The administration, in its initial presentation,
spoke eloquently of the "strategy" required for a War on
Poverty.

There was to be a well-rounded attack on poverty, said administrators and legislators: income tax cuts, civil rights, regional
development, urban rehabilitation, youth programs, vocational
training, and hospital insurance were to be part of the strategy.[2]
And a special office was to be created—the Office of Economic
Opportunity—which would work to create for the poor a new
environment of opportunity, directing aid toward youth and
employable family heads. Those who were poor but not reach-
able through OEO—the aged, families with female heads, poor
farm families—would be reached indirectly.

Three years later, when OEO sought additional funds—a
total of $1.75 billion—it told Congress in prose wondrous for

[2] E. Graham, "The Politics of Poverty," in B. B. Seligman, ed., *Poverty
as a Public Issue*, New York, 1966, p. 232.

Washington jargon that the "Great Society is a society of people who have a conviction of greatness—a society in which each person accepts the invitation to take part in the drama of a Great Nation; to share in equitable measure the triumphs of space travel, the wonder of science and art, the striving for social betterment . . ."[3] Yet these words belied the actual performance of the Great Society on the poverty front.

For in the entire previous year, OEO had at best reached 1.8 million persons, or about 6 per cent of the poor.[4] Others claimed that OEO had reached about five million people, or about 15 per cent of the poor; no one knew what the figures really were. In any case, OEO had demonstrated an inability to touch more than a few of the poor; most had not known at all of OEO or other programs intended to help them. For one thing, the task was simply beyond the restricted resources that Congress had made available. Perhaps this explained OEO's hope that the private sector would become involved in skirmishes against poverty: initially this seemed possible, but private companies became more interested in profits from other skirmishes. Doubtless, war was a factor: after World War II's prosperity and tight labor market five million persons were returned to poverty ranks. After Korea 3.5 million persons went back to conditions of poverty. What would happen after Vietnam? OEO asked Congress in 1966 for less than twice the funds made available in 1964—though it hoped to reach four times as many poor. The evidence suggests that OEO had not become *that* efficient in pressing the War on Poverty.

In fact, there were political components in the War on Poverty that remained unstated. It continued to select certain groups in the society as objects of special aid, rather than providing services as a matter of right and thus identifying the poor. Second, from a sociological standpoint, it became possible to practice "noblesse oblige" in a middle-class manner, a procedure that tended to heighten a sense of satisfaction for those

---

[3] OEO, *Congressional Presentation*, Washington, D.C., 1966, p. 1. For a detailed history of the inception of the War on Poverty, cf. S. A. Levitan, *The Design of Federal Antipoverty Strategy*, Ann Arbor, 1967.

[4] Estimate given to the author by Dr. Joseph Kershaw, then Deputy Director of OEO.

dispensing aid to the poor. In this manner it was easier to direct the War on Poverty into Negro-problem channels, and perhaps to assuage the demands of minority groups for a place in the political sun. Or to use the War on Poverty as riot insurance during the hot summer months when ghettos were likely to erupt. Finally, the War on Poverty provided a mechanism for the discharge of energies of otherwise alienated middle- and upper-class persons whose very ability to articulate and perhaps create a new ideology might have posed a threat of deeper substance than the threat of groups long suppressed.[5]

Few advocates of the War on Poverty were prepared to say that something was awry, say, in the pattern of income distribution. The first congressional presentation by Sargent Shriver, head of OEO, certainly avoided this problem. "On official levels, voices do not openly suggest that a system which distributes economic goods solely on the basis of the individual's present or past functional role . . . may be at the source of American poverty . . ."[6] Any thoughts along these lines were too subversive to be entertained. Congressional reaction would characterize such thinking as "communistic" and thus leave little room for debate. And conservatives are likely to attack any sort of effort, even one addressed to individuals.[7] Consequently, the only attack that remained for poverty warriors was to seek out individual causes of poverty and try to correct them. Thus, if the poor are untutored, they should be educated; if they have no skills, they should be trained; if they withdraw from society, their attitudes must be altered. In the absence of an economic crisis that might affect everyone, the War on Poverty could only assume a politically moralistic note. In that sense it became more of a war on the poor than a war on poverty.

The ideology of those who conducted the war, reflected in such famed reports as that issued under the aegis of Assistant Secretary of Labor Daniel P. Moynihan, sought to establish in the poor the attitudes of those who exercise contemporary "noblesse oblige." But the War on Poverty was not asked for

[5] Graham, *op. cit.*, p. 275.
[6] *Ibid.*, p. 239.
[7] *Ibid.*, p. 241.

by the poor. It was created in Washington by an administration seeking to emulate what purportedly had been done by the New Deal. Lyndon Johnson made poverty a political issue in the 1960's; before that time no one paid much attention to it, except for a handful of sociologists and economists. And it would not be far off the mark to say that it was necessary to convert a civil rights movement into a War on Poverty. It was a substitute for an integrated society and explains why so much of the effort has been directed toward the Negro community when most of the poor are white.

During the 1960's the Negro demanded equality in civil rights. It was this demand—or rather, series of demands—that upset the white majority. As the long denial of civil rights was economic as well as political, it was not difficult to convert political demands into economic ones. It was a simple matter of redefinition and in fact was easily accomplished, so easily that many civil rights activists found it more effective to function within the War on Poverty. This was one of the consequences of the tragic failure of the civil rights movement itself, for not only were Negro organizations warring on each other, but white civil rights activists were moving away from the movement. While Adam Clayton Powell was telling James Farmer to stay out of Harlem with his illiteracy project, CORE and SNCC were pulling away from Martin Luther King and Roy Wilkins of the NAACP. A planning session in 1964 for a White House conference on civil rights turned out to be a disaster: the civil rights leaders were unable to offer fresh ideas and simply quarreled with one another. Much time was taken with a virulent attack on the Moynihan Report. The best that emerged was a demand for more protection for civil rights workers in the South. The militants, graduates of the Freedom Rides and sit-ins, were now in government or business or politics where, like those in the labor movement, they sought to "influence friends and punish enemies." It was a frame of mind, a shift of perspective, which accommodated itself quite readily to the rhetoric of the Great Society.

As Elinor Graham of the Institute for Policy Studies has said, the poverty program thus redefined civil rights in a way that was guaranteed not to upset the power of the dominant majority.[8] How such a transformation could be initiated right at the start of the War on Poverty was illustrated by the experience of the original bill in Congress. The President had the advantage at the time of heading a new administration, albeit one that had inherited in large part the program of its predecessor. It is said that Johnson was more astute in handling Congress, that he paid obeisance to congressional prerogatives while at the same time indulging in strategic "arm-twisting." This was exemplified at the start by the administration's insistence on economy and efficiency in government, even to putting out lights in the White House. It was within this political context that the War on Poverty was born. Yet everyone was called upon to contribute his mite—from the UAW to the DAR. Sargent Shriver, then head of the Peace Corps, was asked to plan the program. He was an apt choice for the job, for his excellent performance in government, his business background, and his connections with the Kennedys were useful assets. The Johnson family even made personal visits to urban and rural slums. It all made a handsome package to advertise the new War.

In the meantime, the bill declaring war on poverty was traversing the usual congressional shoals, only this time the impediments and barriers of legislative tradition were not difficult to overcome. Most of the witnesses before Powell's committee were favorably disposed toward the bill, and the testimony and hearings were well staged by a chairman not averse to stressing economic instead of political disabilities. Most members of Congress had already decided that the War on Poverty was good —for the nation and for them. Moreover, the details of the bill were essentially extensions of earlier legislation, such as the Juvenile Delinquency Act, the National Defense Education Act, and the Civilian Conservation Corps of New Deal days. Thus, Title II of the Economic Opportunity Act was no more than an outgrowth of experience gathered under the Juvenile Delinquency Act, which had viewed social ills as a community problem. Further, it seemed that the bill would be attractive to the constituency to which it was addressed, for it promised a com-

[8] *Ibid.*, p. 246.

prehensive and coordinated treatment of the poverty syndrome. How well this would work remained to be seen.

Six months after passage of the legislation, administrators were still at sea. No miracles had been performed, nor were any on the horizon. Rather the program quickly came under attack: its executives were drawing high salaries; mayors, especially in southern cities, wanted the right to veto community programs. Still, within the first six months the anti-poverty program had enrolled 83,000 jobless youths in the Neighborhood Youth Corps; approved 2,300 loans to small farmers and rural families; and acted on work training programs for 35,000 heads of welfare families with 105,000 dependents. The OEO staff hailed these figures as indicative of an enormous achievement in so short a time. But the poverty warriors were criticized for acting like auto salesmen, promising much and delivering little. Applications for Job Corps camps totaled 200,000, but there were facilities for only a tenth of that number. Placements were impeded by overzealous screening, while wage differentials caused local outcries, especially in the South. And no one knew how to secure the "maximum participation of the poor," a legislative requirement. A year after the program had been initiated, not much improvement was visible. Critics discovered that similar programs had existed long before OEO, in communities such as New Haven, without denting the problem of poverty. Meanwhile, the National Service Corps idea of the Kennedy Administration had been transformed into the Volunteers in Service to America (VISTA) to develop work in slum areas, organize day care centers, and teach the mentally retarded. Other VISTA efforts were simply extensions of current social service efforts. Yet OEO staff people were optimistic. A curious combination of businessmen, labor ex-staffers, journalists, professors, and lawyers, they saw OEO as a unique experiment in social planning— which it decidedly was not, for planning implies perspective in program and coordination, both sadly lacking in OEO programs. Nevertheless, they were able to rationalize their efforts: by incorporating guidance and counseling, said the OEO staff, the War on Poverty was breaking with traditional fragmented programs of the past. Further, the old programs had been con-

cerned with manifestations of poverty—unemployment and
lack of food, clothing, and adequate shelter. On the other hand,
OEO would deal with ignorance, apathy, and hopelessness—
although it was difficult to see how these conditions might be
bettered if only 15 per cent of the poor could be reached.[9]

Despite initial drawbacks, public enthusiasm was high. President Johnson appealed to Americans to "join" him in waging
war on poverty. He provoked an outpouring of American sentiment from the old, tired, young, and eager, from those living in
mansions and those in poverty. Their letters offering to help
numbered in the thousands. But the large mass of thirty million
poverty constituents for whom the program was designed did
not write, for they were unable to do so, being largely illiterate.
The response was that of a guilt-ridden folk, embarrassed by a
new-found affluence and wanting to assuage a middle-class un-
ease by helping. The poverty program itself was determined to
escape the stigma of just another New Deal hand-out. Even the
names of the programs were to accent the positive—no WPA's
or CCC's. There was Project Head Start, Upward Bound,
VISTA, Medicare, and Tender Loving Care. If the warriors could
have replaced "poverty" with an "upbeat" word, they would
have done so. The OEO staff spent many hours devising these
names, all of which are intended to stress the sense of uplift
and forward motion the program imparts.[10] And with these
titles came a frenetic sense of achievement.

Some unkind persons described the early activity as far too
much concerned with public relations. They were all too conscious of Mr. Shriver's merchandising background and were
disturbed by the eager participation of private industry seeking
profit in OEO. So successful was Shriver in convincing others
that something had been accomplished and that still more
needed to be done that the House Education and Labor Committee embarrassed him in 1965 by voting more money than
OEO had expected to spend. A number of observers wondered
how long Shriver would survive, now that the program had met
its critics and come away virtually unscathed. They asked
whether more methodical techniques were not called for.

[9] *National Observer*, January 24, 1965; April 12, 1965.
[10] *New York Times*, April 1, 1964; February 13, 1966.

There were other criticisms of a more substantive nature as well. Congress had mandated that OEO should "coordinate all anti-poverty efforts of all federal agencies." There were some 115 such programs on the books, and it was not likely that HEW or the Department of Labor would surrender its prerogatives to direct these programs. Bureaucratic intransigence was the major outcome: OEO found itself the victim of onslaughts from older agencies. A school dropout could expect attention from the Office of Juvenile Delinquency, the Department of Labor, the Office of Education, the Job Corps, the Neighborhood Youth Corps, and numerous welfare groups. The degree of overlap and duplication was extraordinary, but just par for the course in Washington.[11]

There were many internal problems. Minor questions had to be decided by top-echelon staff; some staff positions were not filled; regional offices remained unopened, causing a backlog of applications in Washington; relationships with universities, essential for the success of a number of programs, had not been evolved. In addition, civil service procedures remained cumbersome in the face of pressure from northern governors and mayors for speed—and pressure from southern politicians for a slowdown. (Everyone accepted the political view that the War on Poverty was mainly for Negroes.) Staff meetings were taken up with congressional inquiries or the problem of suitable ceremonies for opening Job Corps centers. As a result, there was no clear direction during these early days. Programs were started and then pushed at a rapid pace which threatened to reduce their quality. This was evidently the case with such activities as rural conservation centers. On the other hand, the older agencies, the Labor Department and HEW, responsible for important segments of the War on Poverty, had to be nudged to speed up their execution of OEO programs. After sixteen months OEO had spent over $1.3 billion to reach directly or indirectly "several million persons" in 2,900 of the nation's more than 3,100 counties.[12]

[11] *Wall Street Journal,* June 9, 1965; June 10, 1965; *Newsweek,* March 29, 1965.

[12] *Chicago Sun-Times,* February 17, 1966; *Wall Street Journal,* June 4, 1965.

To some extent OEO was successful in assaulting established ways for administering public programs in Washington. It appeared to be part philanthropy and part goad to the rest of the federal bureaucracy. Armed with the power of the purse plus authority to coordinate poverty "work," Mr. Shriver's forces threatened to change existing ways of doing things in HEW, Labor, Agriculture, and other agencies. While there seemed to be no fundamental conflict over ultimate objectives, there was nevertheless much tension over who would determine policy on poverty—Mr. Shriver or someone else, say, Willard Wirtz, or Anthony Celebrezze of HEW. Resentment among the agencies was intensified when OEO came up with programs the other agencies had long wanted but had failed to convince Congress of. The perils of poverty in-fighting were great enough to tarnish Mr. Shriver's image of success. The problem of launching the Job Corps, VISTA, and the community action programs was enormous. As a result, the old-line agencies began to win out—Labor with its Neighborhood Youth Corps, HEW's training for public aid recipients, and Agriculture with its small-loan program. Their autonomy was considerable. The partnership arrangement that Shriver and OEO had wanted turned into unilateral action, with OEO simply providing funds. Administrators had had enough of idea men and wanted to start programs. The turnover of top personnel in OEO reached scandalous proportions. Through all of the turmoil, Sargent Shriver continued on, quite unruffled. Not even the resignation of his top aides disturbed Shriver's equanimity. His sole response was that all this turbulence reflected a marked vested interest in OEO: it was like an old-fashioned New England town meeting. When a task force suggested that the community action programs might be shifted to the new Department of Housing and Urban Development, the President disagreed, in effect lending support to Shriver.[13]

The OEO program began with some $35 million in grants in December 1964. The larger part of $15 million went to begin

---

[13] *New York Times,* April 18, 1965; January 5, 1966; *Wall Street Journal,* December 4, 1964; *Washington Post,* September 26, 1965; October 26, 1965; December 16, 1965; December 26, 1965; January 1, 1966; January 7, 1966.

the Job Corps program, and a sum almost as large was set aside for community action activities. Interestingly, one of the Job Corps centers was set up fifty miles from the LBJ ranch in Texas, under the operation of the President's alma mater, Southwest Texas State College. Altogether some four hundred projects were begun. The attack on poverty went smoothly on some fronts, on others it sputtered. In Massachusetts more problems were created than had existed, stemming in part from organized labor's fears that wages paid under the OEO programs would undercut existing pay scales. Union officials said, not without justification, that they had not been consulted. Other problems arose when communities resisted or did not understand the need for all the federal paperwork. In many metropolitan areas, new agencies established to do poverty work were resented by old-line agencies, as was the case in New York, Detroit, and Los Angeles. In Cleveland, community leaders were unimpressed by OEO's activity, and civil rights leaders were particularly critical of the War on Poverty.[14]

A year and a half later, the best one could say was that OEO represented "creative disorder."[15] Expenditures for the entire War on Poverty represented no more than .1 per cent of the gross national product. The program was ostensibly emphasizing training for youth. While some could question the approach (there are other poor besides youth), the emphasis on training seemed satisfactory, although young people want jobs above all. Others were saying that increasing the payments of existing programs, such as AFDC, would be a more effective way of solving the poverty problem. Yet there was marked dissatisfaction with the older approach, and a politically visible effort such as OEO seemed quite desirable. In any case, how would community action programs be developed without OEO? How else could the administration demonstrate its good faith and intent? How else could local political instrumentalities be created virtually overnight for all mayors to use? How else could a Democratic national administration bypass Republican state governments?

[14] *New York Times*, November 25, 1964; *Wall Street Journal*, January 18, 1965; *Washington Post*, November 25, 1964; January 18, 1965; March 7, 1965; December 28, 1965.
[15] *New York Times*, February 26, 1966.

It was a "grand spectacle, not simply of democracy at work, but of democracy trying to stimulate the response that makes it work better."[16]

Yet, as in other wars, we scarcely knew what we were fighting for. How can poverty be eliminated if by 1975, according to one estimate, family units at the lowest fifth of the income ladder will still have incomes below $3,000 a year? To take them all out of poverty will require personal incomes for the lowest fifth of $38.6 billion in 1975, probably $6,000 per family income. It is unlikely the economy can reach levels high enough to sustain such an average figure, especially when needs will probably exceed available resources by at least $40 billion.[17]

Such prospects have called forth continual criticism of the War on Poverty. Several Republican congressmen were unhappy about the lack of sufficient involvement of the poor. They proposed separation of the rural and urban phases of the program, with even more stress on youth and children, and supported transferring most of OEO's activities to regular agencies. Above all, they said, job creation was an essential element of any War on Poverty, an element that had not been considered important by OEO officials.[18]

In December 1965 OEO proposed to spend $2.5 billion for the coming year. This was cut $1 billion by the Budget Bureau. Some congressmen, notably Adam Clayton Powell, a sudden defender of the poor, thought the budget ought to be closer to $4 billion. But the war in Vietnam seemed to be a factor in the thinking of administration officials, for the latter was running at some $10 to $12 billion a year. The Great Society was prepared to reduce its spending on other programs such as the War on Poverty, and all expenditures for 1966–1967 were to rise very little because of the Southeast Asia affair. Despite the President's disclaimer in January 1966 that there would be no cuts in domestic funds, the Great Society was beginning to dwindle. Individual mayors were quite unhappy, for they had come to recognize that a free-wheeling budget like OEO's could be a powerful political weapon.

---

[16] *Ibid.*
[17] L. J. Walinsky, "LBJ's War at Home," *New Republic*, January 15, 1966.
[18] *Baltimore Sun*, January 7, 1966; *Washington Post*, March 4, 1966.

While the Conference of Mayors resented such a characterization, it did show enthusiasm for *local* programs. Administration officials such as Willard Wirtz and John Gardner denied that any serious cutbacks were contemplated, but when the budget was presented to Congress, only $463 million more was made available to OEO. Although Shriver was to say optimistically that the budget really revealed the President's continuing commitment to prosecuting the War on Poverty, it was obvious that some programs—Community Action and Neighborhood Youth Corps—would not be expanded. The emphasis for the coming year was to shift even further toward youngsters. Head Start was scheduled to gain appreciably in the internecine battles generated by budget upheavals. It was evident that there were to be some programmatic casualties in the War on Poverty stemming directly from another sort of war.[19] In fact, the reaction of local communities was instantaneous: the United Planning Organization, Washington's central local agency, began to clamor at once for more funds on the ground that southern communities had not used their quotas.[20]

Developments such as these apparently impelled the White House to order a tightening of what had become a politically vulnerable program. The President began to wonder whether job creation might not be a more feasible effort, especially for poor youth. It was also suggested that the rural poor be used to help "beautify" the nation, especially the roadsides. Indeed, a project—Green Thumb, costing $1.5 million—was proposed for this purpose, even though it seemed like makework. Nevertheless, the issue of jobs was primary. Poor Negroes in Oakland, California, wanted work, not training for nonexistent jobs. Moreover, ordinary makework carried with it not only a distasteful reminder of the New Deal's WPA, but a political risk as well, for with unemployment generally low the administration wanted to avoid the charge of extravagance. But while training might be good for a young person, it was not likely to help an older person. He simply wanted a job.

[19] *Washington Post*, December 21, 1965; January 2, 1966; January 9, 1966; January 16, 1966; January 26, 1966; *New York Times*, January 12, 1966; January 16, 1966; January 25, 1966; *Washington Star*, January 9, 1966.
[20] *Washington Post*, January 10, 1966; January 12, 1966.

The Administration was anxious also to move away from community action programs that resulted all too often in political warfare between local poverty fighters and state and local leaders. The desire was easier to enunciate than to fulfill, for many congressmen, and particularly the House Labor Committee members, were favorably disposed toward community action. House members acknowledged that so vast a program as the War on Poverty would generate enormous administrative problems, especially in the early phases. Attempts to shift even more parts of the program to other agencies, such as HUD, were for the time being resisted by the administration. The President was said to believe that the poverty effort was too new to be dispersed—yet. Still the criticisms continued—funds were not being released in time, thus generating unnecessary frustration; political patronage appeared to have become an integral part of the decision-making process; and complaints were voiced that the agency was showing signs of bureaucratic rigidity.[21]

Criticism from Congress began almost as soon as OEO started functioning. The Senate Appropriations Committee looked into one program as far back as October 1965. Charges were made that improper procedures had been followed in a Head Start grant to a group in Mississippi; Job Corps training was said to be too costly; Sargent Shriver was criticized for holding on to both the Peace Corps directorship and OEO. And Adam Clayton Powell insisted on a manpower unit directly in OEO, a proposal that made the Labor Department shudder. The idea, of course, came to nought. Ultimately, Shriver surrendered his job as director of the Peace Corps, which he had held since 1961. He was given to believe that the poverty war would be expanded. This proved not to be the case, for it was evident that Congress was determined to become the generalissimo in the War on Poverty.[22]

[21] *Washington Post*, November 4, 1965; *New York Times*, April 12, 1965; April 13, 1965; September 1, 1965; January 7, 1966; February 17, 1966; March 7, 1966; *Wall Street Journal*, February 9, 1966; February 16, 1966; *Baltimore Sun*, December 13, 1966.

[22] *Boston Globe*, January 2, 1966; *Chicago Daily News*, December 22, 1965; January 18, 1966; *Chicago Sun-Times*, December 28, 1965; *Washington Post*, December 10, 1965; *New York Times*, November 2, 1965; January 18, 1966.

At any rate, by the beginning of 1966 angry congressmen were trying to end the freedom of local groups to plan and carry out their own community action programs. Congress argued that planning had been chaotic and organization aimless. More important, the call to anti-poverty action in local communities appeared very much like a call to arms against local political hierarchies. Congress asked for emphasis on job creation and a modulation of "cultural" projects; it wanted intensive on-the-job training for hard-core unemployed, a task easier to be asked for than achieved. Yet the congressmen were merely being practical; they wanted to avoid the dreamy projects of social scientists and reformers, who were apt to be little more than "bleeding heart" Ph.D.'s. Congress wanted to spell out an order of priorities for community action projects in order to eliminate the need for local planning, thus ending skirmishes between city officials and spokesmen for the poor. At the top of the list was job training. Then came health centers, day-care projects, homemaking courses for poor women, and neighborhood clean-up and recreation projects. Congress could count on several old-line agencies plus local mayors and state politicians antagonistic to OEO. Perhaps part of the difficulty stemmed from the habit of OEO staffers of ignoring the calls of congressmen, an expression of political naïveté.

With such hostility it was almost inevitable that the imposing vision of the War on Poverty should begin to fade. Like the war in Vietnam, OEO became a political affliction. Not only did the President begin to talk less about it, but the public too was no longer impressed. A Gallup Poll revealed that only 32 per cent of respondents had expressed favorable views on OEO. The agency had not reached even half the poor and was being attacked even by those who had helped formulate its programs. The middle class of America was no longer inspired, for they felt that nothing much worthwhile was happening. The War on Poverty seemed inadequate as a public welfare program, and it was certainly inadequate as a program to improve "the quality of American life." The middle class saw that the ghettos had not been pacified, and this is what they had really expected: in 1966 alone there had been thirty-eight ghetto riots across the country. Perhaps this was the success of the War on Poverty: a poor person is restless only when his expectations have been aroused, and when they remain unsatisfied, he is likely to rebel. This made the middle class quite unhappy, and they were wondering whether outright suppression might not be a better policy. In the meantime, the War on Poverty itself was coming close to defeat.

The administration had once spoken confidently of a ten-year design to eliminate the ancient plague of poverty. It was now speaking of "holding the line" and cutting the losses stemming from a program that was rapidly becoming unpopular. Conservative critics were having little difficulty discovering cases of maladministration and describing OEO's programs as essentially a hoax. They were not far off the mark, for many of OEO's activities, at least at local levels, had become politically motivated efforts to fend off the protests of the poor while enhancing the power of local political establishments. Critics argued that the War on Poverty was still more promise than performance, with the former rapidly disappearing. Hopeful projects had been started here and there, but these had reached only a tiny portion of the poor, and they were not likely to reach more in the growing climate of retrenchment and reappraisal.

OEO had started in an atmosphere of haste and crash programs, a not untypical American habit. Yet all this merely led to error. While the civil rights movement supplied the idea of "maximum participation of the poor," this only took the program down a highly charged political roadway. Shriver and his cohorts had decided to bypass traditional channels—welfare agencies and state bodies—for they saw no reason to work with the "establishment" that had proved ineffective in coping with poverty over the years. In effect, they set out to battle the establishment, and in doing so sadly underestimated its political strength. Governors, mayors, and social workers started to protest almost as soon as Shriver had fired his shots. Some complaints went directly to the White House, where the President did not care to weaken an important element in his national consensus—more important than new local and as yet politically ineffective groups. It was soon clear that political boats could be rocked only at the risk of having funds denied by Washington. In Mississippi, projects disapproved of by Senator John

Stennis (an important man to keep the consensus) were not renewed. Controversy in Syracuse canceled plans for active, even militant, community action. It became evident that the sort of commitment necessary to eradicate poverty—at least $10 billion a year for at least a decade—would not be forthcoming.[23]

Congress was ready to live a little while longer with poverty amidst affluence, while the President had ceased talking about it at all. The War on Poverty headed for a slow, agonizing demise. One of the most serious difficulties with the OEO program was the inability to measure its progress in any reliable detail. No one could tell with any assurance whether the young men and women enrolled in the Job Corps centers emerged better suited for employment; whether children in Head Start derived lasting benefits from their pre-school experience (evidence suggests that any such benefits do not last long); whether the lives of ghetto dwellers were changed for the better because of community action programs. For here, as in other parts of the administration, there was an enormous "credibility gap." OEO had a powerful publicity operation, the most powerful in Washington next to the Pentagon's, yet many of its claims of achievement and promises of performance were patently exaggerated, and so only served to create frustration. An example of the failure to communicate was Shriver's contention that 80 per cent of the enrollees in Upward Bound were enrolled in higher education. He did not add that over half of them were flunking out of colleges. The major consequence of OEO's first two years may be the curtailment of any serious effort to deal with poverty for years to come.[24]

The political struggle at the national level of the War on Poverty was exacerbated by tensions generated in local communities. Clearly, the direction of the assault on poverty was "necessarily" toward the big cities. In New York, for example, roughly 18 per cent of its eight million inhabitants were poor.

[23] *Springfield Republican*, December 16, 1966; *Washington Post*, December 16, 1966; January 15, 1967; *Wall Street Journal*, February 16, 1966.

[24] *Washington Post*, October 23, 1966; December 16, 1966; January 15, 1967; *Wall Street Journal*, February 16, 1966; *Springfield Union*, December 27, 1966.

Most of these persons lived in some sixteen large areas of poverty, virtually isolated from the rest of the city mainly because their incomes were well below the $3,000-a-year line. The lower East Side, the West Side, Harlem, Williamsburg, Bedford-Stuyvesant, Brooklyn Heights, Brownsville, Red Hook, East New York, Long Island City, Corona, Jamaica, the South Bronx, and Morrisania were among the areas considered "pockets of poverty."

According to federal law the direction of community anti-poverty committees was to remain in community hands, but city officials were nevertheless intent on providing an "umbrella" to coordinate the programs—a euphemism for control. Many persons felt that New York, with the largest concentration of poor—about a million and a half persons—had become a laboratory to discover a solution for poverty. HARYOU-ACT in Harlem and Mobilization for Youth on the East Side were two "demonstration programs" that would help define the nature of community action. So far as New York officials were concerned, citizen participation at the policy level seemed most undesirable. Only pressure from Washington prevented elected officials from exercising virtually complete control of anti-poverty programs. At the top there had been strong emphasis upon participation by the poor, so that a program that was "too official" threatened to provoke dedicated warriors into their own wars on poverty on an unofficial level. Federal officials did not view such developments with equanimity.

Yet it was obvious by late 1965 that city and state politicians were learning to use the War on Poverty as a means of reinforcing their own positions. They disliked the notion that the poor might speak on their own behalf, and officials in Philadelphia and New York and in southern towns were unhappy when they learned that not more than a third of poverty board officials could be politicians. On the other hand, some state officials, such as Governor Rockefeller of New York, made it known they would not endorse programs that would convert community centers into political clubhouses. When state and local officials belonged to different parties, the confusion became overwhelming. Alternative programs, quickly conceived and inadequately evaluated, were often suggested. The Democratic Study Group, an organization of 175 House liberals, proposed measures to deal specifically with hard-core unemployment, while Republicans wanted to rewrite the entire OEO statute. The Citizens' Crusade Against Poverty, a private activist group, insisted that an expansion of the anti-poverty effort was essential; in the meantime, the President was becoming increasingly preoccupied with the war in Vietnam.

In New York the struggle for control of the city's anti-poverty program reached the protest demonstration stage early in 1965. Community leaders in Brooklyn were especially indignant over the mayor's attempt to supersede existing local agencies. Mayors throughout the nation were attempting to exercise the same stringent controls over local programs. They complained that the Labor Department was establishing Neighborhood Youth Corps projects by direct action rather than clearing them through the mayors' offices. The consequence, they said, was uncertainty and confusion. Cities ought to have "umbrella" agencies for community action, because they covered a variety of anti-poverty activities, said the mayors. They insisted that effective program development required coordination at local levels. In no way did they interpret direct involvement of the poor as being independent of a mayor's power to appoint.

The outcome of the struggle was a victory for the mayors. Native poor won some concessions, to be sure, but the mayors won the battle and then threatened to win the war. City halls fought not only the vocal poor but OEO itself and, in some instances, home-town members of Congress. Thus the general principle was established that the poor, while entitled to a "voice" in policy planning, were not to control that policy. It was more than a coincidence that the Watts riots occurred in a city where a struggle for political control of anti-poverty funds seriously delayed certain key projects. The mayor, Samuel Yorty, had failed to reach an agreement with either the vocal poor or the two members of Congress from Los Angeles. The contest for power delayed transmission from Washington of about $22 million, although some money was given to nongovernmental agencies.

A similar problem was beginning to develop in New York, where a number of anti-poverty projects had been initiated prior

to OEO. The President's Committee on Juvenile Delinquency
had sponsored some in 1961, with Mobilization for Youth being
perhaps the best known. MFY worked on New York's lower
East Side. Its perspective was to develop projects that would
make poor kids employable. It stressed self-help and believed
that even the poor were educable. MFY stressed community
action, spurring groups of the indigent into action. Such objectives were to prove its undoing, for an attack along these lines
was far too much for the existing power structure which soon
cried "scandal" and "communism." Such agencies as MFY literally threatened the local establishment, for the police, school
principals, and landlords did not welcome activity that under-
mined their power. In the meantime, the federal government's
program moved to shift power from anti-poverty groups to local
politicians. Kenneth Clark, a leading psychologist active in a
Harlem project, lost out to Adam Clayton Powell. Mayor Wag-
ner attacked MFY as a "slovenly and inefficient" operation.
Washington officials were evasive about the situation, though it
was evident that the mayor simply wanted more control. The
tension was enough to dry up the sources of funds.[25]

What happened to Harlem's project, HARYOU, also illustrates
the enormous difficulties of initiating a grass-roots attack on
poverty. HARYOU, or Harlem Youth Opportunities Unlimited,
had begun as an agency to plan the war on juvenile delinquency
in Harlem, while Associated Community Teams (ACT) was to
actually carry out the plans developed by HARYOU. It was obvious that if the War on Poverty were to fail in Harlem, it would
probably fail everywhere. Behind the attempt to press the war
in upper Manhattan was a drama of heartache and frustration
and, fundamentally, the bitter cost of political ambition. There
was an endless grasp for power, regardless of the consequences
for the community. HARYOU became the most controversial, as
well as the most unorthodox, of the anti-poverty programs. The
agency sought to involve Negroes in the entire society, but it
seemed clear that this was not fully possible. Washington officials criticized it severely but not openly, to avoid offending

[25] H. Krosney, *Beyond Welfare: Poverty in the Supercity*, New York,
1966, Chapter 2; *New York Times*, April 20, 1965; May 3, 1965; July 2,
1965; July 3, 1965; August 15, 1965; August 24, 1965; November 25, 1965;
November 28, 1965; January 7, 1966; February 3, 1966.

Congressman Powell, the powerful chairman of the House Labor Committee. Critics described it as a huge "boondoggle" run by sharp operators at the expense of the poor people of Harlem. Dr. Clark, who had originated the project, later described it as an agency of chaos and confusion.

It all began when the New York Youth Board and Community Mental Health Board contracted with the Jewish Board of Guardians in 1961 to provide psychiatric services. Harlem community leaders were justifiably indignant: they had not been consulted, and the whole proposal smacked of white "welfare colonialism." What was needed, said Harlem's leaders, was not help to adjust mentally but a whole range of social services that might reduce the ghetto's walls. While the JBG plan was sidetracked, the community was eventually forced to take a joint project, HARYOU-ACT, mainly in order to mollify Congressman Powell who was interested in ACT. In any case, the executive director of the combined agency, Livingston Wingate, had once been chief counsel for Powell's powerful House Labor Committee, so that the charge of politics seemed not unreasonable.

Budgeted at over $118 million for a three-year period, HARYOU-ACT received funds from several sources, including New York City, the Office of Juvenile Delinquency, the Labor Department, and OEO. It operated an employment program, a cadet corps in which youngsters paraded to "make them males," after-school study centers, and a youth action program. Its main objective, however, was to stimulate local community action boards to develop an indigenous base of power. The overall program was not very popular with anybody. Politicians recognized that its full development would make men like Powell utterly intransigent. Men like Kenneth Clark, who had been instrumental in starting HARYOU, were deeply disappointed, for in their view the program had been drowned by local politics, by an invasion of the pathology it was seeking to cure. To Clark, men like Adam Powell were manifestations of the social situation of Harlem. Political fear had blinded men to basic problems. On the other hand, defenders argued that only an indigenous program, one that was Harlem's own, not of "the man" downtown, would be acceptable to the residents of the ghetto. Hence any attempt on the part of the city administration to take over the program, warned Wingate, HARYOU's director, would have to reckon with Washington—that is, with Adam Clayton Powell. And President Johnson was catering to Powell, for he did not want to jeopardize the entire OEO program.

Subsequently, Clark went his own way. In early 1967 he founded the Metropolitan Applied Research Center to coordinate fact-finding, analysis, and program development on behalf of low-income groups. The agency, MARC, would operate widely in northern metropolitan areas and would concern itself with urban problems and civil rights. Clark wanted Negoes *and* whites to grasp the complex implications of such issues as "black power." As he put it, civil rights implied good transportation, balanced taxation, job training, decent education, and good housing. Financing was to be secured from private sources so that the contingencies of local politics might be avoided.

Meanwhile, there were the public programs to consider. One reporter visited a HARYOU-ACT program on pre-employment training. There were 250 youngsters in a dingy building on West 137th Street. For $20 a week they were attending classes in reading, arithmetic, speech, and deportment, all intended to help them get a job and hold it. The teachers led spelling drills and taught the use of rulers. Students read papers asserting that Hannibal, Beethoven, and Haydn had Negro blood. When asked why they were in pre-employment classes, one boy replied that his mother wanted him to go; another answered, "Twenty dollars."

Internal politics in Harlem raged. Clark broke with Powell, accusing the latter of wanting to use HARYOU for patronage. The charge seemed not far off the mark, for soon thereafter Wingate was appointed executive director, mainly through Powell's efforts. Washington officials, always ready with a quick response, remarked that the atmosphere of crisis stemmed mainly from too headlong a dash into fighting the War on Poverty. Much had to be done quickly and errors in judgment were bound to occur, said the officials.

As time went on, questions began to be raised about the agency's accounting and administrative practices. A number of law enforcement officers began to examine these practices, including the District Attorney and OEO itself. Wage payments seemed irregular, and funds from the city and federal government were commingled, contrary to law. A considerable sum had been spent for uniformed guards to watch the offices. HARYOU administrators saw nothing amiss, although one or two watchmen would have been sufficient. Investigators from accounting firms and Congress came upon the scene, but it was difficult to make sense of HARYOU's books. Bank overdrafts of over a half-million dollars suddenly appeared. The tangle was so complex that Wingate was forced to take a ninety-day leave of absence—at full pay. Throughout all of this mystery, Powell stayed aloof; despite his promises, his investigators were rarely on the scene. HARYOU's controller was discharged, and OEO asked the Department of Justice to review the findings of the auditors. Washington was determined that better controls be instituted: additional funds were held up in 1965 until the poverty agency accepted new management and fiscal policies. In the meantime, it became evident that the actual program was seriously lacking. A report prepared by a panel headed by James Dumpson, former Welfare Commissioner, discovered files and records either inadequate or missing, so that no evaluation could be made. In all the turmoil, little had been done for the poor.

HARYOU responded that such was not the case. Despite lack of funds, it had helped some ten thousand residents of Harlem through its Project Uplift and its Narcotics Institute. Some 2,700 youths had been placed in employment through its efforts, not counting the employment of 1,800 youths through the Neighborhood Youth Corps. Wingate warned that Harlem's youths would rise in violent revolt if anything happened to HARYOU-ACT. So far as he was concerned, the agency represented a last chance for Harlem, and it was not to be relinquished without a struggle. Other observers thought Wingate had been indulging in power politics, using the agency for his own objectives. Wingate was quick to retaliate against his opponents: he charged that the city had held up funds, that his enemies were politically motivated.[26]

[26] Krosney, *op. cit.*, Chapter 3; K. B. Clark, *Black Ghetto*, New York, 1965; *New York Times*, October 11, 1965; October 13, 1965; October 20, 1965; November 3, 1965; November 9, 1965; November 25, 1965; November 26, 1965; December 11, 1965; December 30, 1965; January 18, 1966; February 3, 1966; March 9, 1967; *New York Herald Tribune*, October 9, 1965; October 10, 1965; *Chicago Daily News*, April 10, 1965; *New Republic*, December 18, 1965.

The impact of local political struggles on the War on Poverty was further illustrated by what happened in the area of education. In 1965 there were some nineteen million people over the age of eighteen who had less than an eighth-grade education, according to the Census Bureau. About three million persons over the age of fifteen were completely illiterate. Obviously, a major objective of the War on Poverty was to overcome "functional illiteracy," to prevent undereducated persons from losing their jobs, and to prepare others for training courses so they could find jobs. This was the need in the urban ghettos as well as in Appalachia. Head Start, the Neighborhood Youth Corps, and the Job Corps could not reach these people; a basic adult education program was essential. Nevertheless, the effort, at a total cost of only $35 million, was minuscule. At such a rate it would take three to four decades to make the nation's population functionally literate. No funds were provided for recruiting students: could uneducated persons be expected to respond to printed brochures or notices that they could not read in the first place? Tentative projects to cure illiteracy were initiated in Mississippi, yet no more than a thousand persons could be accommodated. The District of Columbia had 33,000 illiterates, but as of March 1965 there was no program to deal with the problem. Private companies were trying to obtain OEO funds to develop volunteer training classes where tutors could teach reading skills. By March 1965 nearly thirty states were ready to launch anti-illiteracy programs; they were delayed by OEO's failure to issue guidelines and funds.

One of the more promising ideas was a proposal by James Farmer, former head of CORE, to eradicate illiteracy in Harlem. He asked for a grant of $780,000 for literacy classes in eighteen centers, with federal funds to be used to train instructors and provide teaching materials. In January 1966 OEO almost approved the project; ultimately it never did, for it was reported that Adam Clayton Powell was opposed to the project. Powell thought it would be a "mistake" to establish another group in New York to wage war on poverty. He was perhaps protecting his own favored project; in any case, Sargent Shriver did not seem anxious to challenge Mr. Powell. The congressman himself would not explain his stand other than to suggest that illiteracy education should be done by HEW, and that job training for illiterates seemed more urgent. So Farmer's project was never funded.[27]

Thus, despite a torrent of legislation sent to Congress by the President, the education problem could not be dented. As spending by the Office of Education mounted from an annual average of $700 million to $4 billion, educational appropriations threatened to become a greater source of congressional "pork barrel" projects than the regular rivers and harbors bill. The immediate beneficiaries had been teachers, school administrators, textbook publishers, and school suppliers. It was, however, difficult to determine to what extent the children of America had benefited from the Great Society's largesse. The school dropout rate in the Cardozo section of Washington was as high in 1967 as it was in 1964—20 per cent. The basic problems of reforming an outmoded curriculum and improving vocational education had not been solved. The federal school-aid program remained fragmented and amorphous. The elementary school effort had been spread too thin to be really helpful, allocating about $140 per child. Whatever gains had been made by Head Start were washed away through lack of follow-up when youngsters entered the regular school program, which was inadequate anyway. Local school authorities were sidestepping the requirement that poor children be reached, claiming that the education bill had been vague on the issue. In some districts teachers' aides were placed in wealthy areas before schools in poor sections were staffed. Local people could not fight the paper war of state and federal authorities. Some states were using funds for construction, although specifically prohibited to do so. The good intentions behind these programs were not to be denied, but they were foundering on local, state, and federal politics.

The education bill itself, a $1.3 billion aid program passed by Congress in April 1965, was far too complex and literally did not spell out how the nation's educationally deprived were to be helped. Administration officials said its fuzziness was intentional, in order to allow local communities to work out their

27 *New York Times*, March 21, 1965; December 12, 1965; March 5, 1966; *Washington Post*, March 7, 1965; March 24, 1965; February 9, 1966; March 8, 1966.

own programs. The important objective, they argued, was to get a bill on the statute books, committing the federal government to educational assistance. Aid was supposed to focus on poor schools by providing over a billion dollars for public schools located in poor neighborhoods. Its intent was to stimulate shared-time classes, educational television, remedial study, health services, breakfasts, and counseling services. Allotments of funds were to be based on the number of school children aged five to seventeen from families with annual incomes of less than $2,000. Another title of the bill allocated $100 million for supplementary educational centers.

Francis Keppel, Commissioner of Education, thought this was an opportunity for new cooperation between the schools and the community. Educators ought not to feel threatened by all the Great Society programs, he said. Private schools entered the fray: by January 1966 twenty-nine of them had planned four- to eight-week programs for poor kids. Even private foundations were entering the field: in April 1965 the Ford Foundation announced a grant of some $4.5 million for educational projects to help the poor.[28] Yet the major effort had to come from public sources, and there red tape and chaos reigned.

Other cities did no better than New York in escaping local politics, in education or in other areas of the anti-poverty program. Although Washington, D.C., has a most affluent appearance, slums and deprivation are a gigantic problem. The poor are no poorer than they were in the 1940's or 1950's, but the rich have become a good deal richer. Washington has not managed to cope with either its own good fortune or its poverty. Juvenile delinquency is highest in low-income areas. The worst of its housing is desperately overcrowded; housing construction has failed to keep up with needs, especially for low-income families. Land planning in the surrounding suburbs has become a subtle expression of class hostility, for the suburbs have drafted plans so as to exclude families below a desirable level of income. As for public assistance, Washington falls far behind other cities. One of the world's great medical centers, its Children's Hospital, teeters perpetually on the edge of bankruptcy. Virtual illiteracy in the schools is common, and with

28 *New York Times*, April 11, 1965; April 13, 1965; January 12, 1966; March 7, 1966; *Washington Post*, April 20, 1965; January 17, 1967.

more college degrees per capita than any big city, Washington still has no major institution of higher learning. Hardly more than a southern town before World War II, Washington has become a symbol of wealth, power—and poverty.

To deal with Washington's poverty, a central agency was formed—the United Planning Organization—which later became the city's anti-poverty "umbrella" institution. Yet once the local War on Poverty was under way, difficulties ensued. Within a short time five top officials resigned as a result of policy differences with the director. A management survey suggested that UPO be reorganized, that it was top-heavy with officialdom. Some of UPO's officers thought the agency should have taken a firm pro–civil rights position, and they were troubled by the director's conservative administration and reluctance to take sides in controversial public issues. Mainly activists, the staff thought UPO had the opportunity to establish political entities to teach the poor how to use legal power; they kept thinking of the New York experience. So did the director, James Banks, and, supported by a predominantly white board of directors, he preferred to move slowly and cautiously. Projects began to duplicate each other, and there appeared to be little direction to the overall program. It was not long before OEO officials were holding up funds for UPO or cutting back on requested grants. The local anti-poverty agency complained it was being starved, but the mills at OEO in another part of Washington ground slowly. The bureaucratic maze crippled local efficiency, especially when Congress had so much to say about local affairs. The federal government had become so involved with itself that it could not care for people living at its doorstep.

It took a mother's death in the winter of 1964 to make the District Commissioners realize that a person evicted from her home could walk the streets of Washington seeking help until she died. The Department of Health, Education, and Welfare said in one report that local anti-poverty agencies simply faced demands that exceeded their capabilities. Neighborhood centers run by UPO could not do the job, for they lacked both talent and resources, said the report. In the Cardozo area, one of the most depressed in the city, citizen advisers were wrangling with UPO over the establishment of day-care centers. The Cardozo residents wanted such centers to care for young chil-

316   *Ben B. Seligman*

dren to give jobless mothers time to work. UPO feared such
operations would be emotionally damaging to the children, but
residents felt that UPO was simply unresponsive to the needs
of the neighborhood.

By late 1966 staff morale in UPO had reached a low point.
As a result of lack of funds and pressure from OEO, the agency
reduced its staff, mainly administrative workers. Executives and
specialists with education and experience were the first to go:
they could find other jobs more easily than someone who had
just come from the public assistance rolls or who had been
recently unemployed. Upsetting as it was, UPO was on notice
to cut back its spending on community action to $385,000 a
month, a rather sharp drop from the $675,000 a month it had
expected to spend between 1966 and 1967. Such reductions
meant fewer people on hand to operate the various community
action programs in Washington. Anti-poverty agencies in the
suburbs, once working through UPO, would have to deal directly with the federal government, because UPO did not have
enough staff members to provide technical assistance. And
other essential projects were simply postponed.

As a result of this turmoil, part politics and part inefficiency,
local neighborhood centers contemplated splitting away from
UPO, which did not object since it was OEO policy to encourage neighborhood anti-poverty agencies to become independent.
The theory was that such a center could be more responsive to
an area's residents than a central organization. The Cardozo
center became CHANGE, the Cardozo Heights Association for
Neighborhood Change and Enrichment. Residents objected to
some of the projects: they preferred jobs and money. UPO's
employment center was successful in getting jobs for about half
its applicants. Considering the lag in job creation and development, it was not a bad record. Of the approximately twelve
thousand persons placed by UPO, some five thousand had
Neighborhood Youth Corps part-time jobs; there were also some
one thousand Job Corps trainees and 1,500 pre-vocational trainees. The rest were placed in low-paid, dead-end jobs. Many
applicants were uninterested in such undignified jobs as cham-
bermaids, porters, and janitors.

The two thousand or so persons working directly for UPO
were terrified at the prospect of cutbacks, for many of their jobs

had no counterparts in government or industry. Where would *they* go? Despite UPO's plea for a full budget for 1967, there was little OEO could do. Congress had ordered a reduction in community action. UPO spending, at an annual rate of $9 million, was to be cut in half. UPO might reduce all of its neighborhood programs across the board; or it could cut the number of centers it was supporting; or selectively cut back some programs and not others. It was an unhappy dilemma for the Washington anti-poverty warriors.

The explosive potential of local tensions was illustrated in Cleveland, where the city's inability to start solving problems of discontent and poverty forewarned a sequel to the five-day riot of 1965. There was no leadership in City Hall, in the business community, or among the "responsible" Negro organizations. While a Negro militant shouted that the white man was a "beast" to be overcome, white youths on motorcycles charged through Negro ghettos flailing residents with chains. Little was accomplished in Cleveland because the mayor and the federal government were at odds. Of all the slum renewal projects planned in recent years, only one had been completed. Little had been accomplished because the mayor and business groups were at odds. A businessman's committee created after the 1965 riots accused the mayor of "playing politics with the well-being of Cleveland." Little had been accomplished because the mayor and Negro organizations were at odds. The NAACP and the Urban League could not get Negroes into building trades jobs and had become *personae non gratae*. For his part, the mayor complained that he could not get enough money for projects and that Washington was utterly unfair in its dealings with him. But the plans for placing the poor in jobs moved slowly. Two thousand persons were to be placed by June 1967; the plans had been announced in March. In the meantime, Negro groups were planning further militant action even as White Citizens' Councils were organizing a "white backlash."[29]

Local political struggles were most apparent and intense in

[29] *Washington Post*, October 30, 1965; November 1, 1965; November 2, 1965; November 3, 1965; November 4, 1965; January 7, 1966; February 6, 1966; March 3, 1966; December 15, 1966; December 16, 1966; January 23, 1967; February 25, 1967; *Christian Science Monitor*, February 18, 1966; *Wall Street Journal*, March 14, 1967.

the South. It was only in March 1966 that the Child Development Group in Mississippi had its budget approved, after one of the most prolonged political hassles in the entire life of OEO. For a long time classes for youngsters were operated on a voluntary basis, while OEO officials debated whether to provide funds for the project. Had it refused, OEO would have alienated a major segment of the civil rights movement and invited the wrath of the Citizens Crusade Against Poverty which was interested in the Mississippi project. Needless to say, approval aroused the indignation of the state's congressional delegation, many of its newspapers, and the segregationist organizations. The lines of battle had been drawn when Child Development, operating under a $1.4 million OEO grant, hired about thirty of its 1,160 teachers from SNCC, CORE, and the Mississippi Freedom Democratic Party. Senator Stennis denounced Child Development's connection with civil rights groups and charged huge discrepancies in its finances. He attacked the qualifications of its teachers and the quality of the materials they used. Child Development responded that it had saved tax monies because in the first year it taught two thousand more students than had been anticipated.

Yet generally the South was laggard in its opportunities. It did not ask for its share of the available poverty funds, and without applications there was little OEO could do. Southern communities were unwilling to provide the necessary 10 per cent local portion. They were suspicious of the intent of the program, and white leadership preferred to forfeit federal grants rather than accept integration or extend leadership to Negroes. Hence, while Alabama stood eleventh in the nation in the number of poor, it was twenty-third in the amount of monies it received from OEO. The only southern state that seemed to hold its own was Arkansas, nineteenth in the number of poor and thirteenth in the amount of anti-poverty money received. Mississippi was not very interested, while Georgia would have had a poor record if OEO had not made exceptions for them. The richer states received the major share. California, ranked third in the number of poor, was getting more than any other state, followed by New York (second in the number of poor). New Jersey and Michigan were well up in the rankings of money received. It was evident that not all the states were alert and demanding of their rightful share of anti-poverty funds.[30]

Further north, the local power centers wanted money, but they also wanted control. In Chicago, Mayor Richard Daley argued that the poor could not help the poor. Responding to the charge that all he wanted was patronage, he said there was nothing wrong with politics if it did some good. Yet the poor of Chicago were resentful, for they wanted to do their own thinking and their own planning of the local War on Poverty. Daley maneuvered so that the welfare machine, a mammoth creation of big city life, was firmly in command of anti-poverty efforts despite federal prohibition against such tight control. Maximum participation of the poor was new and far too revolutionary for welfare programs, which had in any case failed to create jobs and housing for the poor. Chicago would have none of this: welfare officers drew up the anti-poverty blueprints and then called in residents of poor areas to serve as "advisers." Of the twenty-four members of the anti-poverty steering committee appointed in 1964 by Mayor Daley, eighteen were directors of public agencies or businessmen who had served as chairmen of city commissions. None of the twenty-four represented a private welfare agency, and none represented a neighborhood or community organization. It was at least a year before any Negro appeared as a member of the steering committee, but those appointed were safe middle-class Negroes. The committee was supervised by the Chicago Committee on Urban Opportunity, with membership virtually identical to that of the Joint Youth Development Committee. The latter's record included failure to obtain approval for most of the anti-delinquency proposals submitted to Washington. Involved in this power center were twenty-five chairmen of city government agencies, nine businessmen, five aldermen, four union officials (who almost never attended meetings), and one judge. None of them were poor or represented the poor, and all were considered safe by the Daley machine.

Local neighborhood poverty leaders discovered that persons they sent for job interviews were being given short shrift. An applicant needed a sponsoring letter from an alderman—the

[30] *New York Times*, April 14, 1965; January 2, 1966; March 7, 1966; *Washington Post*, November 21, 1965.

poverty program in Chicago had become a tool for powerful legislators to control the poor. Aldermen used the program as they had used public housing and public aid—as devices to maintain their power. They controlled thousands of sub-professional jobs in the Urban Progress Centers that were to be the backbone of Chicago's War on Poverty. But it was not clear what these jobholders would do, although it was presumed they would recruit applicants for job training and literacy classes, uncover families in need of counseling, and investigate reports of building code violations. The Chicago political machine tried to assure its critics that it would seek "responsible" persons and that it would be "objective." Opponents, notably Saul Alinsky, were skeptical: they had learned that anyone who complained was "irresponsible" and "negative." Private social welfare workers were beginning to wonder when, in all the conflict, the War on Poverty was going to help its first poor person in Chicago.

Despite the attempt to challenge Daley's rule, his power in the anti-poverty effort was almost absolute. He was even able to act contrary to Washington's wishes. Anti-poverty money made jobs, and Chicagoans employed by the city at various kinds of social work moved into higher-salaried jobs at federal expense. The faithful moved up all along the line—not difficult considering the city had received over $15 million in anti-poverty grants. To be sure, there were community advisory committees for each Urban Center, but the chairman was selected by the mayor's deputy. Businessmen, like the mayor, recognized that activity of the poor was a potential threat to the established order, and they joined him in resisting this threat. One banker told a local church group that if it pressed for a job training program he would not help raise funds. Large companies such as Sears, Roebuck and Ryerson Steel were reported to resist local neighborhood training projects. Comment from local community groups, such as The Woodlawn Organization, were rejected. From the standpoint of these groups, the War on Poverty had become the ancient war *against* the poor. They observed that advisory committees should be resisting the middle-class habit of keeping the poor dependent. The conflict eventually reached the House Labor Committee, where representatives were shocked that the motives of politicians would be impugned.

A year later rallies were held in Chicago to celebrate the progress of the War on Poverty. These were not much different from time-honored block rallies and ward meetings. Aldermen, judges, and city commissioners quoted Lincoln, Roosevelt, and Kennedy, while praising significant advances. Yet the accomplishment had been limited, if only because the program had become so enmeshed in local politics as well as in a conflict with Washington. Daley insisted that his program had to set standards and criteria, even if these were not spelled out in the law. Thus the issue of control was double-edged: the Chicago machine versus local poor and Daley versus Washington. Local organizations such as Woodlawn's TWO asked whether public funds could not finance basic reform by going to independent groups to organize the poor, instead of the monies being used to perpetuate the status quo. They contended, with some justice, that the local War on Poverty was being used to "buy off [their] rage against being confined to the ghetto." It was a rage against the last of the big city political machines.[31]

In Los Angeles a searing race riot in the summer of 1965 revealed the weaknesses of the Great Society's poverty program in the City of Tomorrow. In November 1965 OEO gave Los Angeles over $17 million; it doubled, from 400 to 840, the number of poor persons who could be hired at $4,000 a year to aid their neighbors in such areas as Watts. It was hoped that services to young people would be expanded. Yet in Los Angeles, too, local politicians used the War on Poverty to advance selfish ends. Mayor Samuel Yorty resisted federal requirements to involve the poor in program planning. The administrative structure of the War on Poverty became a jungle in a region which included a county government, seventy-six mayors, fifteen members of Congress, and thirty-two school districts, all spread over an area of four thousand square miles.

The poverty program in Los Angeles operated under an

[31] *Chicago Daily News,* April 5, 1965; April 7, 1965; April 8, 1965; April 9, 1965; April 14, 1965; *Chicago Sun-Times,* April 22, 1965; January 11, 1966; January 19, 1966; *Washington Star,* February 24, 1966; *New York Times,* April 14, 1965; July 23, 1965; January 2, 1966.

armed truce called the Joint Powers Agreement. While the
Watts riots had brought the politicians together on paper, there
was no real peace among them. The poor were supposed to
have a voice in the poverty agencies, but the election of their
representatives was impeded because politicians gerrymandered
voting districts. It was possible that Watts itself would have
no representation. Yet the election district lines could not be
changed without the unanimous consent of the politicians.
Some politicians wanted to abandon the elections outright, a
violation of the Joint Powers Agreement. There was opposition
to job training and a demand for "instant jobs." Such advocates
remembered the state law that required dropping heads of
families from the relief rolls when they undertook job training
for compensation. Congressmen investigating the program in
Los Angeles felt it had "bogged down in nine different direc-
tions."

As if to prove Yorty's point, the election of local representatives to poverty boards in 1966 drew pitifully few of the eligible
voters. Although the poor had shown a similar lack of interest
in poverty program elections in other cities, officials had hoped
results would be better in Los Angeles, particularly because of
the program's link with the Watts riots. A corps of six hundred
volunteers had been organized to familiarize people with the voting. On election day, chartered buses helped people to the polls.
Yet only 2,700 voted to select seven representatives from the
fifty-four candidates. The turnout was less than 1 per cent, compared with a 2.4 per cent turnout in Philadelphia and 6 per cent
in Hartford. But voting in Los Angeles was limited to persons
with annual incomes of less than $4,000 and to heads of house-
holds. Poor persons are reluctant to identify themselves in this
manner. Election day was cold, and city officials perhaps knew
also that poor people won't leave home on the day their relief
checks are delivered. In any case, the poor were not much interested in an election conducted by middle-class institutions
for what they construed to be middle-class objectives.[32]

[32] *Washington Post*, November 25, 1965; *New York Times*, June 17,
1965; January 24, 1966; March 4, 1966; *Chicago Daily News*, March 3,
1966.

Meanwhile in Boston, payroll irregularities were reported for some of the poverty programs. Joseph Slavet, the director of Boston's umbrella anti-poverty agency, was tied to the city administration through one of his aides, who was also the mayor's liaison officer. Although the mayor had no well-knit organization of his own, Slavet helped him in the handling of municipal affairs. Youths who did not qualify for the Neighborhood Youth Corps were hired nevertheless, and payrolls were padded with fictitious names. Finally, Action for Boston Community Development, at the insistence of OEO in Washington, discharged Slavet on grounds of administrative oversight.[33] In Newark the local conflict was resolved in favor of local politicians who had set up an organization parallel to that of the native poor to provide the overall "umbrella" for anti-poverty efforts. They did not want local groups to apply to Washington for aid without their knowledge. Syracuse rejected the assistance of Saul Alinsky of Chicago Woodlawn fame. For politicians he was much too dangerous a man, because his objective was direct involvement of the poor, and the politicians wanted nothing to do with measures that would require the poor to exercise their own power. The feud between the poor and the establishment in Cleveland paralleled Chicago's squabble. Denver's Community Action Programs limped along, crippled by political infighting between its director and the poor themselves: Spanish-Americans and Negroes were charging favoritism, while, as in other cities, politicians were trying to keep the pot from boiling over. And in Oakland, "downtown" and the ghettos were separated by deep-rooted antagonisms.

All over the country a fantastic power struggle was going on to decide who was to control anti-poverty funds. In the meantime, those who were supposed to be helped continued their miserable existence in the ghettos and rural slums of America.[34]

[33] *Washington Post,* January 7, 1966; *New York Times,* November 21, 1965.

[34] *New York Times,* April 15, 1965; December 22, 1965; January 17, 1966; January 24, 1966; *Washington Post,* November 21, 1965; *Christian Science Monitor,* December 22, 1965; *Wall Street Journal,* December 19, 1966.

FOR FURTHER READING

There is no full-scale study of the politics of poverty, although some aspects will be explored by Sar Levitan in a forthcoming book. The implications of national policy for the poverty program are explored by Elinor Graham in "The Politics of Poverty" and "Poverty and the Legislative Process" in Ben B. Seligman, ed., *Poverty as a Public Issue* (New York: Free Press, 1965). Insight into the nature of the local political struggle may be gained from Kenneth Clark's *Dark Ghetto* (New York: Harper & Row, 1965) and from Herbert Krosney's *Beyond Welfare: Poverty in the Supercity* (New York: Holt, Rinehart and Winston, 1966).